the series on school reform

Patricia A. Wasley
Coalition of
Essential Schools

Ann Lieberman
NCREST

SERIES EDITORS

Joseph P. McDonald
Annenberg Institute
for School Reform

This series also incorporates earlier titles in the
Professional Development and Practice Series

What's Happening in MATH CLASS?

Reconstructing Professional Identities

VOLUME TWO

Deborah Schifter, EDITOR

FOREWORD BY PATRICIA WASLEY

Teachers College
Columbia University
New York and London

This work was supported by the National Science Foundation under Grant No. TPE–9050350. Any opinions, findings, conclusions, or recommendations expressed here are those of the authors and do not necessarily reflect the views of the National Science Foundation.

Acknowledgment is given to AIMS Educational Foundation for permission to print the sorting, tallying, and graphing sheets from Primarily Bears, Book 1.

Published by Teachers College Press, 1234 Amsterdam Avenue, New York, NY 10027

Library of Congress Cataloging-in-Publication Data

What's happening in math class? / Deborah Schifter, editor : foreword
  by Suzanne Wilson (v. 1); foreword by Patricia Wasley (v. 2).
      p.   cm. — (Series on school reform)
  Includes bibliographical references and indexes.
  Contents: v. 1 Envisioning new practices through teacher narratives —
v. 2. Reconstructing professional identities.
    ISBN 0-8077-3482-9 (v. 1 : cloth : acid-free paper). — ISBN
0-8077-3481-0 (v. 1 : paper : acid-free paper). — ISBN
0-8077-3484-5 (v. 2 : cloth : acid-free paper). — ISBN
0-8077-3483-7 (v. 2 : paper : acid-free paper)
    1. Mathematics — Study and teaching.   I. Schifter, Deborah.
  II. Series.
  QA11.W465   1996
  510'.71'2 — dc20   95-25216

ISBN 0-8077-3483-7 (paper)
ISBN 0-8077-3484-5 (cloth)

Printed on acid-free paper
Manufactured in the United States of America

03 02 01 00 99 98 97 96   8 7 6 5 4 3 2 1

To Virginia, Jill, and Janet,
carrying on with the work.

Contents

Foreword

"If a math teacher says to me one MORE time that girls aren't good at math, I'm gonna blow! It just makes me SO mad!" said Ellen, a senior student at a small northeastern high school.

"Math is boring. We do the same thing every day. The teacher stands at the board, goes over our homework, shows us how to do a new problem, then we work on those for the rest of the period and for homework," said a group of sophomore students.

"Yeah, but the hardest part is that some teachers are good at explaining it and others aren't. I had to get a tutor last year because we couldn't make any sense of what the teacher was talking about or from the book either," added Jeremy. "A whole lot of us had tutors."

"I don't know why the schools don't do something about math," complained Ms. Helprin, a parent of several children in a Southwestern high school. "Two of my kids and any number of their friends are just stumped by it. We've had to get tutors for both of our kids and that really strapped us financially."

For the last three years, colleagues and I followed 150 students through high school in different parts of the country. All of the schools were working to change daily practices, structures, and requirements to improve students' learning. We heard more complaints from students and parents about math than about any other subject. The kids complained that it was boring and hard to understand. When we pressed them about what *boring* meant, they suggested that their classes were too routine and that they had no sense of the pertinence of math to their daily lives, to the world in which they lived. Parents complained that students had too much trouble with math and that something—besides suggesting that they should pay for tutors—ought to be done. The parents were generally enthusiastic supporters of the changes their high schools were making, but found it frustrating when they saw little evidence of it in math classes.

When we shared these findings with math teachers, they first suggested that they were prevented from working differently with students by standardized tests, like the SATs, that govern their students college admittance. After a lengthy exploration of the tests and the relationship of the tests to what happens in classrooms, they discovered that the more serious impediment to changing practices was that they had no images of what a different, more powerful mathematics classroom might look like.

This book, full of examples from elementary classrooms, provides such a set of images. It is exciting to read. In all of the classrooms the teachers are working with their students to be mathematical thinkers. There is no evidence that the kids are bored by a repetitive skill and drill approach, or that their confusion might go unaddressed.

This volume—written by teachers about their own work, project director Deborah Schifter, and several additional math scholars—is an important book for two reasons: 1) it clearly illustrates a different approach to learning mathematics, and 2) it is self-conscious about the process teachers must go through to get there.

The book moves in a refreshing sort of developmental sequence. Dr. Schifter first describes the project she and her colleagues designed to help elementary math teachers strengthen their own understandings about mathematics and as a result, improve their teaching techniques in line with current research on learning. The book then provides first-hand accounts from teachers who participated in the project. Each set of essays deals with a new dilemma: teacher's own math experiences, trying to teach differently, conducting classroom-based research, taking students deeper. After each set of teacher narratives, a math scholar looks across their stories to draw out common themes and to determine what they teach us about the need for change in elementary mathematics education. The structure is very deliberate, thoughtful, and creates important relationships for our heightened understanding about the current mathematics reform movement.

So, what kind of images do these essays provide? Two, in particular: They show us teachers in new professional roles and they show students working quite differently. All too often, as teachers hear news about new techniques or strategies, for lack of helpful images, they interpret these as descriptions of what they already do. (What traditional math teacher would suggest that she does NOT teach kids to be good mathematical thinkers? And yet, most traditional approaches do not push students to demonstrate their thinking or their understanding.) Unfortunately, this undercuts the potential for growth since it allows teachers to think that no change is needed at all! We see what it really means for teachers to be "managers of learning" instead of "deliverers of instruction." They build exploratory projects that enable students to see the pertinence of numbers in their daily context—like counting all the books in the room, or using the sixth graders' graphs from the hallway display to push third graders' thinking. They look beyond a text for activities that exist in the everyday world; they take advantage of what exists around them rather than relying solely on books and worksheets. They show us what it is like for teachers to be real researchers: to set a problem—like kids' understanding of what it means to count, to gather data, to analyze the data, to revise approaches based on their analysis, and to write about one's findings. Jessica Dobie Redman discovers that many children in her classroom do not understand that there is a one-to-one relationship between what they count and the numbers they use to describe them! What an important discovery for a teacher to make so that she can help correct her students' grasp of mathematics. And we see students discover ways to do skip counting, grapple with a variety of answers. We see them grow as they learn that, while there is generally a correct answer in math, there may be a variety of ways to get to the answer—another very important discovery that fosters both critical thinking and flexibility.

In addition, this book suggests a whole set of fresh, but important relationships. It reinforces the need for interdisciplinary approaches for both children and teachers. By engaging in the writing process about their understandings of mathematics, we see both students and teachers gain important insights they may not have achieved had they not moved from mathematics to words. We see a new kind of partnership between university-based scholars and teachers. While analyzing the teachers' learning experiences, these critical friends help to further plumb what we know by making connections, clarifying what the narratives teach us, and reminding all of us about important areas for further investigation. (Susan Jo Russell gave me much to think about when she suggested that the mathematics reform movement is wrong when it suggests that kids need more "real life" math, that what it really needs is a different kind of math context within the classroom—a sense that math is everywhere in our common environments and that there are interesting problems to tackle all around us.)

What's Happening in Math Class?, Volume 2 is a book that gives me confidence that important transformations are occurring in elementary mathematics education, and provides me with hope that it might eventually make its way to high school classrooms. Imagine what we might be able to accomplish as a country—balanced budgets, economic recovery, welfare reform—if the majority of the students in our schools found math class as stimulating as, say, listening to music! Imagine what it might be like to have parents who were terrifically enthusiastic about what's happening in math class!

Pat Wasley
Coalition of Essential Schools
Brown University

Acknowledgments

When I received word four years ago that the National Science Foundation would fund the Mathematics Process Writing Project (MPWP), the project that produced this book, my first reaction was elation; my second, panic. After all, I had been teaching mathematics, or mathematics education, for 17 years. Could I suddenly become a writing teacher?

I turned to Rebecca Faery, the then new director of the writing program at Mount Holyoke College, for advice. "Of course you can teach writing," she reassured me. "After all, the principles of learning that guide the teaching of writing are the same as those for teaching mathematics." And she was—to some extent—right.

But I relied on other resources as well. Rebecca had organized a faculty writing group that met weekly to discuss members' work-in-progress. The feedback I received on a just-begun writing project of my own was to contribute significantly to the final product. But the opportunity afforded me by that group also required that I think about such questions as: Which of my fellow participants' comments are helpful and which are confusing or irrelevant? Where was I being defensive and what allowed me to hear criticism? What did my own emotions—pride, satisfaction, anger, frustration, annoyance—indicate? I took this experience with me into the MPWP and it helped guide me as I responded to project participants.

I also frequently called upon what I had learned from Lesleá Newman and Michael Thelwell, teachers with whom I had studied fiction writing. For although the MPWP teachers were not writing short stories, they needed to develop the feel for the telling detail, the sensitivity to nuances of speech and gesture, that give this genre its truth-telling power.

However, the crucial learning came from building this project together with its participants. The first wave—Kathleen Bridgewater, Virginia Brown, Anne Hendry, Rita Horn, Nina Koch, Nancy Lawrence, Jill Lester, Barbara Anne Miller, Valerie Penniman, Margaret Riddle, Rosemary Rigoletti, Janice Szymaszek, Lisa Yaffee, Joyce Zippe—were willing to help me figure out which classroom structures worked, what assignments were useful, and what pace it was reasonable to set. At the start I had only vague notions of what their papers could be; it was these teachers, pursuing their own visions, who showed me what was possible.

Thus, by the time I met with the next two groups, we had a base to work from. Their critiques of their predecessors' written work helped us come up with alternative topics and formats. And although I had learned much from that first wave about how to teach writing, their successors continued to give me valuable feedback. Many thanks to Christine Anderson, Marie Appleby, Kathy Baker, Virginia Bastable, Maria Buendia, Elizabeth Clark, Mary Flynn, Allen Gagnon, Catherine Ginsberg, Humilia Gougeon, Perrie Graveline, Vicky Gruneiro, Robin Gurdak-Foley, Virginia Hawley, Caryl Isenberg, Peter Kostek, Doris LeBlanc, Donald Lennon, Jill Lester, Michael Lipinski, Michelle Mather, Joanne Moynahan, Donna Natowich, Deborah O'Brien, Anne Marie O'Reilly, Jessica Redman, Sherry Sajdak, Donna Scanlon, Jan Schott, Karen Schweitzer, Alissa Sheinbach, Mary Signet, Geri Smith, Susan Smith, and Nora Toney.

I regret the space limitations that prevent inclusion of all the teachers' papers in this book and its companion volume, *What's happening in math class?, Volume 1: Envisioning new practices through teacher narratives*. Together, the two contain the words of fewer than half the project's participants, but all are represented in spirit—all 48 contributed to the discussions about teaching, learning, mathematics, and writing that formed the backdrop of this work; all offered thoughtful responses to their colleagues' writings; and each helped in the creation of a space safe enough to allow risk taking and encouraging enough to support serious, time-consuming effort.

Once the papers were completed, the feedback I received from pre- and in-service education students at other institutions helped me to see how these writings could be used in a variety of settings. Many thanks to Cathy Fosnot, Lynn Hart, Ron Narode, and their students.

Deborah Ball, Virginia Bastable, Lynn Goldsmith, and Marty Simon helped me think through the organization and presentation of this body of work. The essays written by Deborah Ball, Ruth Heaton, Steve Lerman, and Susan Jo Russell add a significant dimension.

Thanks to Sarah Biondello, Brian Ellerbeck, and Karl Nyberg, editors at Teachers College Press.

And more than thanks to Alan Schiffmann, who has applied his heart and intelligence to the development of ideas presented in this book, as well as to the sustenance of its editor.

Introduction: Reconstructing Professional Identities

Deborah Schifter

> In the last four years I have begun to question just what it means to be an effective teacher. I have discovered that my students, who appeared to be successful, were often lacking insight and true understanding of the very concepts that I thought they had . . . learned. This realization caused me to question what it means to teach for understanding. (Gagnon, 1993, p. 1)

Out of a convergence between changing social needs and two decades of research in cognitive psychology, a new vision of mathematics instruction has emerged in the United States. In contrast to the traditional classroom, in which a teacher broadcasts material that her students then rehearse individually, the proposed pedagogy emphasizes students working together—posing questions, formulating conjectures, discussing the validity of various solutions—while the teacher, guided by close analysis of her students' thinking, frames appropriate problem-solving contexts for them, facilitates discussion of their mathematical ideas, and steers them toward confrontation with important conceptual issues (Mathematical Association of America, 1991; National Council of Teachers of Mathematics, 1989, 1991, 1995; National Research Council, 1989, 1990).

Clearly, the kind of change implied in this contrast cannot be merely, or even primarily, a matter of introducing new instructional techniques—cooperative learning, say, or the use of manipulatives or computers; nor can it be this plus a "teacher-proof" curriculum designed by "experts" for transmission to students. Instead, the new mathematics pedagogy—whose vision is paralleled by analogous movements for reform in writing and reading, science instruction, social studies, and art (Cobb, 1994; Lord, 1994; National Council for the Social Studies Task Force, 1993; National Research Council, 1994)—can be enacted only if teachers construct for themselves practices appropriate to its principles.

In posing some of the questions he and his colleagues face as they work at new ways of being mathematics teachers, high school department chair Allen Gagnon testifies that this process is neither simple nor straightforward.

1

I have come to realize that my old view of teaching (presenting the material in a clear and concise manner) was too narrow in scope and did not take into consideration how learning takes place. As I struggle to gain insights into how my students learn, my teaching changes. . . .

In considering how to teach, there are many questions that must be answered. What is learning? How does learning occur? What is the role of the teacher in the learning process? What is the role of the student in the learning process? How do I assess what my students understand and how do I use what I learn to provide them with experiences that allow them to advance those understandings? What are my obligations to all my students, including the best and the so-called "worst"? Where does the need to follow the "curriculum" fit into the puzzle?

These questions are a source of great concern to me. If I am going to continue to feel effective in the classroom, then these issues must be given both thought and action. Reflection has become a powerful tool in my daily attempts to bring about a metamorphosis in my teaching. Yet, in reflection on these questions, other concerns surface. Should students work regularly in groups? Do they need to be active in the exploration of math concepts? Should they be encouraged to develop problem-solving strategies? Do I need a better understanding of the mathematics I am attempting to teach? Am I required to make better connections between the ideas and concepts I deal with? Where is the time to accomplish all of this going to come from?

How do I prevent all of these issues and questions from overwhelming me and making me ineffective? My head spins when I try to think of all the things I need to consider. (Gagnon, 1993, pp. 1–2)

PROFESSIONAL IDENTITIES AND THE CHALLENGES OF REFORM

In this book, nine teachers tell stories of change. At a point, earlier or later in their careers, the authors of these stories were offered a glimpse of a way of teaching mathematics consistent with the ideals that drew them into the profession and some help in making that way of teaching their own. But if the common premise of their stories is the struggle to construct new practices, as these teacher-authors tell us about their experiences—sharing with us thoughts, feelings, and insights; frustrations, failures, and successes—these stories equally become narratives of changing professional identity.

Or, more precisely, "identities" in the plural—for these teachers enact multiple identities: as mathematical thinkers, as managers of classroom process, as monitors of their students' learning, as colleagues, and as members of the wider education community. "Identities" in this sense—more a matter of what one does than who one thinks one is—are constructed in and realized through practices. And it is in this sense that new practices imply transformed practitioners: creative rather than rote and limited mathematical thinkers; facilitators of students' mathematical thinking and discussion, instead of conveyors of computational routine; inquirers into children's mathematical constructions, instead of talliers of right and wrong answers (these three addressed in this introduction); members of collegial "communities of inquiry" into issues of instruction, rather than isolated candidates for burnout; producers and disseminators of knowledge about learning and teaching, not just consumers and objects of the research of others (these last two the theme of the conclusion).

As mathematical thinkers

While mathematics teachers are necessarily mathematical thinkers, far too many, especially at the elementary level, have an impoverished grasp of disciplinary content and modes of thought. Formed in the very classrooms they are being asked to change, they endured mathematics then, and relay it now, as a sequence of fact and unmotivated computational routine, rather than as an historically dynamic body of ideas that they and their students can explore, analyze, and debate. How can teachers who dread mathematics learn to reason mathematically—to follow an argument and assess its validity—so that they can track their students' thinking and, by skillful questioning, help them deepen their understandings? And how can such teachers become sufficiently confident of the mathematical terrain—its connections among concepts, their representations, and the various contexts in which they may be embedded—to select tasks that are grounded in what students already know but still give them access to new ideas? Indeed—and, for achieving these goals, crucially—how can teachers learn to use, and be helped to use, their mathematics instruction as a site for their own ongoing development as mathematical thinkers?

As managers of classroom process

In a traditional mathematics classroom, the teacher faces her students, who watch and listen as she broadcasts the day's algorithmic routine, posing questions to see if they are following her explanations, and repeating them if they are not. Then, having assigned a series of repetitive exercises to fix the routine in memory, she checks answers to establish that the point of the lesson has been understood (that is, that the routine has been accurately memorized), before moving on to the next topic.

In the classroom centered on student thinking and discussion—the classroom envisioned by mathematics education reformers—the children regularly disperse into small groups where they work together on problems, while the teacher visits around the classroom listening for significant mathematical issues and considering what types of intervention, if any, are appropriate. And when the children reassemble to compare their ideas and solutions, her questions facilitate discussion. How do teachers learn to manage the logistics of, and how do they and their students learn to redefine and assume responsibility for, a classroom process so much more complex and so dramatically different from the one they were socialized into? And, as they learn to do these things, how is their experience of the source and nature of mathematical authority transformed? In the traditional classroom, mathematical authority is felt to come from elsewhere—the text, the brain of the expert, or, ultimately, perhaps a heaven of timeless truths only awaiting discovery—and to be inarguable; the answer matches the one at the back of the book or beyond the clouds, or it's wrong. How, in the new mathematics classroom, can teacher and students acting together construct and sustain a discourse rigorous and powerful enough to bear that authority in itself?

As monitors of student learning

Central to the new mathematics pedagogy is the principle that students working to understand a concept bring to its interpretation a body of ideas—theories, beliefs, images—deriving from their personal histories. As a corollary of this principle, it follows that that body of ideas endows students' mathematical constructions—even when wildly unsound—with a kind of sense. If teachers are to facilitate student construction of richer mathematical understandings, they must learn to make sense of their students' sense-making. Monitoring student learning thus can no longer be a matter of checking to see whether students have "received" and "retained" what they have been shown and told, but demands sustained inquiry into their thinking. Now teachers must ask themselves: What are the grounds of my students' constructions? What traces of logical process can be identified in the thoughts they express?

In order to begin to hear their students' ideas, teachers must break deeply rooted habits of listening for answers. How do they learn to suspend judgments of correctness long enough to be able to explore student reasoning? And how do teachers learn to adjust their own lesson planning and moment-to-moment decision making in order to follow up those ideas?

*   *   *

In issuing these challenges to the professional identities of teachers of mathematics, the reform process denies a pervasive assumption of extant school culture—that experienced, competent teachers have by and large finished learning and know all that they need to: From their own years of schooling they derive the requisite knowledge of the discipline; from preservice courses, their lesson-planning strategies; and from their student teaching and first year or two in their classrooms, the skills needed to manage day-to-day routine, monitor student learning, and deal with parents and administrators. As the example of countless teachers, veterans like Allen Gagnon as well as relative novices, demonstrates, acceptance of that assumption does not preclude teachers' working hard at their mathematics instruction. But an algorithm-based instruction whose goal for students is accurate recall of computational procedures does not produce in its practitioners *the need* to continue learning. By contrast, the practitioner centering mathematics instruction on student thinking must continue to develop as mathematical thinker—making new mathematical connections as he or she engages students in exploration and discussion; as manager of classroom process—inventing new ways to leverage students' powers of reasoning as he or she is confronted with their surprising notions; and as monitor of student learning—discovering new aspects of children's mathematical thought.

As practitioners of the new mathematics pedagogy successfully negotiate the traumas of initial dramatic shifts, what questions move to the heart of their teaching? What goals are appropriate to an instruction that can never become routine?

NARRATIVES OF CHANGING PROFESSIONAL IDENTITIES

Although the stories told in this book are personal and each is unique, teachers whose histories are grounded in similar traditions of mathematics instruction—both as students and now as teachers—are likely to face similar challenges to their professional identities as they embark on the process of transforming their instruction. Thus, these narratives from the mathematics education reform movement offer some coordinates to those about to venture into unfamiliar territory. They enumerate starting points: authors' own experiences as mathematics students, their sense of dissatisfaction as mathematics teachers, and their desire to change the way they teach. They indicate directions: a determination to engage their students in problem solving, to listen to their students' mathematical ideas, to learn and understand mathematics for themselves. They identify way stations, recognizable achievements: when students become so excited by a mathematics problem they don't want to stop, when one student's mathematical insight builds on another student's ideas, or when the teacher achieves mathematical insight for herself. And they describe the many obstacles encountered along the way.

These papers represent nine of the 49 narratives produced in an experimental project designed to support teachers' writing about their own mathematics instruction. The project was conducted by SummerMath for Teachers, an in-service program for teachers of mathematics, grades kindergarten through 12, located at Mount Holyoke College in South Hadley, MA (Schifter & Fosnot, 1993). Each year for three years (1990–1993), 14 to 19 teachers who previously had attended at least one SummerMath for Teachers offering were invited to become teacher-writers in a one-semester course. Some participants had been working with SummerMath for Teachers for as long as seven years; others had attended an introductory course the previous summer and were just now beginning to work through what it means to enact practices based on a constructivist view of learning.

To help frame the nine teachers' papers presented here, I have solicited essays from four teacher educators, each of whom was asked to read two, and in one case, three, of these papers and to comment on a theme of my choosing which the narratives exemplify in common. Thus, this book assigns the 9 narratives, plus the essays, to four chapters, each organized around challenges to teachers' professional identities posed by the new mathematics pedagogy.

Chapter 1 invites the reader to consider two personal histories of mathematics mis-education for the issues they raise concerning how teachers committed to the reforms can develop as mathematical thinkers equal to their new ambitions for their mathematics instruction. In Chapter 2, a pair of vivid accounts of the difficulties of establishing a classroom process centered on student thinking and discussion provide context for exploring the sorts of new authority teachers must take on in order to teach this way. For Chapter 3, the theme of learning to listen for the sense in students' mathematical constructions frames a trio of narratives—two by veteran teachers—that register their authors' excitement at discovering that children have mathematical ideas. Finally, two narratives by teachers who have weathered the difficulties of the initial shifts supply the pretext for the question posed by Chapter 4: what kind of practitioner emerges from these processes of professional transformation?

In this book's companion volume, *What's happening in math class?, Volume 1: Envisioning new practices through teacher narratives* (Schifter, 1996), which contains an additional 13 narratives produced in the same project, the emphasis shifts from the struggle to become a new kind of practitioner to explorations of aspects of the new mathematics instruction. Issuing from the conviction that what is needed at this stage of the reform process is a wealth of images that can provide grounding for discussion of the meaning of its rhetoric, the book offers interpretations of such rhetorical motifs as "facilitating students' construction of their own mathematical understandings," "students becoming powerful mathematical thinkers," "mathematics classrooms as communities of inquiry," and "teaching mathematics to *all* students." These interpretations touch on such issues as implications for instruction of constructivist perspectives on learning, concerns about the mathematics content brought to the classroom, strategies for introducing students with traditional expectations for instruction to a new classroom culture, the challenge—and possibility—of reaching all students, and the role of novel instructional techniques and technologies in support of mathematical inquiry.

The narratives contained in this volume span grades kindergarten through 6. Some of the classes described have been grouped by ability; others are heterogeneous. Most of the authors teach in public schools.

The papers reflect the demographics of western Massachusetts. Mount Holyoke College, the sponsor of the project, is located in South Hadley, a college town with a sizable working-class population. Close by are Amherst and Northampton, also homes to well-known colleges. Just south of South Hadley is Holyoke, a small city with many of the problems endemic to this country's depressed urban centers. Until mid-century, Holyoke was a thriving mill town, but it has since suffered continuing economic decline. The school population is about 70% Hispanic, mainly immigrants from Puerto Rico, and 30% Anglo. The surrounding hills are dotted with small towns, each containing only one or two elementary schools. One author, who drove across the state each week to participate in the project, resides and teaches in Roxbury, a predominantly African-American section of Boston.

Characteristic of all the papers is their specificity. Most include explicit descriptions of classroom events, including dialogue. Teachers used various strategies to capture dialogue—some tape-recorded their mathematics lessons; others took notes during class, transcribing them later; still others reconstructed discussions after the school day ended. Most writers tried to provide depictions as true to the events as possible; a few chose to create composite characters or composite classes in order to protect the anonymity of their students. All student names are pseudonyms.

The stories teachers tell contradict the assumption that competent teachers already know how to teach; the message they convey is that learning is never complete. And by voicing their rejection of that assumption, they break through the isolation so characteristic of the culture of teaching. Some readers will feel reassured that they are not alone with their confusions and doubts. Others may learn how to support teachers as they work to fashion professional identities adequate to the new mathematics pedagogy.

REFERENCES

Cobb, N. (Ed.). (1994). *The future of education: Perspectives on national standards in America.* New York: College Entrance Examination Board.

Gagnon, A. (1993). Struggling. Unpublished paper.

Lord, B. (1994). Teachers' professional development: Critical colleagueship and the role of professional communities. In N. Cobb (Ed.), *The future of education: Perspectives on national standards in America* (pp. 175–204). New York: College Entrance Examination Board.

Mathematical Association of America. (1991). *A call for change: Recommendations for the mathematical preparation of teachers.* Washington, DC: Author.

National Council for the Social Studies Task Force. (1993). *Curriculum standards for the social studies.* Draft. Washington, DC: Author.

National Council of Teachers of Mathematics. (1989). *Curriculum and evaluation standards for school mathematics.* Reston, VA: Author.

National Council of Teachers of Mathematics. (1991). *Professional standards for teaching mathematics.* Reston, VA: Author.

National Council of Teachers of Mathematics. (1995). *Assessment standards for school mathematics.* Reston, VA: Author.

National Research Council. (1989). *Everybody counts: A report to the nation on the future of mathematics education.* Washington, DC: National Academy Press.

National Research Council. (1990). *Reshaping school mathematics: A framework for curriculum.* Washington, DC: National Academy Press.

National Research Council. (1994). *National science education standards*. Draft. Washington, DC: National Academy Press.

Schifter, D. (Ed.). (1996). *What's happening in math class?, Volume 1: Envisioning new practices through teacher narratives*. New York: Teachers College Press.

Schifter, D., & Fosnot, C. T. (1993). *Reconstructing mathematics education: Stories of teachers meeting the challenge of reform*. New York: Teachers College Press.

CHAPTER 1

As Mathematical Thinkers: Confronting One's Own Mathematics Mis-Education

What must teachers learn in order to enact the new mathematics pedagogy? As the reform movement addresses this question, we dare not ignore what teachers have already learned—and not just about the doing and teaching of mathematics—as products of the very education they are now being asked to transform. In narratives that describe how they were schooled into becoming fearful and incompetent mathematical thinkers, Lisa Yaffee and Nora Toney vividly show us why we cannot ignore their experiences as mathematics students. Yaffee, who grew up in the suburbs of Boston, MA, looks back from the perspective of a fifth/sixth-grade classroom in a college town. Toney comes from a predominantly African-American section of Boston; at the time this chapter was written, she was teaching fourth grade in the school system she had attended as a child.

In a teacher development setting that encouraged them to locate their capacities for mathematical thought, freeing those capacities necessarily entailed overcoming their histories of mathematics mis-education. And as they learned to exercise their new powers, their own elementary classrooms became available to them as sites for learning the mathematics they needed in order to teach their students mathematics for understanding.

Deborah Loewenberg Ball's concluding essay registers how all too commonly teachers' own mathematics education demeans their capacity for mathematical thought. While soberly assessing the challenge such histories pose for the reform effort, Ball is able to draw hopeful lessons from Yaffee's and To-ney's progress in reconstructing their identities as mathematics thinkers.

+   −   ×   ÷

PICTURES AT AN EXHIBITION: A MATHPHOBIC CONFRONTS FEAR, LOATHING, COSMIC DREAD, AND THIRTY YEARS OF MATH EDUCATION

Lisa Yaffee

The new math arrived at our suburban Boston elementary school one sixth-grade afternoon in 1963. Mr. Brimm, the long, lean, impeccably clad principal, strode forcefully into our class that Friday, just 15 minutes before the end of the day. He had in tow two white men who looked very much like him, both in suits and ties: "the G-Men" we dubbed them, mostly because they carried matching black attaché cases. It turned out that they were MIT professors who had invented something called School Mathematics Study Groups (SMSG), which they were piloting in our school. They told us that SMSG would be really fun and would completely change the way we thought about mathematics. They waved a fat, xeroxed manuscript at us to punctuate their enthusiasm. They were sending home permission slips, and they hoped every child would fill one out and return it to school.

On Monday the G-Men were back, each breezing in with a pile of xe-roxed manuscripts under his arm. I was scared. Mr. Baker asked us to give the aliens our attention. We did so and one of the men read a list of names. The Chosen were bidden to rise and to bring a sharpened pencil. I thought about driving this projectile through the right frontal lobe of my brain, but in-stead walked carefully with my back straight, head high, and eyes forward as I was sure Marie Antoinette had done in her hour of truth. We followed the men down the polished wooden hall to Miss Edgeberg's class. Her kids were out at recess, where I desperately wished I could be. In this small group of what I thought were very smart kids and in the presence of two MIT profes-sors, who were supposed to be smarter than most other types of professors, my shameful stupidity would be discovered. Although I knew I was dumb in math, I really didn't want anyone else to know. My credibility as sixth-grade class president would be completely shot.

I have no idea how long the first session lasted. The subject was set nota-tion and Venn diagrams. We were told to open our xeroxed books (this was novelty enough, since most of us had never seen a xeroxed anything before) to the first page. Leslie Ross read the definition of a set that appeared in print before us. It said something like, "A set is a group of related objects."

"Does everyone understand?" one of the G-Men asked us.

Everyone claimed to. I didn't. "Do you mean like brothers and sisters?" I asked fearfully.

"Yes!" he shouted. I couldn't figure out why he sounded so happy. "Or dogs and cats and elephants, or the set of foreign cars . . . "

"Or the set of states in the U.S.!" the other one added. "Or the set of classrooms in this building. . . . "

I was getting more and more confused. What did this litany have to do with mathematics?

We then went on to drawing sets inside of circles and to writing U's and upside-down U's to denote sets united or intersected. I could do all of this without a problem, but wondered why we were doing it at all.

At the end of the period, we were praised for catching on so quickly. The taller man with the crew cut and thick glasses asked if anyone had any questions. Without even thinking, I said that I had one. "Why are we doing this?" I asked. "What does it have to do with math?"

The question fell like a dead thing into the quietly breathing room. The G-Man narrowed his eyes and stared at me. Bringing his head down to my level, he peered right into my face and countered, "Why do you think?" His tone implied my inanity. A couple of my classmates tittered. I had no idea, but I knew when I had been humiliated in public. The tears sprung, and I jumped up and walked out. "Wait a minute, girl, come back here!" The tone was urgent.

"She's crying," Leticia Plock was happy to point out. I ran as fast as I could to the girls' bathroom. I can't remember who came in after me.

In a couple of weeks the G-Men vanished and we were expected to work in our SMSG books, with support from our classroom teacher. Someone began calling the program "Some Mathematician Sure Goofed" and the name caught on. Mr. Baker even called it that. Gradually our SMSG time eroded from five days a week, to three, to one, and then slid noiselessly into oblivion with our other post-Sputnik attempts to compete with Soviet superiority in math and science. I was delighted to see it go.

What replaced it was team teaching with Miss Stahl, who had been my fifth-grade math teacher, and life regained its comfortable tedium. Change classes, walk down the hall toting math text, ruler, pencil, eraser. Sit at your borrowed desk in its place in the row (denoted by masking tape brackets on the floor), write out your heading (name, grade, school, date) in cursive, fold your newsprint paper into eight boxes and copy the problems from the board, one into each box. Raise your hand when you finish. Miss Stahl would come to correct your work, and if you were unlucky enough to finish early, you would get to rework in public, on the board, a problem you got. Old Gerta was careful not to put me up there more often than anyone else, but whenever she was looking for the only student in 22 who got problem 10 wrong, it would be me.

I received my first Cs in eighth-grade math, where we were lumbering amidst the ill-defined precincts of pre-algebra. My teacher was young, elegant, and funny, the opposite of Miss Stahl. She cracked sophisticated, oblique jokes about sex and dating, and made fun of our eighth-grade traumas while making it clear that she experienced the same problems in her own life. We adored her. She was the first "girl," as opposed to female battle ax, that I had ever met who was good in math. I know she considered me hopeless, but she never held it against me. She would stay after school on Wednesdays to help Leda Farmer and me. I couldn't bear to tell her that I didn't understand her explanations, because I knew she would blame herself instead of my stupidity. I worked really hard and pulled a B for my final grade, but didn't have a clue as to the nature of what we were studying. I wondered about it, and also about why it was important for eighth graders to be able to solve for the unknown, but the biggest unknown of all was how negative numbers related to me, personally. At this point in my math career, however, I knew better than to ask.

Ninth grade was another story entirely. Fat Zak, as we referred to the instructor, was a nasty, abusive man who hated his job and kids our age. He spent most of our class time locking horns with the two smartest boys in an attempt to unman them. Every student in the room was aware that this power struggle was going on, but we were all afraid of him. He yelled at people, and at one point actually threw chalk at Ron Ash's face when Ron was looking out the window instead of at the board. The putative subject of this class was Algebra I, where the universal goal was to remain unnoticed and thereby to avoid the wrath of Fat Zak. Since he was unit leader, a kind of subadministrator responsible for running one of the nine "houses" at our high school of 3,000, he handed out in-school suspensions liberally. I never got one, but I was berated for being a "dimwit." He thought he was expressing fondness for me.

In this course I got Cs and Ds with an occasional F. I refused to stay for extra help after the first time, when Fat Zak sat at his desk, his right hand propping up his ample jowls, his left hand drumming on the table impatiently while he stared out the window and waited for me to complete the example he assigned. When I got it wrong, he asked what my problem was. Wayne Yastemsky's courageous, "You are an asshole," was still ringing in my ears from that morning's class, but I bit my tongue. I wanted to go to college and couldn't afford a three-day suspension. I admitted meekly that I didn't understand what algebra was. I knew it was about patterns, but I couldn't see any structure or logic to them, I told him.

"Whadya wanna understand it for? Just do it!" he bellowed, rising from his chair. It was clear that after-school help was over. I never went back.

It was at this point that I dropped from honors-level math to "A-level," which was described to my mother by the school guidance counselor as the section for kids who would never get into a so-called "good" college. I was not allowed to change teachers, just to compete with "dumber" kids. The daily routine was to take out our homework, trade papers, and go around the room calling out the answers on the page in front of us, to which Fat Zak would grunt, "Right" or "Go to the board." If compelled to approach the board, we were supposed to copy the solution, as written, and to explain why we thought the person had gotten it wrong. Then we had to name the idiot whose paper we held, at which point Fat Zak would scribble something in his grade book. After that we would go on to "new material," the presentation of which would be read from the text. Then Fat Zak would do on the board the example that was already done for us in the book and ask if anyone had any questions. Nobody ever did.

Since math was the class right after lunch, it didn't take us long to decide who we were going to trade answers with in advance and to compare papers as soon as we had bolted our food. It was unusual for two people to get the same problem wrong, but it did happen occasionally. In order to keep the teacher from getting suspicious, we agreed to leave a few problems wrong on our own homework papers, but to make sure we had copies of the correct solution to each problem on scrap paper when we went to the board, so we wouldn't affect anyone else's grade. Zak never noticed the number of times people would claim to be copying a solution off someone's paper, only to have that person get the problem marked wrong on their homework when the papers were passed back the next day. We knew we were being dishonest, but no one felt guilty. It was clear that Zak didn't care if or what we were learning. We soon came not to care either.

In tenth grade, the wind shifted again. We studied geometry with a now-and-happening first-year teacher. It didn't matter to us that Mr. Grazzi talked like "dis dhere." We were intrigued by the fact that he wore a slicked-back, fifties, West-Side-Story-type hairdo, even though it was *totally* uncool to do so in 1969, and by his equally alluring fake pocket handkerchief, a well-starched, three-pronged cloth butterfly stapled to a bit of cardboard, which he filed in the left breast pocket of his navy blue polyester suit.

I can't go so far as to admit that geometry was fun, but it was comprehensible. There were pictures you could follow when the explanations were too abstract, and you could argue about the answers. In fact, the answers implied argument, since whether or not a proof was valid depended a lot on how you stated it. I was good with words and was a fairly logical thinker, so for the first time in my life I found myself doing well in a math class. I didn't feel like an impostor. I felt that I understood, pretty much, what was going on. Finally, I had math under control. It was wonderful!

Eleventh grade meant Algebra II and Trigonometry, which for me was the beginning of the end. My teacher was nice enough, although he had a very sarcastic sense of humor. You could tell that he enjoyed kids and really liked being a high school math teacher. He tried to make class fun. He even tried to explain things so that Leda Farmer and I would understand them, but he couldn't. When I asked questions about the polynomial expressions swimming across the page, Mr. C would look at me like I was deranged. Then he would sort of peruse my face to see if I was being a wise guy. I wasn't. I really wanted to know what those expressions meant. Were they describing the speed of light or the trajectory of a headlight beam as it hurtled through space? I knew it had something to do with relationships and with change, at least when we were filling in functions charts. Why couldn't anyone tell me what algebra was about? I needed to know in order to want to learn it. I could catch occasional glimpses of the connections between algebra and the regular math I knew, but whenever I would try to exploit these parallels, I was discouraged from doing so.

The most stunning example of this was when Mr. C announced that there was a problem in the textbook he had been unable to solve. "If anyone can show me how to do this problem, I'll give them an A for the term." He then laboriously copied a very complex polynomial onto the board. We were supposed to simplify it, if I recall correctly. The class sat intently studying what he had written. In 30 seconds I saw the solution. My hand shot into the air. "YOU!!?" Mr. C intoned. "I don't believe it."

I jumped out of my seat and almost ran to the board. "It's easy!" I could hear my joyous voice proclaim. "Just take the square root of the whole thing and factor out the 12." I worked deft magic with the chalk and sat back down.

Mr. C stared at the board in stunned silence. Scarface Dave the Rave, our smartest classmate, eyeballed my solution. "That's it, Mr. C. Good work, Yaffee. You finally get an A in math!" I laughed delightedly.

"How did you see that?" Mr. C asked incredulously.

"Well, I just used what I remembered about fractions. Whenever you reduce one, you factor something out. I couldn't see anything to factor immediately, so I tried taking the square root. The rest was obvious."

Mr. C seemed angry. "Well, I can't give you an A," he told me in front of the whole class. "You don't deserve it. You are a C/D student." I could feel my face fall and fought for control of the tears.

"But that was an A moment," David protested. "You're not going to act like other teachers, are you Mr. C?"

"Turn to page 367," was the grim response. I got a C— as usual that term, and the heart went out of me. I worked as hard as I could, flunked at least half the tests, but got a B− on the midterm and so ended the year with a C+. I vowed never to take another math class again.

This pledge was fulfilled when I enrolled in a college that had no math requirement. There, I ducked gleefully all pursuits remotely numerical, including conventional math, the lab sciences, economics, statistics, and computer studies. This left me with limited options, but I was pleased, having disposed of mathematics completely, antiseptically, and painlessly. No more suffering. (No more future.)

Seven years later, I found myself in graduate school and subjected to a math course once again. This one wasn't too objectionable. It was taught by a spacy but maternal woman, and was designed for aspiring teachers of grades K–2. This was fine with me. I had a great time predicting how many seeds would be inside a given fruit and then hacking it up to see. I enjoyed finding six ways to count kids in the room, or petals on a daisy. We measured our desks in pinkies, in Kleenex, in forearms, in coke bottles. We tried to calculate the number of sleeping teachers that would fill the classroom. We graphed everything. It was exciting and sensible, but there was something missing. I couldn't quite tell what it was.

The next snapshot was taken two years later, at a high school for emotionally disturbed teens. As an assistant in the math room, I mostly taught rote procedures for using various fifth- and sixth-grade algorithms to kids as old as 22. It was depressing to see how little I had to give them. What I did have were a bunch of recipes, the formulae of my youth, which I had memorized but never understood. Whenever I had asked for explanations there weren't any, and this time was no exception. The head math teacher had no idea why taking a fraction of something meant to multiply it, when the physical reality indicated by such a problem was obviously division, but for the first time I heard a math teacher say, "Gee, I don't know. What a good question. I never thought of it before." All of a sudden, not knowing seemed like something positive, or at least hopeful. To not know meant that you could think about it some, play with it. To not know meant that you had permission to explore and to argue, which meant you *could* know. It was a turning point, but I was still totally clueless as to how to teach math. I was equally clueless about how to learn math, and I wasn't sure that the two issues were related.

Five years after that I stumbled into the least likely of all scenarios, my own classroom! Imagine my surprise, nay HORROR, when I realized on the second day of school (not a moment sooner, mind you) that I would be expected to teach mathematics to 22 fifth and sixth graders who were much smarter than I was in every way. Mathphobia—fear, loathing, nausea, clammy palms, rank odors, cold sweat pouring off the brow—these were familiar and therefore comfortable sensations compared with what I felt at that moment of epiphany. What was I going to do? I didn't know the first thing about math, or about teaching, for that matter. How was I going to figure out what each kid already knew? What about the kids who couldn't speak English, or the kids with learning problems who were mainstreamed into my classroom? WHAT ABOUT FRACTIONS?! They were the centerpiece of the fifth/sixth-grade curriculum, and an ancient talisman of my incompetence as a math student.

When in doubt, take action. I sat down abruptly in the middle of my classroom floor, put my head between my knees, and took several deep breaths to fight back the waves of panic breaking over me. Then I rose courageously and walked briskly down the hall.

"Hey, Ingrid!" I called into room 145, "does this school have any math textbooks?"

"Sure, check the closet across the hall from your room," said the lady with the dazzling smile. "The purple one's fifth grade and the brown is sixth. Are you okay?"

"Yeah, I am now," I told her staunchly. At least I had a place to start.

Several weeks later, it was time for math.

"Oh gawd, do we have to do math?"

"Math is stupid. Ya never use it for anything."

"It's so boring to just work out of the book every day."

"You hate it and we hate it, so why do it?"

"I like it," objected Max in a squeaky, little-boy, embarrassed-but-proud tone of voice. "I'm in the seventh-grade book and it makes me feel secure when I get all the answers right."

"Oh shut up!" retorted David. "Your mom's a math professor anyway. Of course you're gonna like it."

"Look, we live in a math-based society," I listened to myself telling them. "If you intend to participate in a way that allows you to control your life and make your own decisions, you're going to have to know math. If you permit yourself to become a math bozo, you will foreclose your options and give other people the power to tell you what career you can pursue or what job you can hold."

But I heard my kids, I really did, and I knew that I was failing them. They were at risk and it was my fault. If I had taken math more seriously and tried harder to like it as a student myself, then I wouldn't be imparting my own hatred of the subject to the next generation. I felt angry, guilty, and devastated. How could anyone have allowed me into a classroom to perpetrate the same math crimes of which I had been a victim? Why weren't psychological tests given to prospective teachers to find out what kind of damage, witting or otherwise, they could inflict on kids? To make matters worse, it was only the third week of October. The year would be a long one, and the kids were already bored and restless. In desperation, I signed up for a workshop entitled "Making Math Learning Stick." If this Ellen Davidson woman and the teachers from our system could stick it to me without getting it stuck in my craw, then maybe I would be able to do something constructive for my students.

As the workshop date approached, I began to get nervous. Would I be able to admit to my peers the enormity of the atrocities committed? After all, it wasn't just that I couldn't teach math; I didn't understand it either, and yet I had been arrogant enough to suppose that this didn't matter, that I could be a "teacher" anyway. I felt miserable but put it aside. It was too late to listen to such affective clatter. It was time to focus on mathematics.

What happened over the course of the next five Thursday afternoons is a bit of a blur, but I remember walking into a school cafeteria and seeing piles of junk on the tables. Some of it looked familiar. We had built "trains" out of Cuisenaire rods in grad school ("And for this you get credit?" my mother gaped incredulously), but I had never seen unifix cubes or base-10 blocks before. The atmosphere was enthusiastic and inviting. There was food. People were talking and actually listening to each other. They sounded happy. Someone came over to talk to me. I wasn't scared anymore. I tried to figure out why but couldn't. Then I noticed coincidentally that there were no men in the room and found that strange. I had never been involved in a unisex math class before. I wondered if that was why I felt "safe."

After the hubbub died we were shown a videotape of a sixth-grade boy in the process of trying to solve word problems on a board. We were told that he was an A$-$ student in an excellent public school system in New York State. As the boy worked a fraction problem, Marty Simon, then director of the SummerMath for Teachers Program at Mount Holyoke College, interviewed him about what he was doing and why. The boy was floundering. He made several false starts and couldn't verbalize why he chose to multiply. He kept saying he couldn't *remember* why multiplication was appropriate in this context. Finally he gave up on that problem and asked for another. "I used to know how to do that one," he told Marty.

There was silence when the VCR was switched off. Since no one volunteered a response after Ellen waited for one, she began to ask questions. "What was this boy's problem? What did he know about math? What did he need to know in order to solve the problem assigned?" I couldn't think about that. The boy in the video was me at his age, and every single kid in my math class. I wondered why I couldn't bring myself to say it. I wondered if anyone else had felt a flash of recognition.

The discussion adjourned to a problem-solving session in which we were given problems like, "Gertie's job was to mow ¾ of the lawn. If she does ⅔ of her job now and ⅛ of it after she takes a lemonade break, how much will she have to do after dinner?" We were supposed to solve these problems as a group and be able to defend our solutions using manipulatives.

It was interesting to watch what happened. Everyone began working independently. Some people wrote equations on their paper, others grabbed some blocks and started building. I didn't know what to do, so I asked meekly, "Aren't we supposed to work together?" A couple of people looked up and replied, "Yeah, you're right." The other half of our group ignored us and continued working on their own. "Why doesn't someone read the problem?" one woman suggested. I did so, gladly. It would be the only contribution I could make to the group.

When we were called back to the circle, I was shocked to see that (a) 45 minutes had passed, (b) we had two answers that seemed right, (c) we couldn't prove either one of them, although both had their selling points, (d) we were delighted with ourselves and felt that we had accomplished a lot, and (e) we had been having fun! Although I felt kind of stupid a couple of times while we were thrashing the problem around in the group, so did the other group members. Instead of an isolating experience, feeling dumb had brought us together and had forged a group resolve to carry on rather than to give up. It was affirming to be confused, not negating, and this was an educational first for me. What did it mean?

The other four sessions were much like the first. We would begin by using manipulatives to solve word problems in a small group, then would gather to verbalize what we had learned. In the last session we were allowed to ask questions of the presenters. I wanted to know what these teachers' classrooms looked like at math time. All of them said the same thing, and it blew me away.

"They look just like this one."

"You mean, no textbook?"

"No textbook."

"The kids work in groups?"

"Most of the time."

"Where do you get all the word problems?"

(A big smile here.) "We make them up."

"You what? How do you find the time?"

(Shrug.) "There are some commercial ones available that are pretty good: the Lane County Problem Solving in Mathematics series and other Dale Seymour publications. The Middle School Math Education Project has some good ones, but mostly we make them up."

"How do you know if a problem is good?"

Ellen responded, "Let's talk after class."

The implications of all this were horrifying. I knew now what had to be done, but didn't know how to do it. Worse than that, I didn't think I could do it. I was a first-year teacher in a school system that chewed them up and spit them back bloodied and quivering. I was struggling, without a set curriculum, with how to teach writing, reading, health, social studies, science, and study skills to a combined-grade, mainstreamed group. I couldn't give up the math text. I was already splayed and splattered. But, I realized suddenly, I could introduce a "Problem of the Day" with which to begin each class. After the kids solved and talked about it, they could go back to working in their books.

The next day I threw the first problem at my students. It was one of those where you have a given number of species, heads, and legs, and you have to find out how many of each kind of animal there are. I read the problem out loud to the group, trying to suppress my excitement.

"A farmer has some hens and some rabbits. Zeb counts 50 heads and 140 feet among them. How many rabbits and how many hens does the farmer have?"

Then I looked up. No one cracked a facial expression or said a word. I could feel the gloomy tension in the air. Finally Max asked quietly, "Why do we have to do this?"

Taken aback, I sputtered, "Well, I thought it would be fun for a change. Everyone is always complaining about how boring math class is, and about how they hate to work out of the book. Here's a chance to do a problem where the answer isn't obvious, nor is the procedure for finding the answer. I thought maybe you could work with a partner or with a bunch of friends and come up with some answers. Then maybe we could figure out as a group which one is right."

"Don't you already know the answer?" demanded a skeptical Amber.

"Well, I have one answer, but I'm not really sure if it's right," I replied, truthfully.

Jeff snorted his contempt. "Some teacher!"

David, who was a classroom leader, had been quiet till then. "I think we should give this a chance. Yaffee's trying to be a better math teacher and she needs our support. I'm going to do this problem, even though it looks pretty hard. I think most of you are too afraid to try. Go ahead and be wimps, if you want to, but anyone who wants to be in my group, let's meet on the floor."

"Thanks, Dave," I nodded. "Anyone who wants to be in my group can meet at the back table."

"Do we have to work in groups?" asked Jake. "I usually do better on my own."

"No, do what you like. Let's meet in 15 minutes."

After a few moments of quiet discussion, the room erupted into a blur of sound and motion. Arms were gesturing, fists were pounding tables, kids were trying to shout each other down.

"I need some drawing paper," one boy came over to inform me.

"You know where it is. Go get some."

"Can I use the board?" came another request.

"By all means."

Back in my group I could hear Erica moan, "But I don't even know where to begin!"

"In my other school the teacher used to say, 'Figure out what the problem is asking you to do. Then figure out what you already know,'" Noah offered.

"That's sound advice," I agreed.

"Okay," began Amber. "You know there are 50 animals because that's how many heads there are."

"Oh, yeah," smiled Erica. "You also know that some of the animals have two legs and others have four."

"No you don't," countered Noah. "My dog only has three legs. He got hit by a car and one had to be amputated."

"How can he run?" someone wanted to know. The discussion whirled around and around. The 15 minutes were up immediately.

"Does anyone need more time?" I asked.

"No amount of time would help me," Jake admitted. He hadn't gotten very far by himself, but everyone else was ready. We all met in a circle, where arms were flailing and kids were calling out.

"Can we go first?"

"No, *we* want to!"

"Yeah, but we finished first, so we should get to talk first."

"This isn't a race," someone parroted me neatly.

"Let's just go around the circle," I suggested. "Mike, why don't you start."

The five groups came up with four different answers. We had just enough time to present and explain all of them before the period ended.

"Aw, do we have to stop?" Noah whined.

"Can we finish the discussion tomorrow?" David wanted to know.

"Yeah, I want to see if I'm right," admitted Max.

"Sure," I replied.

"Erica's cheating!" Peter called out.

"No, I'm not." Erica glared at him. "I'm copying down *all* of the answers and as much of the explanations as I can remember. I want to think about this tonight at home. Also, tomorrow it will be easier to figure out where we left off."

"Thanks, Erica. That's a great idea. Anyone who wants to take this problem home tonight and think about it, or talk it over with parents and sibs, go right ahead. That's not cheating; you might learn something."

The kids were now looking forward to math every day. I had ordered some books from Dale Seymour (P.O. Box 10888, Palo Alto, CA 94303) and was assigning a problem to kick off each class. As the students felt more confident and became proficient, this part of the class ended quickly, and we went back to working in our textbooks for the rest of the period. It took only a couple of weeks for them to begin groaning every time we had to turn from problem-solving to the text.

"Can't we do those problems all the time?" asked Jake. "That's real mathematics, you know—all that pain in the brain. Mathematicians don't sit around and play with numbers. They let computers do that for them.''

Naturally, he was right, and I thought back to that math workshop in which teachers told me they used no texts. For a few moments I fantasized about what it would feel like to be one of those teachers, then I picked up the telephone and called Mount Holyoke College, where they had a program for People Like Me.

''My students are at risk in mathematics!'' I blurted into the receiver to the unsuspecting soul who answered.

''Oh. Uh, does this mean you'd like us to send you some information about SummerMath for Teachers?''

''Yes!'' I revealed gratefully. I was already blathering. Many teachers had told me that the course was intense and demanding. These were not welcome adjectives for a math course, in my experience. There was other bad news. Students had to keep a daily journal in which they responded to everything that happened to them (kind of like psychotherapy with no one listening, I remember thinking). They had to take dance and tennis, but worse even than that was the fact that we would have to write two papers in a two-week period. About what, I wondered? How do you write papers about math?

Ellen Davidson, Deborah Schifter, Jim Hammerman, and Paula Hooper were beaming at us, their arms full of boxes. Uh-oh, it wouldn't be pretty. I knew that much by my second SummerMath day. Our instructions were to meet with our predesignated group and to calculate how many boxes of a chosen rectangular size it would take to fill the irregularly shaped, many-alcoved room we were sitting in. As a dyslexic, this project was my idea of hell. There was no way to simplify it that made sense, I realized, looking around for floor tiles you could measure in box faces or geometric patterns on the walls. Of course you could always lop off the alcoves and guess how many of *them* would fit in the main body of the room, then calculate the latter's capacity in Kleenex or cereal boxes, but for some reason that didn't seem fair. I hadn't learned yet that you could define math problems, like all of life's other little dilemmas, any way you wanted to. I still felt that Teacher Knows Best and that she or he alone understands what I was supposed to get out of this experience. In other words, I didn't have enough control over mathematics or confidence in my own learning process to realize that this activity was designed to be a classic pain in the brain of the kind Jake had described, and that I, in fact, was supposed to take control of the situation and make it manageable! What a revelation that was when I wrote about it in my journal later on. How stupid I felt not to have noticed this all along. Naturally, any time I used math-related procedures in real life (building bookcases, bouncing checks, praying I had enough gas to make it to the next exit), I modeled, simplified, estimated, guessed. Why had I been so hesitant to use these techniques in a place where you were supposed to practice them? Mostly, I surmised sheepishly, because

I hadn't realized that these were math skills. How completely embarrassing. I knew now that I would have no trouble writing math papers. Mathematics was a lot bigger than I thought it was.

My first SummerMath experience was exhausting. For two weeks we had been bombarded with alien stimuli and thrown into chaos. The megaproblems (like the one in which we filled the room with empty boxes—what better metaphor for previous math education experiences than that?) were so big and ill-formed that we didn't know where to begin or if we had finished. Then there were the nonroutine word problems that seemed vaguely familiar but frustrating because the void algebraic poetry of our collective youth did not apply. Next there was Logo, which was totally new. It required a much more structured type of thinking than I was used to, and there was no context from which to make sense out of the procedures. We were also thrown the Xmanian challenge in which we had to devise a number system and be able to operate in it for the digits A, B, C, D, and 0. It was horrifying to discover that as adults we couldn't do paper-and-pencil, four-place subtraction with zeroes and borrowing in Base AO. Was it appropriate to expect second or third graders to do the same in a base just as alien to them?

At the end of the first week I wrote:

> This week I learned what it feels like to be a pre-operational and concrete-operational kid contending with formal-operational expectations.
> It's hard, frustrating, overwhelming, infuriating, demeaning, terrifying, and depressing. A cursory glance at this list of adjectives suggests that learning is FOR SURE an affective process. . . . Support systems are extremely important. Learners can feel smarter in a small group situation, where an individual's idea is more likely to be noticed and appreciated, than in the larger fray. This is especially important for girls, who have been socialized to be less aggressive and self-confident than boys. It's up to the teacher to create an affective climate in which learning can happen for EVERY student, but how to pull this off is another issue.

When you get right down to it, this is the only issue as far as public education is concerned, and as our society becomes increasingly diverse, creating an environment that feels positive for all students is critical to our harmonious survival. It was, by now, August 12 or so. I would have about three weeks for ponderings—moral, metaphysical, pedagogical, political, and mathematical. By September 8, I would have to have a plan.

Luckily, there were some familiar faces. Three of the kids who were in my fifth-grade class reappeared as sixth graders. One of them was Jake, who had a pretty clear idea of what I was trying to accomplish. The other two were divergent thinkers who routinely came up with simple and elegant solutions to the most complex problems. Among the new students were six very smart girls, only one of whom was willing to challenge the boys, and an intimidating, dominating boy with a laser wit, ever ready to put the rest of us down. Scattered amidst them were six ESL kids, four from mainland China who had an astonishing grasp of math algorithms but who didn't understand math concepts very well and who were just learning English, and five children with diagnosed severe learning and writing problems. All of them were very bright. Only six claimed to like mathematics.

After giving the students a textbook placement exam to find out what they knew, and concluding that the test told me nothing, I manufactured a worksheet that had some computation problems involving basic operations. I wanted to have the kids solve the problems on the worksheet in groups using base-10 blocks, but I knew that most of them had never used the blocks before. We needed some kind of introductory activity first, so I arbitrarily decided to build a block city. Each group had to construct a building, name and label it, and know how many units were in it. When they were finished with the structure they would tour the city, determine how many units were in each edifice, and figure out how to record this information. Then we would argue about the answers and about what we might have learned.

At no point do I remember making a conscious decision to throw the textbook away. I knew it had to be done. In fact, I had known that for a whole year before I just kind of did it spontaneously. As things turned out, the students had such a good time building their city and inventing sensible ways to count and keep track of huge numbers that all of the year's activities just evolved naturally from that first experience. Once we figured out what base-10 blocks were, we used them to determine what addition, subtraction, multiplication, and division are. I spent weekends writing "problem sets" consisting of 15 or so multistep word problems about the children themselves, their habits, and their obsessions. Deborah Schifter, who was providing follow-up from the SummerMath program for me, would come to observe once a week and would throw in some wonderful challenges like, "Can anyone figure out how to subtract from left to right instead of the way we usually do it?" These questions would keep us going for days and would lead to some interesting subsidiary discussions. For example, "Why DO we subtract from right to left? Whenever we do a subtraction problem with the blocks, it's natural to start with the big numbers, the thousands, first. Why do you teach us to do it backwards in school?"

We worked on basic operations until November, by which time one student could dump a pile of blocks in the middle of the floor and arrange them a bit, and the other students could write a word problem that this arrangement posed. I gave the kids a conventional test, with a couple of appended essay questions, and they did fine. The next order of business was fractions. I had no idea where to begin. I tried to think of a way we could use base-10 blocks as a bridge to learning fractions, but their three-dimensionality might prove confusing to some of the students, I thought, and it seemed much too early to deal with the issue of relative wholes, which is implied by the blocks' uniformity of scale. What I mean by this is that before the kids even got a chance to understand that $\frac{1}{4} < \frac{1}{2}$, they would have to confront the fact that a unit, a rod, and a flat can all equal $\frac{1}{10}$. This idea seemed unavoidable, pretty abstract, and potentially confusing if examined before other, more basic concepts could be explored.

When I turned to Deborah for help, she suggested that the kids make their own manipulatives. We had a healthy supply of oak tag, so we measured and cut it into fraction bars. The children voted that a whole would be $18'' \times 3''$ and the teachers decided that students would need to make two wholes, four halves, three thirds, four fourths, five fifths, six sixths, eight eighths, nine ninths, ten tenths, and twelve twelfths. Sevenths and elevenths were optional.

What came out of this exercise was fascinating. For starters, about half of the fifth and sixth graders didn't know how to use a ruler. After we got past that hurdle, it became clear that even though we had done some background activities (folding and cutting paper, working with towers made of unifix cubes and trains made of Cuisenaire rods, coloring in shapes on graph paper, writing fractions, talking about what the top and bottom numbers in a fraction mean, etc.), most kids still didn't understand what a fraction was. When dividing an 18-inch whole into fifths, for example, the children would come up with five 3-inch sections and would then have a chunk left on the end. I'd look at the results and say, "Gee, you have six pieces there. How can that be fifths?" The kids would shrug and wait for me to tell them what to do. I'd walk away. Finally someone came up with the idea of dividing the leftover piece into fifths too, and then tacking one of those fifths onto each of the original three-inch segments. Lia eventually realized that if she had simply divided 18 inches by 5 to begin with, she would get $3\frac{3}{5}$ inches, which is how big each fifth would be. "Oh, my God!" she exclaimed as she hit herself on the head, staring at her fraction pieces, "that's what a remainder *is*, that little piece on the end you have to divvy up and deal out." The other kids looked at her quizzically, not really understanding the model she had just constructed for herself, but, of course, many of them had other things to worry about at that moment.

By the time these issues were resolved and the fraction bars were finished, most of the children had a pretty good idea of what equivalent fractions were, and all of them knew why the value of the fraction got smaller as the number in the denominator got larger. When we started playing games with the pieces, many of the students had moved, conceptually, well beyond what those activities could teach, but were perfectly willing to do them anyway, having found, as Stella put it, that "you never know when you're going to learn something amazing about something you already know." So we arranged the pieces in some kind of pattern and tried to guess what the governing rule was; and we had prizeless, unacknowledged contests to see who could come up with the most ways to combine their fraction bars so that they formed a whole. We discovered early that we had done such a sloppy job with measuring and cutting out the fragments that we couldn't rely on their physical accuracy, so we got into the habit, almost from the beginning, of writing an equation for everything we did. Even though most of the kids didn't know what a common denominator was, they could tell by looking at their pieces on the floor that $\frac{1}{4} + \frac{1}{8} + \frac{1}{8} + \frac{1}{2} = 1$. A few weeks later we would move to problem sets in which the answers didn't add up to a whole, and the students would have to find a way to understand what $\frac{1}{4} + \frac{1}{8} + \frac{1}{8}$ meant.

The final picture at this exhibition is formulating as we speak. Although it has been four years since I felt compelled to confront my endemic fear and hatred of mathematics, I am still sitting in class at Mount Holyoke every Thursday night and I am still writing word problems about my students every weekend. The math class I find myself in tonight has a shape much different from the ones depicted previously. It comes disguised as a writing workshop, and its purpose is to generate some descriptions of what math teaching and learning can be for people, younger or older. As the members of this class read and marvel at each other's work, Deborah points out that we are providing "windows" into the state of math education at this specific moment in the latter twentieth century. What amazes me is how different the view is through each, although the assumptions about what constitutes learning and teaching are pretty similar.

The larger picture is even more exciting to contemplate. It seems almost coincidental that the National Council of Teachers of Mathematics (NCTM) has recently come out with standards that affirm the ideas we have been struggling to implement in our quiet corner of west-central Massachusetts. We know that teachers all over the country and, in fact, all over the world have been working to create a meaningful context in which their students can learn and use powerfully the web of concepts that is mathematics. It's time for us to share what we've learned in the interest of promoting universal math equity and literacy. Everybody, not just the lucky few with "math minds," should be able to feel good about themselves as math problem solvers. No one should have to suffer the foreclosure of options engendered by not knowing how to think mathematically. Math is not arcane. Anyone can learn it. Anybody can teach it, too, but not until they confront the gaps in their own understanding.

For those of us who learned by the book, this process of confrontation might require throwing the textbook away and turning to our colleagues for help. We are all smarter as group members than we are as individuals, and right now the group of teachers interested in increasing the accessibility of mathematics to everyone is growing. Windows are being opened, admitting welcome blasts of fresh air. People are jumping out, leaving their 30-year-old flotation devices behind on the ledges. There is a lot of commotion down there. Swimmers thrash about, changing direction in midstream. Cries of "You're joking!" or "I can't believe I didn't see that before!" punctuate the harried sputterings. "What if the students can see I'm wrong?" "I don't want to start all over again." "Word problems? I always HATED word problems . . . " A few people, too few it would seem, are providing ballast for the rest of us as we deal with the torrential outpouring designed to help us meet the *Standards*. I say, look to your colleagues. We're the ones reinventing math education.

+   −   ×   ÷

FACING RACISM IN MATHEMATICS EDUCATION

Nora L. Toney

Racism is a virus. . . . And since nobody's really looking too hard for a cure it reproduces itself over and over again.

> Marita Golden, *And Do Remember Me* (1992)

I was one of those students who never really had a complete grasp of mathematics. I achieved superficial successes—I was able to earn above average grades in math all through my schooling (with the exception of Geometry and Algebra II)—but never realized continuity and growth in my mathematical understanding. This is a thought I have pondered over and over again for the past 25 years.

I now believe this lack of growth was due to the inadequate, inferior, and racist instruction I received from the underfunded, segregated, inner-city public school system I attended from kindergarten through ninth grade. When I try to visualize mathematics instruction during my elementary and middle school years, it is basically a blur—perhaps because of negative experiences that forced me to block math classes out of my memory.

However, I do recall reading stories from a worn and torn basal reader series about Dick, Jane, Sally, and Spot. I thought it strange to be reading stories, to which I could not personally relate, about white middle-class siblings and their trusty dog, stories that did not have themes similar to those of my own culture. Also, I wondered why there were only two African-American teachers in my school when 99% of the student body was African-American. I noticed that my elementary school building was 100-plus years old and renovation of the building was unheard of; basic maintenance was considered a luxury. I remember attending French class for the so-called brightest students in grades 3–6 in the school auditorium. Several broken window panes had been replaced with sheets of cardboard and at least three other classes were being conducted simultaneously. At first, I was excited by this special opportunity, but soon began to question the validity of learning a foreign language that seemed irrelevant in the wake of the growing population of Spanish-speaking people in my community and our country. As I look back now, all of these types of neglect seem like a form of racism.

In my school system, African-American children were punished for minor infractions by further limiting their already limited opportunities to learn. When I was in the fourth grade, two sixth-grade girls were placed in my class for several months as punishment for misbehaving. I felt sorry for these girls, because their mothers were unable to come to the school and grieve such punitive measures. Simply because these parents viewed themselves as powerless or were unaware of their rights as parents, they were not afforded a formal hearing or conference. Even at nine years old, I knew this punishment was harsh and unfair, and I also knew that my parents never would have tolerated any such treatment of their children. In fact, I wished that these girls had parents like mine—parents who would stand up for their child's rights and challenge arbitrary decisions.

Then, in the eighth grade, Mr. Freeley, my homeroom and history teacher, told my friends and me that we were a well-organized gang because we dared to question a curriculum that did not include the many contributions of African-Americans to our country's history. When several of our concerned mothers arrived at the school to question him about this statement, he told each of them that *her* child was not a part of the gang. We couldn't help but wonder who, then, constituted the gang.

I also remember when Mr. Freeley had my classmate, Donna, removed from the college prep program because her mother could not come to a parent–teacher conference and advocate on Donna's behalf. As a single parent and sole provider for her family, Donna's mother could not afford to take time off from work—she simply could not chance getting fired. Of course, I felt the pain and rage that Donna felt and shared this concern with my mother. We both surmised that because Donna's mother was unable to fight this injustice, Donna would remain in the lower track of instruction. Subsequently, Mr. Freeley did this to students as often as he was able to get away with it. Although Donna was bright and determined and vowed to achieve academic success no matter how many obstacles were placed in her way, my friends and I were not fooled by her hard demeanor and nonchalant attitude toward this injustice. We all knew that she was hurt and spiritually beaten down. In my opinion, Donna was never the same open and optimistic person she once had been. She was hardened by this experience and mistrustful of the authorities who represented the system.

I was a well-behaved child and did not suffer such setbacks. In fact, when I completed my minimal tasks, I was rewarded with the special privilege of running errands for the teacher. I thought going on errands for the teacher was great, until I mentioned this fact to my mother and her reaction was that of dismay and anger. She recognized that I was missing out on invaluable instructional time in the classroom. However, I, like the other African-American children, was not expected to learn. We were given few challenging academic learning activities. Nor were we allowed to work with ideas or issues that pertained to us and our lives.

By the end of eighth grade, the message was clear. The Boston public schools didn't care about what I, an African-American female, learned. They thought nothing of boring or abusing me and other students like me. Therefore, my parents decided to remove me from the Boston public schools and sent me to Worcester, MA, to live with my grandparents and attend school there. But I hated going to school in Worcester. I didn't have any friends; my new school was cold and unwelcoming; and I felt lost and alone. By the third day of class, I had broken out with huge red hives and I vowed to never go back. When my mother realized how unhappy I was, she relented and let me come back to Boston and attend one more year in the system. But my parents were disillusioned. They knew that I, along with my brothers and sister, was being shortchanged on a decent education. This eventually would limit my options for college and, consequently, for a career. As a result, when a new busing program gave my parents the opportunity to place me in a suburban high school ranked second in the country for providing students with an excellent education, they gladly did so.

The advantages of being exposed to an excellent school system were offset by the discriminatory practices directed at its students of color (whether intentional or not). We were referred to as "Metco students" instead of "Jefferson High students." We were placed in average- or low-achievement ability classes. Whenever there was an altercation involving students of color, we were blamed. Teacher expectations were low, and we were considered complainers and troublemakers. In fact, we simply spoke up about injustices and demanded to be taken seriously. Even though I usually received good grades, I was told by math teachers, directly and indirectly, that I did not need to know how to do math. Not a single one of my math teachers took the time to help me understand a concept.

I can remember, in tenth-grade geometry class, trying to make sense of an abstract explanation for a theorem. I raised my hand and told my teacher that I did not understand why the theorem worked the way it did. His response was to push his glasses up on his nose, shrug his shoulders, and repeat his previous explanation. His body language suggested that he had done his job by explaining the theorem and there was nothing more he could do. Needless to say, I never asked for clarification again.

The not-so-subtle message was, "I do not expect you to do well in mathematics. You are not intelligent enough, because you are a female and, worse, you are an African-American female and you do not count." I was outraged that individuals, supported by society's norms, could have such power to impose their will on my educational pursuits and my life. But, in fact, my experiences were and are shared by students of color throughout the country.

I was frustrated and discouraged, because I knew I had been cheated, and I also knew why. As difficult as it is to admit this, there were justifiable reasons, given the tracking system, for putting me with the low group. My inferior mathematics and science backgrounds were no match for my new school system's standards. But once I had been placed in the low group, teachers were not invested and had no interest in helping me move forward. If I showed interest, behaved myself, paid attention, attended class, passed in all of my homework assignments (even if they were incorrect)—in other words, if I didn't cause any problems—then I would receive a passing grade. I told myself that math didn't matter, but I knew it did. I wanted desperately to understand geometry, algebra, trigonometry, calculus, and statistics. I always wanted to know why a certain formula worked the way it did or what a theorem meant. I didn't want simply to accept a rule or procedure; I wanted to understand why we followed such steps. Although I was unable to obtain a level of mathematical understanding that satisfied me, I never gave up hope. I truly believed that as long as I applied myself and was taught in a way I could understand, I could achieve a reasonable level of success. And, more important, I believed in myself and held fast to my faith in myself.

These feelings of self-worth and my whole network of beliefs and values were formed through my experience of a strong support system. From the time I was a young child, I heard the echoing voices of my grandparents and parents saying, ''Get a good education. Always do your best no matter how great or small the task. Take pride in what you do. Be thankful for what you have. And remember to help those who are less fortunate than you.'' They gave me not only constant encouragement and reinforcement, but also love and understanding. So, no matter how much the world beat up on me or discouraged me, I always knew I could depend on my family for acceptance and affirmation. My support base included certain teachers (though never math teachers), extended family, ministers, church members, community workers, mentors, and friends.

Unfortunately, the encouragement, affirmation, and love that I received were still not enough to help me acquire the academic skills—particularly in mathematics—that I needed in order to grow educationally and professionally. In spite of my negative experiences with mathematics, I did quite well in other areas and a handful of teachers (particularly Mr. Johnson and Mr. Finn) in those disciplines supported me and my efforts to learn. At that point I rested on my laurels, dismissing my confusion and frustration with mathematics as insignificant and irrelevant.

Later on, during my undergraduate studies, then as a teacher and graduate student, I was blessed with meeting and forming relationships with professors and administrators who were caring and understanding. These individuals had open minds, held high expectations for my professional growth, and were extremely supportive in helping me to achieve my educational goals. Hence, I was able to successfully complete my undergraduate studies in early childhood education (which didn't require high-level math courses). Within a few months of graduating from college, I was working as a teacher in the system that I had once attended as a youngster and early adolescent.

Unfortunately, I found the salient aspects of racism to be more pervasive than ever. During my first year of teaching in Hyde Park, a Boston neighborhood, I took my class of white kindergarten students outside to play in the schoolyard. When we were ready to file back into the building, some white youths appeared on top of the roof. They yelled racial slurs at me and told me to go home and get out of their neighborhood. Then they threw beer bottles at me from the roof, almost hitting some of my students. We were all horrified by what happened, and as soon as I calmed my students down, I reported the incident to my principal. My principal's response to the incident was, "Do not take the children outside to play anymore."

During my second year in the system, I taught in a school in the West Roxbury section. Knowing that I was in my classroom working after school, white youths would hang out on the fire escape, banging on my door and yelling out racial remarks. Several times they spray-painted the door with "nigger." My principal's response to this was, "We all leave right after school around here; I suggest that you do the same."

During my fourth year teaching at a school in Roxbury, a white male coworker matter-of-factly referred to African-American and Hispanic children as "nothing but a bunch of animals who are pathological menaces to our society." Another colleague in the same building referred to a second-grade student as "amoral."

In contrast to these experiences, I did receive professional support from important individuals. Specifically, during my sixth year of teaching I acquired two important mentors. One was my principal, a caring and nurturing African-American female, who encouraged me to go to graduate school. The other was my professor and academic advisor, an Irish-American male, who held high expectations for me. I felt compelled to meet the challenge.

As my teaching career progressed, I was somewhat satisfied with my students' achievements and development—but only somewhat, because I felt that my mathematical understanding was lacking and that, therefore, my mathematics instruction was at best adequate. I sensed a need to improve my own mathematical understanding so I could better instruct my students.

When a new principal, a vibrant, energetic, resourceful, and visionary leader (an Hispanic/African-American), came to our school four years ago, he immediately encouraged teachers to participate in a variety of professional development courses—cooperative learning, math, science, whole language, computer technology, self-esteem, and so on. He implemented after-school projects and created a program for males placed at risk by our society's systemic racism. He organized a new computer lab to help improve student reading and math skills, purchased new textbooks, and mandated that all children achieve success in spite of the odds. Naturally, when he asked me to be a participant in a two-week summer math workshop, I consented. Basically, my reasons for doing so were that I respected and believed in my principal's vision for educational excellence for all students and that I knew my own mathematical understanding needed improvement. I hoped this workshop would help make my mathematics instruction more effective for my students.

As I sat attentively in a mathematics workshop on a pleasant summer day in mid-August, I sensed and experienced something totally different from anything I had known before. The 22 participants in the workshop were inner-city elementary public school teachers from the Boston area, most of whom had been teaching for 10 years or more. Fifteen were white; five, African-American; one, Hispanic-American; and one, Portuguese-American. All but three were female. It was a safe environment to learn in, and the atmosphere was open and inclusive. The focus of the workshop was to engage us actively in the process of learning math. It was apparent that the instructor believed in her ability to teach all students and, in return, expected all students to engage in the activities and learn.

She began by telling us a story about a faraway civilization called Xmania. The people there had a number system that was not very efficient. Therefore, a group of mathematicians were working diligently to try to develop a new system that was less problematic and more manageable. Finally, a certain mathematician designed a successful number system that used only the symbols 0, A, B, C, and D. In this system one could add, subtract, multiply, and divide. Also, one could represent any number, no matter how small or large. Before the mathematician could explain her new number system, she died. However, she did leave behind some Xmania blocks. The instructor then held up a small cube, a rod, a flat, and a large cube (all from a set of base-5 blocks) and explained that our task was to use the blocks to design an Xmanian number system based on the information given. There were no clues as to how to start.

We were divided into groups of four, and the instructor distributed the blocks. At times, all four of us worked together; other times, we worked with a partner or individually. We were not asked to follow a conventional procedure or formula, but rather we were encouraged to illustrate our ideas by constructing representations with the manipulatives. We thought out loud and discussed one another's ways of solving the problem. We wrote symbols and tables, and drew diagrams. We also were asked to develop a group chart to represent our Xmanian number system to the others. Then each group explained its chart, and the whole class discussed the various systems. I was able to see how some systems were more efficient than others, and I developed a new appreciation for the complexity and cleverness of our place-value system.

More important, perhaps, we were introduced to a new way of thinking about mathematics. This approach felt right to me. It was natural, liberating, and affirming. I found I was able to discover meaning and understanding in a more concrete way. Being asked to write in our journals on a daily basis allowed me to reflect on my thoughts and on our discussions and investigations. At the end of each week we wrote a synthesis paper about how our mathematical understanding was developing. All of these perspectives facilitated my learning process. For the first time in my life, I was experiencing success in learning mathematics. I found myself making mathematical connections that had been absent during my schooling. I discovered why we invert denominator and numerator when dividing fractions and why the size of the whole is so important in comparing fractions. I was motivated, challenged, and inspired by an insatiable desire to learn more and more about this new exploratory approach in mathematics education.

A logical question to pose at this point is, "Why did I experience success?" I realize now, although I didn't at the time, that this instructor was honoring my cultural learning style. What is a cultural learning style? Well, first of all, everyone has one, whether it be Eurocentric, African, Hispanic, Native American, Asian, or a combination of cultural backgrounds. A cultural learning style is simply what one is exposed to in the home setting, based on the family's ethnicity, which is usually passed on traditionally and socially from generation to generation. For instance, in my home, learning was fostered through rich family discussions and debates in which we analyzed various views and topics, balanced with quiet time for thinking and rethinking ideas. There was much activity—counting and classifying objects, baking, sculpting, drawing, making crafts, doing daily chores, and writing thank-you letters. We regularly perused family albums, and the older generation frequently recounted family history. We all engaged in storytelling, performed in talent shows, danced, sang, and played a variety of physical and mental games. We also solved problems using mental math and read silently on a daily basis. My mother constantly stressed the importance of us children helping one another and solving academic as well as life problems together. Also, much of the learning that took place in my home was in pairs (my brother and I, my older sister and brother), groups (all of the siblings problem solving to secure funds for holiday or birthday gifts for our parents), and the entire family pooling our thoughts and ideas together to solve problems that affected all of us.

In contrast, formal schooling consisted mainly of paper-and-pencil activities, sitting at a desk 90% of the day, listening as the teacher imparted her knowledge to us, or watching as skills were demonstrated at the board. A tranquil and rigid classroom atmosphere was valued, as was individual seatwork.

Students working in groups or with partners were considered cheating, and informal interactions between the teacher and students were taboo. I quickly learned the school culture and made the necessary adjustments, but for many of my peers this was a difficult task. They were unable to sit still, control their desire to speak out of turn, or refrain from interacting with peers and teachers. As a result, they were labeled children who "acted out" and were judged "culturally deprived" or "ineducable."

I realize that a teacher is responsible for being aware of the many different cultural learning styles of his or her students and must make an effort to understand and respect such styles. But my teachers and those of my siblings and friends perpetuated institutional racism through a lack of flexibility or acceptance of cultures other than the dominant one. I learned through painful experiences that racism doesn't have to be overtly about race, but rather can be about "attitude."

I was amazed that this instructor (white, Jewish, female) had challenged my intellectual framework while honoring my culturally defined African-American learning style. By structuring math activities in which I interacted with materials, moved around a lot, worked in pairs and in small and large groups, explored, tested, reasoned, argued about, and reflected independently, she set up a situation in which I learned particular mathematical ideas. She also created an atmosphere of inclusiveness. The irony of it all is that I was being challenged in *mathematics*, the realm where total success had never been mine before.

As the instructor posed questions about my ideas, those ideas (mine!) suddenly made sense. This exploratory approach to mathematics afforded me the opportunity to make pictorial, written, kinesthetic, auditory, interactive, verbal, and mental connections with concepts and ideas in mathematics. My individual learning style was encouraged and supported along with my personhood. I realized that the thinking process employed in exploring a problem was as important as finding the right answer. Also, my instructor possessed high expectations for all students. She did not equate cultural diversity with deprivation. In other words, just because I had a different cultural background did not mean that I had been deprived or that I could not learn.

Since I could see how this exploratory approach to mathematics honors different cultural learning styles, I wanted to implement it in my own classroom. I viewed this way of teaching mathematics for understanding as offering ALL students success. My new goals for teaching mathematics (and really all subjects) included providing investigative problem-solving opportunities that would allow students to identify many of their own strategies.

I teach in a medium-sized, inner-city public elementary school in Roxbury with a large Spanish-bilingual population. My school services more than 620 students and their families through Spanish-bilingual, monolingual, special education, and kindergarten programs. Also, we have a Parent Center that is coordinated by two dedicated individuals who are successfully increasing parental involvement in our school.

Within the monolingual program, I teach a self-contained fourth-grade class of 19 students in what my school system terms an advanced work class (AWC). Most people who are familiar with the program see it as tracking, providing at least some students with the best the system has to offer: foreign language and language arts enrichment programs, class size limited to 20 students, the same teacher for two years. Workshops and professional development opportunities are made available to AWC teachers. Most of the students in my classroom have the support of their families, have been exposed to many experiences, and are more focused and goal-oriented than most of their peers. I would not consider them advanced children, but rather intelligent children, with unlimited potential, who have a reliable and caring support system. My students represent families of mixed socioeconomic backgrounds (low, middle, and upper-middle income). Also, it is apparent that academic success is highly valued by all families.

Thus, I began the past school year reflecting on my own mathematical thinking and understanding, reconsidering the nature of mathematics, working to change my personal relationship to mathematics, and encouraging my students to do the same. I have tried to orchestrate activities that engage my students in mathematical thinking. I allow my children to pose their own questions and to follow them up in explorations. Overall, I am earnestly trying to teach mathematics for understanding.

I am also trying to honor, in a variety of learning situations, my students' culturally defined learning styles. I provide cultural, historical, and scientific field trips; a self-esteem component; and additional time for the arts, oral presentations, and group discussions, large and small. I incorporate contextualized material rooted in students' past and present experiences, which offers them a sense of familiarity and relatedness and allows for deeper understanding. This is no easy task, since the cultural composition of my classroom is diverse: nine African-Americans (from various ethnic groups), four Latinos (Puerto Rican and Venezuelan), one Asian (Korean), and five whites (from various ethnic groups). Five of my students were not born in the United States. There are 12 females and seven males. As guidelines, I try to incorporate the eight most common features of the African-American learning style, which I believe are useful for all children (compiled from the work of Shade, 1990, and Kuykendall, 1992).

1. Students learn best through observing and modeling the activity, not by being told what to do.
2. Learners have a high energy level and need a variety of tasks and much movement.
3. Learners function best if the material is contextualized; in other

words, the material must be rooted in and validate the students' experience, thus providing a relationship between curriculum and the familiar.

4. Learners process material kinesthetically (writing, physical games, role playing); visually (photographs, charts); auditorially (records, music); interactively (group discussion); and haptically (drawing, painting, sculpting). Print-oriented approaches (reading assignments) are also important.

5. Children prefer to demonstrate their knowledge in action rather than in traditional testing situations. They are always and foremost performers. Children enjoy showing what they know through oral presentations and oral exams, class projects, group assignments, singing, dancing, rapping, dramatic performances, verbal dueling, debating, and traditional oral storytelling. In fact, they seem to thrive in such a natural and challenging setting. Furthermore, culturally biased tests have never been able to measure or reflect the true ability of African-American students or other students of color.

6. Children are highly creative and imaginative, and demonstrate excellent physical coordination; this suggests that art and physical education must become integrated aspects of the cognitive curriculum, not just frills.

7. Children are vivacious, expressive, and excited by the prospect of engaging in verbal dueling, even with the teacher.

8. Children demonstrate a thinking style that might best label them as parallel processors and intuitive thinkers.

As a result of these efforts, it's gratifying to see that my students have progressed in their mathematical thinking since school began. Initially, they were impatient when they were expected to listen to each other's thinking and were interested only in seeing how fast they could find the correct answer. They were not accustomed to reflecting or writing in journals about their ideas, nor did they realize that they could pose their own questions for further exploration. Now I find that my students are earnestly searching to make sense of their past knowledge as they integrate new information into their mathematical-conceptual framework. All students are progressing in a reasonable manner at their own developmental rate. They are learning to respect their peers' mathematical thinking and are able to articulate their own ideas in more profound, mathematically sound, and thoughtful ways. I am encouraged by a student's reflection in her journal.

From listening to other people's answers, I learned how those people got their answers. I also learned other ways to solve a few problems. I like learning lots of other different ways to do things, so that I am not always doing things the way I do things. I don't want to always be stuck with the way I do things, because I think that later on in life, I will find that I will want to do things differently.

In conclusion, as I have examined my own learning experiences, I have discovered the ingredients necessary for me to learn and achieve success: high teacher expectation, fairness, inclusiveness, engaging contextualized material, constant monitoring and feedback, discussions/debates, and reflective writing. Generally speaking, I need numerous opportunities to connect my thinking and ideas to new concepts and ideas. These factors facilitated my *learning* of mathematics, so now I am trying to incorporate these same factors into *teaching* mathematics.

I believe that the current reforms in mathematics education can address the learning styles of many groups that historically have been excluded from mathematical pursuits. However, a focus on theories of learning and innovative teaching strategies will not be sufficient. Individuals must accept and deal with the fact that racism—systemic and individual—is alive and well in our country's educational system. If attention is not paid to it, the national mathematics education reform movement will become stagnant and ineffective.

REFERENCES

Golden, M. (1992). *And do remember me*. New York: Doubleday.

Kuykendall, C. (1992). *From rage to hope: Strategies for reclaiming black and Hispanic students*. Bloomington, IN: National Educational Service.

Shade, B. L. (1990, September). Engaging the battle for African American minds. A commissioned paper for the Charles Moody Research Institute.

CONNECTING TO MATHEMATICS AS PART OF LEARNING TO TEACH

Deborah Loewenberg Ball

Most teachers and teacher educators acknowledge that teaching mathematics for understanding depends on knowing mathematics well oneself (e.g., Wilson, Shulman, & Richert, 1987). Yet this is not common. That many elementary teachers' prior experiences have left them feeling inadequate, fearful, and uninterested in mathematics is widely recognized (Simon, 1993). Even secondary teachers who, on the whole, have been more successful in school mathematics, often have not developed deep understandings of mathematical ideas (Ball, 1990). Still, opportunities for teachers to learn mathematics are not central to most professional development activities. Somehow, habit in both teacher education and policy leads to proxies for understanding: coursework or tests. And attention is drawn away from what Lisa Yaffee and Nora Toney so poignantly show us: that teachers' histories with mathematics learning powerfully shape their sense of themselves as mathematical knowers as well as their dispositions toward the subject. Setting new requirements alone cannot ensure adequate attention to the need for teachers to connect with mathematics personally in order to help their students make connections.

Lisa Yaffee and Nora Toney provide us with two vivid stories that illustrate the depth of feeling embedded in what teachers bring to learning to teach mathematics. Toney has crafted a potent account of growing up African-American and female in schools that do not serve either students of color or girls well. Writing with conviction, she boldly describes what it was like to experience school as the "Other." Schooled on reading books that portrayed the lives of white middle-class children, Toney soon grew furiously aware of the hollow nature of the American commitment to democracy and opportunity for all children. Her school building was decaying, the curriculum seemed distant and meaningless, and her teachers did not seem to care what she or her classmates learned. When her geometry teacher did not offer Toney an explanation she asked for, the message she heard was, "I do not expect you to do well in mathematics. You are not intelligent enough, because you are a female and, worse, you are an African-American female and you do not count." Although Toney had support and encouragement from family and friends, the messages of school were louder; for lack of reasoned instruction, she graduated without mathematical understandings and skills that later proved to be crucial to her ability to create for her students the kind of classroom that she envisioned.

Yaffee shares with Toney the experience of mathematics instruction that denied her capacity and, eventually, her capability. Unlike Toney, however, Yaffee's theme is less explicitly grounded in who she is. Her story points at who her teachers were: people who could not or would not help her make sense and who sometimes ridiculed both her requests to do so and Yaffee herself. When Mr. C, her Algebra II teacher, exclaims, "YOU?!! I don't believe it!" at her sudden flash of mathematical insight, and then berates her as a C/D student in front of the rest of the class, Yaffee resolves to take no more math. Made to feel incapable, like Toney, her career choices were consequently circumscribed, closing paths that required mathematical study. Like Toney, she coped with this in part by deciding that mathematics was useless. But her experience had scarred her nonetheless. And, later, when she became a teacher, she felt as helpless as did Toney, worrying about the mathematical legacy she would bequeath her students.

Both teachers, as participants in the SummerMath for Teachers program, engaged in mathematical activity in ways that enabled them to reconstruct their sense of themselves as knowers (Schifter & Fosnot, 1993; Simon & Schifter, 1991). Program leaders presented challenging problems and encouraged the teachers to work together, and to draw flexibly on what made sense to them. Toney writes about the powerful sense she had that the instructor believed in her, and Yaffee recalls the climate that supported her as she gradually began to take risks. Toney and Yaffee both emphasize the feelings of support and safety, of being encouraged to draw much more broadly on their own resources, of feeling affirmed as competent. For both authors, the opportunity to learn mathematics in ways that felt more natural was, in Toney's terms, "liberating." They felt successful in mathematics for the first time. This experience of success fostered the confidence they needed to begin changing their approach to teaching mathematics. The experience also gave them images of a pedagogy of mathematics that could engage and support all students in being successful.

Understanding the histories that teachers bring to their learning and their practice is crucial to creating worthwhile opportunities for teacher learning. And learning is at the heart of making change (Heaton, 1994). The visions for improving mathematics education are ambitious and complicated: to help all students develop mathematical skill, learn to work flexibly, understand mathematical ideas, and engage in mathematical discourse within a classroom community in which diverse perspectives and modes of expression are respected (National Council of Teachers of Mathematics, 1989, 1991). Creating a practice toward these ends is an uncertain and challenging task and not merely a matter of implementation (Ball, 1991; Cohen, McLaughlin, & Talbert, 1993; Lampert, 1985). It is all the harder given the gap between this vision and teachers' own experiences in school. Ironically, the challenge to realize this vision rests with teachers, themselves products of the very system the current reforms seek to change (Cohen & Ball, 1990).

Fervently committed to changing school mathematics, both Yaffee and Toney found themselves caught in a tangle of frustration that thwarted their efforts. When their students complained about the uselessness and boredom of math, or demanded to understand, neither teacher was equipped to respond. Yaffee felt guilty when she saw herself knowing how to do little else than what she had experienced. Toney, too, felt unprepared to help her students really understand. Simply recognizing the inadequacy of the instruction they had received, however, was not sufficient to support these teachers' efforts to do better for their own students. To do more would require returning to mathematics themselves, to rebuild their sense of themselves as mathematical knowers and to make connections to mathematics as an arena of ideas and human activity. Toney and Yaffee show us how essential this odyssey is to the agenda of change. Their stories also raise issues that are crucial to the venture. I take up three: subject matter learning and teacher education, the role of curriculum, and who teachers are and the agenda for change.

SUBJECT MATTER LEARNING: DIFFICULT CHOICES IN TEACHER EDUCATION

Yaffee and Toney came through school without crucial understandings of mathematics. Although both sought to learn, their efforts to make sense were rebuffed. Consequently, they rejected mathematics and came to view themselves as uninterested in and poor at math. And Yaffee and Toney are not alone; most elementary teachers have had similar histories with school mathematics. With secondary teachers, the challenge is shaped by the fact that although they, too, often lack conceptual understanding, they feel more competent and also more complacent. If teacher educators aim to prepare teachers who can teach mathematics for understanding, they must create opportunities for teachers to build connections with mathematics, not just as teachers but as knowers themselves. What does this entail?

Toney and Yaffee both describe their experiences learning mathematics as participants in the SummerMath for Teachers Program. What stands out in their accounts? Yaffee describes the work as "hard, frustrating, overwhelming, infuriating, demeaning, terrifying, and depressing." She felt inept. But, encouraged by the instructors to work with her peers, Yaffee tackled word problems, invented a new number system, and sought to figure out how many boxes it would take to fill the room. She speculated that working in a small group helped her to overcome her feelings of inadequacy. "Learning is FOR SURE an affective process," she reflected in her journal. Toney, involved in similar experiences, recounts how she felt successful in mathematics for the first time in her life: "I discovered why we invert denominator and numerator when dividing fractions and why the size of the whole is so important in comparing fractions." Most of all, the experience showed her what it could mean to affirm a variety of "cultural learning styles"—ways of knowing embedded in different cultures. Discussion and debate with others, independent journal reflection, and working with concrete materials—all these afforded her opportunities as a learner that meshed well with her own style. They affirmed who she was as a person and made it possible for her to feel smart.

What Yaffee and Toney seem to have learned, however, highlights a dilemma for teacher educators. On one hand, teachers need opportunities to delve into some mathematics in depth, to engage in mathematical reasoning and problem solving, to compare and validate alternative solutions and methods, and—as Toney and Yaffee report—to experience a mathematical learning environment. On the other hand, this need is in tension with the need to explore with their students the vast territory of mathematics for which teachers are responsible. Cheated out of a rich mathematics education, teachers need opportunities to explore fractions *and* integers, probability *and* geometry, algebra *and* number theory. There is a lot of mathematics that they must help their students learn. So teacher educators face a dilemma familiar to teachers everywhere, a dilemma between depth and coverage.

Beyond this issue of scope lies a second tension: one of respect and integrity. Yaffee and Toney make clear how important it was to them to feel validated as mathematical thinkers. The value placed on diverse ways of knowing is lauded particularly by Toney, who writes compellingly about the need for schools to honor different cultural learning styles. Clearly, for both Toney and Yaffee to build connections with mathematics, this feeling of being respected was crucial. Still, not all ways of thinking are mathematically valid. Ideas that are sensible and imaginative may nonetheless not work mathematically. Treating teachers with respect means attending to the integrity of the mathematics in which they engage. Valuing multiple ways of knowing is not enough if it leads to solutions that are reasonable but do not hold up to mathematical scrutiny. How to respect learners' ideas and ways of thinking while attending also to the integrity of what they are learning is another familiar dilemma of teaching.

What did Yaffee and Toney learn from the mathematical experiences they had in SummerMath and where are they headed with that learning? Their accounts suggest that they developed a profound appreciation for a learning environment that would support students' intellectual activity. Although they mention the mathematics problems they explored, the feeling of the experience seemed more important. After years of feeling inadequate, they felt validated as mathematical thinkers. Reconstructing who they were as mathematical knowers, they discovered that they could learn and enjoy mathematics. And this inspired both teachers to reconstruct how they engaged their students in mathematics. Midstream in their efforts to make change, they do not, however, offer glimpses of the challenges they face with mathematics beyond what they explored in SummerMath for Teachers. Do they feel prepared to help their students learn other topics meaningfully? Does Yaffee feel that she is more able to answer, "Why do we have to do this?" Does Toney ever find herself perplexed about whether a student's idea is mathematically sound? I am curious as to what is going well and what is difficult. Building on the foundation that their experiences at SummerMath for Teachers provided, what is the current trajectory of the authors' subject-matter learning?

THE ROLE OF CURRICULUM IN TEACHING MATHEMATICS FOR UNDERSTANDING

Dilemmas of subject-matter learning in teacher education imply that teachers will need to go on learning mathematics over time. An important question is how that learning can be supported. In addition to further professional development, curriculum materials may offer opportunities for learning content. Yet it seems that such materials are often marginal in teachers' efforts to teach for understanding. New to her school and grade level, Yaffee was relieved to find the math textbooks; they gave her a place to start. Yet, through a mathematics workshop, she encountered and was attracted to an image of teaching in which teachers did not use textbooks. Similarly, Toney strives to use problems situated in contexts that matter to students as the medium of learning. She also seeks to use their own questions and problems. At this point, it seems that, although they may draw on supplementary materials, neither teacher uses a textbook to teach mathematics. Is an opportunity being missed? What role can curriculum materials play in helping teachers learn— and helping their students learn—mathematics?

In order to design materials, curriculum developers steep themselves in mathematical ideas and explore multiple approaches through which those ideas might be encountered. The materials they create can offer teachers access to a greater breadth and depth of connections and meanings. In the explanations they write, both content and pedagogy can be explained. It would seem, as a result, that curriculum materials could serve as a rich site for ongoing teacher learning. Furthermore, providing curricular guidance could help to ensure that students encounter key mathematical ideas and ways of thinking.

Still, it is not clear whether most curriculum is written with teacher learning as a goal. Perhaps most curriculum developers have their eye on students rather than on teachers. To what extent do they aim to help teachers learn mathematics through the materials they write? Moreover, if a key element of the kind of teaching to which Yaffee and Toney aspire is responsiveness to students' ideas, can curriculum materials adequately anticipate students' mathematics? Perhaps this kind of teaching cannot, by definition, be guided in the abstract.

Yaffee offers an example: When she asked her students to divide an 18-inch strip into fifths, many would cut five 3-inch sections and have a sixth 3-inch section left over. Crucial was her response: "Gee, you have six pieces there. How can that be fifths?" Yaffee had to know a great deal in order to create and use this problem. Among several key elements was the particular choice of numbers: She needed to predict that $18 \div 5$ might challenge her students and that they might solve it by cutting six pieces. She needed to be able to invent a response to this solution that could push them to confront the concept of "fifths." Could curriculum materials have helped her to do this?

Questions about the role of curriculum materials go beyond their value to the teacher. What becomes of students whose teachers, engaged in new learning, bypass crucial ideas while delving into less central ones? One role that curriculum materials might play is to serve as maps of the territory of learning. Navigating the vast expanses of mathematics is no small challenge.

Where, for example, on some map of the curriculum does the problem 18 ÷ 5 lie? What is the next good problem? What mathematics are students having opportunities to explore? How do opportunities become realities—that is, *do* students connect division and fractions through this cutting problem?

As teachers build their own understandings and relationships with mathematics, they chart new mathematical courses with their students. Whether and how curriculum materials can be designed to support teachers' exploration of mathematics—their own and their students'—is a question worth fresh consideration. Given the expanse of mathematics to be learned, and the multiple ways in which it can be explored, creating materials that offer alternative paths and that also signal key ideas could provide both opportunities for learning and curricular guidance for teachers. Such materials might also offer insights into how students might think about particular ideas, preparing teachers to hear and to respond more effectively. Curriculum materials might be designed to support both teachers' and students' learning, and could, once again, be seen as important tools in trying to teach well. (For examples of such efforts, see such current NSF-funded curriculum projects as Education Development Center, in press; Lappan, Fitzgerald, & Phillips, in press; TERC, 1994; Wagreich, in press.)

IMPLICATIONS OF WHO TEACHERS ARE AND WHAT THEIR EXPERIENCES WITH MATHEMATICS HAVE BEEN

I would like to step back from the ostensible questions about subject matter and curriculum, and return to the authors themselves. In many ways, what is most powerful about their writing is what they help us see about who they are and what that means for their learning, their practice, and the agenda for change. From the outside, much is the same about these two stories: two women teachers who, on reflection, recount school experiences that stripped their sense of themselves as mathematical knowers and left them with a profound distaste for and disconnection from mathematics. Their stories make plain that the choice of teaching was made more convenient because that choice did not involve any further mathematical study. Both encountered problems as teachers, for they wanted to teach mathematics in ways that respected their students as thinkers and yet they found that they lacked resources to do this. Theirs are histories that underscore the need for teacher education to take seriously what teachers bring to learning to teach (Ball, 1988). Teachers like Toney and Yaffee need opportunities to explore mathematics, to reconstruct their views of themselves as mathematical knowers, and to develop the resources they need to teach for understanding.

That Toney and Yaffee construct their stories as differently as they do is worth contemplating, however. Toney situates her account within a larger picture of a racist system of schooling of which the mathematics instruction she describes is but one part. This system comprises a pedagogy and a curriculum made from and for the white middle class. In telling her story, Toney writes out of her identity as an African-American woman. In school being black and female shaped what she encountered and took away with her; now it shapes her retrospective account of her mathematics experience as well as her ambitions as a teacher. Yaffee's story is more pointedly a focused critique of mathematics education. She writes with a critical—at times, sardonic—perspective on the men who were her mathematics teachers. Beginning with the professors who brought the seemingly pointless "new math" into her sixth-grade classroom and continuing through Mr. C, who, in eleventh grade, considered her mathematically hopeless, Yaffee's teachers consistently rebuffed her efforts to understand. Yaffee stops short of questioning their qualities and qualifications, conveying instead the frustration that marked her relationship to mathematics.

Toney's experiences are framed by the lack of worth and respect that she felt in school, by the messages school communicated to her. Her ambitions as a teacher are, in turn, framed by her drive to make schools places that work responsively and responsibly for all students, particularly students of color. Mathematics is part of this agenda, but it is not its whole. For Yaffee, a lack of worth was communicated, but it seems to have been localized to mathematics. In turn, her aim seems specific to mathematics and the improvement of mathematics instruction, although there are a few subtle hints that she is particularly concerned about girls.

These two stories highlight questions about the role of gender and race in teachers' personal experiences with mathematics in school. While Toney makes race and culture an explicit issue, gender remains largely implicit across the two stories. Toney comments that she was aware of being African-American *and* female when her teachers made her feel marginal; Yaffee notes the absence of men in the math workshop she attended and wonders how that may have contributed to the "safe" nature of the environment. Although neither teacher makes gender the central issue, the stories pulsate with it. Would a parallel set of men's accounts of their math classes and teachers so predictably reveal feelings of worthlessness? Of being made to feel dumb? Of seeking reason and explanation and being waved off time and time again? That an overwhelming majority of elementary teachers are female makes gender crucial to understanding the challenges of teacher learning and of teachers making changes in mathematics education. Yet, oddly, the burgeoning literature on feminist pedagogy, on women and mathematics, and on girls' experiences of school, is rarely linked to issues of mathematics *teacher* education. How race and class interact with gender issues in the context of mathematics teacher learning is also vital, for, as Toney's story underscores, the experiences of women of color are not identical to those of white women.

If we are to take seriously teachers' personal histories, we need to understand the economic, cultural, political, social, and personal factors that combine to shape those histories, in and out of school. Without such understanding, we are likely to treat symptoms rather than causes. Ultimately, working to change schooling requires a deeper understanding of the society in which schools are embedded and of the school experiences in which teachers have been immersed. It is one thing to create experiences that respond to what individual teachers bring: to help them come to know differently and develop a sense of intellectual power and self-worth. It is another to change the system that has shaped what they bring (Deever, 1990; Weiler, 1988).

CONCLUSION

Nora Toney and Lisa Yaffee write vividly about their experiences in mathematics classes and how those experiences shaped what they brought to teaching. They describe the changes they are now working to make in themselves and in their practice. These stories depict an unusual insider perspective on efforts to make connections with mathematics as part of learning to teach, and they make plain the critical need to support change. Looking backward, their stories underscore the need for dramatic change in the nature of school mathematics. That both women found mathematics classes so alienating should remind mathematics educators—who themselves typically were successful with math in school—of how poorly much mathematics instruction serves most students, and particularly girls and students of color.

Looking forward, along the trajectory—which we only glimpse here—of the two teachers' learning, their stories highlight the complicated challenges posed by the current reform agenda. Constructing multiple structures that can support teacher learning must become a priority. Simplistic ideas about subject matter credentials for teaching will not address the pressing need. We need to uncover more about what it takes to teach mathematics for understanding, in ways that are responsible to the subject matter and the curriculum and responsive to a diversity of students. The roles that might be played by programs of professional development, curriculum materials, or writing—as Yaffee and Toney have done—need to be explored. Teachers, as Yaffee proclaims proudly, are "the ones reinventing math education." It is clearly they in whom we must invest. The two narratives remind us that it is crucial in designing supports for their learning that teachers' stories be heard; their experiences, respected; and their views, solicited. This view inside is a helpful beginning.

REFERENCES

Ball, D. L. (1988). Unlearning to teach mathematics. *For the Learning of Mathematics*, *8*(1), 40–48.

Ball, D. L. (1990). Prospective elementary and secondary teachers' understandings of division. *Journal for Research in Mathematics Education*, *21*, 132–144.

Ball, D. L. (1991). Implementing the *Professional Standards for Teaching Mathematics*: Improving, not standardizing, teaching. *Arithmetic Teacher, 39*(1), 18–22.

Cohen, D. K., & Ball, D. L. (1990). Relations between policy and practice: A commentary. *Educational Evaluation and Policy Analysis, 12*(3), 249–256.

Cohen, D. K., McLaughlin, M. W., & Talbert, J. E. (Eds.). (1993). *Teaching for understanding: Challenges for policy and practice.* San Francisco: Jossey-Bass.

Deever, B. (1990). Critical pedagogy: The concretization of possibility. *Contemporary Education, 61*(2), 71–76.

Education Development Center. (in press). *Connected geometry.* Dedham, MA: Janson.

Heaton, R. M. (1994). Creating and studying a practice of teaching elementary mathematics for understanding. Unpublished doctoral dissertation, Michigan State University, East Lansing.

Lampert, M. (1985). How do teachers manage to teach? Perspectives on problems in practice. *Harvard Educational Review, 55,* 178–194.

Lappan, G., Fitzgerald, W., & Phillips, E. (in press). *Connected mathematics project.* East Lansing: Michigan State University.

National Council of Teachers of Mathematics. (1989). *Curriculum and evaluation standards for school mathematics.* Reston, VA: Author.

National Council of Teachers of Mathematics. (1991). *Professional standards for teaching mathematics.* Reston, VA: Author.

Schifter, D., & Fosnot, C. T. (1993). *Reconstructing mathematics education: Stories of teachers meeting the challenge of reform.* New York: Teachers College Press.

Simon, M. (1993). Prospective elementary teachers' knowledge of division. *Journal for Research in Mathematics Education, 24,* 233–254.

Simon, M. A., & Schifter, D. (1991). Towards a constructivist perspective: An intervention study of mathematics teacher development. *Educational Studies in Mathematics, 22*(5), 309–331.

TERC. (1994). *Investigations in number, data, and space.* Palo Alto, CA: Dale Seymour.

Wagreich, P. (in press). *Teaching integrated mathematics and science project.* Chicago: University of Illinois Press.

Weiler, K. (1988). *Women teaching for change: Gender, class, and power.* New York: Bergin & Garvey.

Wilson, S. M., Shulman, L., & Richert, A. (1987). "150 different ways of knowing": Representations of knowledge in teaching. In J. Calderhead (Ed.), *Exploring teachers' thinking* (pp. 104–124). Eastbourne, England: Cassell.

CHAPTER 2

As Managers of Classroom Process: Inventing New Patterns of Authority

In the design of the usual in-service offering, whether the one-day workshop to acquaint teachers with new lesson ideas or innovative techniques, or the more intensive experience lasting several days or even weeks, ensuring smooth and rapid implementation is a high priority. But, as narratives by Karen Schweitzer and Anne Marie O'Reilly attest, teacher development initiatives conceived in the spirit of mathematics education reform are disruptive of familiar and deeply entrenched classroom management routines.

At best, then, the workshop or institute supportive of the reform process can propose a vision, set an agenda for change. The real work, our teacher-authors tell us—figuring out how to translate the vision into day-to-day instruction—will be neither smooth nor rapid, but arduous, sometimes scary, and sometimes exhilarating.

In this chapter, Schweitzer and O'Reilly, second- and sixth-grade teachers, respectively (in rural schools in western Massachusetts), describe their struggles, during the three months following an intensive two-week summer institute, to reconcile their determination to center instruction on student thinking and discussion with their longing for the book, program, or expert whose recipes will guarantee success.

In an essay exploring aspects and consequences of such efforts to redefine and resituate responsibilities for students' mathematical development, Ruth Heaton underlines the risks this project poses as teachers reconstruct their identities as managers of classroom process.

What's Happening in Math Class? Volume 2: Reconstructing Professional Identities: Copyright © 1996 by Teachers College, Columbia University. All rights reserved. ISBN 0-8077-3483-7 (pbk.), ISBN 0-8077-3484-5 (cloth). Prior to photocopying items for classroom use, please contact the Copyright Clearance Center, Customer Service, 222 Rosewood Dr., Danvers, MA 01923, USA, tel. (508) 750-8400.

$$+ \quad - \quad \times \quad \div$$

THE SEARCH FOR THE PERFECT RESOURCE

Karen Schweitzer

I have always believed that children learn best by doing and discovering, and that it is important for children to have some amount of choice and control over what they do. I've also always thought that children have to have real purposes for their work and that their work must have meaning for them. Most important, I believe that if children are going to live in the world in a more respectful, thoughtful, and inquisitive way as adults, they need to learn how by practicing as children.

I have spent the past 11 years teaching in small, rural New England schools. The student population in these schools has tended to be racially and ethnically homogeneous and economically diverse. My concentration over the past six years has been in kindergarten through second grade.

Merging philosophy and technique has been a struggle for me over these past years of teaching. Although I've never used a basal curriculum in any subject, I've not been completely satisfied with all of the programs that I have used. I spent many years concentrating on changing and improving my language arts program and was beginning to realize that my math program was calling out for attention. I was intrigued when I heard colleagues talking about an in-service program called SummerMath for Teachers.

I am now trying to understand and clarify the changes that I've gone through in the past nine months since I became involved in that program. I hope that through this narrative, I can communicate clearly what has been an unclear process.

BUT HOW WOULD I TEACH MATH?

I muddled through last year, my first year teaching second grade, with a class of 12 children in a very small classroom. When I first found out that I would be teaching second grade, I became anxious. I was eager to stretch my kindergarten language arts program to meet the needs of the second graders that I would be facing, but how would I teach math? One of my close colleagues, Susan Smith (see Chapter 5 in the companion volume, Schifter, 1996), had previously attended a SummerMath for Teachers Institute and I was beginning to understand a bit of what she was doing. I said to myself, "Well, I sort of already get the philosophy—if I could just get a grasp on what was actually happening in her classroom. What I need is for someone to tell me what activities to do." So I gathered suggestions for activity books that

would help me. The books had interesting ideas and some fun games, and between those books and a few conversations with Susan, I made it to the spring.
During that year, I learned that it was important for kids to figure out how to
solve problems and that I had a role as a questioner. However, I also knew
that things weren't really working the way I wanted them to. I was generally
dissatisfied but I hadn't yet articulated why.

That spring, when I received the SummerMath for Teachers Institute application, I looked at the essay question that asked me to write about my philosophy of teaching and about how I taught math. A year earlier I had received
the same form for the same institute, but had been so overcome by anxiety
about putting those ideas in writing that I never filled it out. Now, when faced
again with the same task, I thought of the school year, my math program, and
how I was feeling, and I thought, "That's it. This year I really have to do
this. But it'll be okay. I'll go to SummerMath, they'll tell me what to do, and
my worries will be over." I thought that I would go to the institute and get a
list of problems for my second graders to solve, or at least a recipe for how
to write them, and a list of questions to ask the kids. Then my math program
would be all set.

The process of filling out the application should have been my first hint
that it would not be that easy. In order to answer the questions posed, I really
had to think about my overall math program and how my philosophy was being applied, which was something that I was unaccustomed to doing. That first
task of reflecting critically on my math program in writing forced me to look
at my classroom and take note of some things.

For example, that was when I first articulated for myself the inconsisten-
cies between my math and language arts programs. My language arts teaching
reflected my philosophies that children need to be invested in what they do,
that they need to work at their own levels of understanding, and that it is important for them to have practice not only in the skill areas, but in identifying
the strategies they are using as readers and writers. My students had time to
practice reading and writing, and to share their ideas and accomplishments
with others. I held reading and writing conferences with the children. Most
important, I let myself learn from them where they were and where they
needed to go next. I was also in the process of realizing that there was not one
right way to run a literature-based language arts program and that each teacher
has to find the way that works for her or him.

On some level, I was becoming aware that most of these practices never
carried over into my math curriculum. I understood that children learn best by
doing things and manipulating objects, so I had a lot of math manipulatives in
my classroom. But the children always used them to do things just the way *I*
wanted them to, in the way that made sense to *me*. I used the manipulatives
to explain things and they used them to practice and reinforce what *I* had

taught. I still believed I had to teach math in the prescribed sequence and, of course, that the children had to use manipulatives to develop a concrete understanding of the concepts. Besides, the manipulatives made math more fun and that motivated the kids.

When I received my acceptance to the SummerMath for Teachers Elementary Institute, I was elated. I was finally going to find out how to "do" what my colleague had been doing and what I'd been hearing people talk about. Based on what I'd heard, I knew that the institute was set up so that the structure and the activities reflected the philosophies of the program. The instructors would teach us using techniques that we could use with our own students. As I said earlier, I also expected some "how to's," such as how to write word problems, how to teach place value, and how to set up the classroom.

The two weeks at the institute were both exciting and disappointing. I was eager to soak up all that was offered because I was sure there were answers there somewhere. I listened carefully and waited patiently. I dutifully wrote down almost everything that was said in those two weeks. After all, who knew when I would need to refer to these spoken gems? At the institute, I learned the power of reflecting on my own learning processes, and I learned the importance of "probing questions"—those questions that help people look for their own answers and for their own next questions.

But I was disappointed that they didn't give me a list of those probing questions to pull from, and in a way I felt cheated because I wanted the instructors to tell me what and how to teach. I kept expecting to get to the day when they would give out lesson plans, but instead I found out that, like the children we were going to teach, we were not going to be given direct answers. Toward the end of the institute, one of the instructors did give us the names of some resource books that we could use to help give us ideas. I felt some satisfaction.

The institute ended and school became more and more imminent. So did teaching math. As I thought about what I would do and how I would do it differently than I had in past years, I began to feel sort of panicked. So I got out my notes and ordered one resource book that had been recommended, *A Collection of Math Lessons from Grades 1–3* by Marilyn Burns and Bonnie Tank (1988), and another book by Marilyn Burns, *About Teaching Mathematics* (1992).

When the books arrived, I read some of the activities and thought they sounded interesting. Not only that, but they seemed to fit with the philosophy of letting children create meaning by solving problems for themselves. Now I felt equipped to deal with teaching math. I did wonder what I would do when I ran out of activities in the books, but I thought that perhaps I would have gotten the hang of creating my own by then.

AND SO SCHOOL BEGINS

The first time we had math was during the second day of school. I had intended to start my math program on the very first day with such an exciting and inviting math activity that the children would be captivated and hooked on math for the rest of the year. I wanted to be inspired and to create this magnificent problem by myself—to apply all the things I had learned in the institute. But I never quite figured out what that perfect activity was, so I just skipped math that day.

That afternoon, after the kids had gone, I decided that I couldn't skip math for the rest of the year just because I couldn't think of the perfect activity. Besides, I had already agreed to take another class through the Summer-Math for Teachers Program, one in which we were going to write about our math teaching, and I had to have something to write about. I realized that perhaps I was not quite ready to create all of this from scratch, and that maybe this was one wheel I did not have to reinvent. I turned to the experts and started reading *A Collection of Math Lessons*. I thought, "Maybe I can find something meaningful to *my* kids, something from *their* environment, something that emphasizes many different ways to do things, and something that will encompass the wide variety of ability levels in *my* room." I read several lessons, but none of them fit all of these criteria. Something was missing. "Now what do I do?" I wondered. "Stay calm," I answered myself, "there has to be some math for us here someplace." I thought back to what we had done so far on that first day of school.

As an introduction to the classroom, the 12 second graders in the class each had shared an observation about the room and something they had wondered about. I noticed that three of the questions were "how many" questions. (How many blocks are there in the block area? How many books are there in the room? How many seashells are there on the theme table?) If "how many" was what the children were wondering about, I thought that a discussion of these might be a good place to begin.

On the second afternoon, I announced that it was time for math. One little girl said, almost as if she was asking permission to be excused, "I don't really want to do math." I knew that she was talking about "papers" with counters and endless problems, and so I answered, "I think second-grade math will be quite a bit different from first-grade math, so don't worry yet." She looked momentarily appeased, but her face told me that she wasn't quite ready to believe me. We all sat down on the carpet in the meeting area and several more children voiced their dislike for math. I again said, "Wait. Don't decide yet. See what it's like, first." After hearing what they thought of "math," I really felt the pressure to do something that met all my criteria for the perfect math lesson. So I took a deep breath and said, "I noticed that some of the things that you wondered about yesterday sounded like they had to do with math."

"Yeah," agreed John, and he proceeded to read all of the how-many questions from the chart. "So much for discussion," I thought, "and where is the prob- ing question in here anyway?!" But I figured that I had to go somewhere with it and added, "Why are those math questions?"

John answered, "Because they are counting."

"Is math only counting?" The children slowly began to throw out ideas about what math was.

"It's like putting 3 and 4 together."

"It's when you put unifix [cubes] together to add."

"Could math be patterns?" I asked. "Uh-huh," they agreed, and they began to make patterns with the unifix cubes that were in the middle of the circle. I made sure to emphasize and affirm all the different ideas.

I then returned to the question of how many books were in the room. (I chose that item mostly because I thought it couldn't hurt to focus our attention on books.) "How could we answer that question?" I asked. "It's easy, just count them," they told me. I said that we were going to get into groups of three and figure out lots of different ways that we could count the books. (Even though I wasn't sure that there was any merit to this activity, I wanted them to go through the process of talking to each other in small groups.) Then we would get back together and share all the different ideas, and after that we would count the books.

I really thought that all was going well now. They would go through this process, I would ask lots of great questions, they'd learn a lot, and we'd be off to a great start. Except when I mentioned breaking up into groups, all of a sudden, two children had stomach aches and one child started to sneeze. "But we can't stop here, before we really get started," I thought, and I pushed on.

When the children finally settled down in their groups, they were all quiet and seemed shy about talking to each other in this way. I hadn't expected this task to be as difficult as it was. And when we got back together and they shared their ideas (count by 2s, by 5s, by 10s), I found that the probing ques- tion, "How would you do that?" fell flat on its face. We had been working for 35 minutes when I decided to leave the actual counting until the next day, so I recapped how many different ideas there were, and that was our first day of math.

I ended that day frustrated and disappointed. I had wanted to dazzle them, to show them that math is interesting and inviting. Instead, by the end of the lesson, we all ended up a little unsure. Our nerves were showing, theirs and mine, and none of us were sure what lay ahead this year. I wanted to follow through on the activity since we had started it, although I was no longer cer- tain of the importance or wisdom of counting the books.

The next day, we counted the books. The air was filled with excitement as the children spread out through the classroom, three or four of them stationed in front of each bookshelf and display case. Everyone was busy and the happy sounds of counting filled the air. Although the number of books was too large for them to understand, they were delighted to be tackling such a large number. One child, who had difficulty with the task, remarked at the end of the session that it was the first time in two years he'd had fun doing math.

I chose to write about this experience for the first meeting of the writing class I was attending. After reflecting on the activities of those two days, I was able to write:

> I guess I realize that I can't change their expectations about math in one day but that each lesson needs to emphasize in some way the things I want them to notice as being different from the kind of math that they are used to doing.

The following week we continued math with more counting. As part of my assignment for the writing class, I was listening to the dialogue that was happening. As I was doing this, I began to notice that although the children were active, were solving problems, and were verbalizing to me when I posed questions to them as they worked, some were not talking to each other while they were solving problems, and most were not listening to anyone during class discussions. It's not that important things weren't happening—the children were learning that math was different in second grade, and they had even solved a few interesting problems—but I guess I wanted it all to happen at once.

I decided that I needed to create a problem that would focus them on listening to each other in a discussion, and I designed one that was centered around our lunch count. In the morning each child puts her or his name tag into one section of a three-section box, depending on whether she or he is having hot lunch, cold lunch, or cold lunch with milk. The children were curious when they saw the box brought out in the afternoon at math time. We began by counting the names in each section and then we counted the names of the children who were absent. Next, the class figured out how to show that day's lunch count with their unifix cubes. When they felt comfortable doing this, I presented the problem I wanted them to solve: "I want you to show me what a day would look like if I came in and I had lost some of these cards and the only thing that I knew for sure was that 5 people were having hot lunch, 1 person was having milk, and everyone was here."

I put the children in pairs and they began to work. I worked with two children who were having a hard time figuring out what they were being asked to do, and most of the others seemed actively involved with their unifix cubes and their partners. I could hear the buzz as I conferenced with the two boys, and I was excited by what I heard. Voices sounded excited by discoveries being made; active bodies grouped around their unifix cubes. A comment from

Lisa caught my ear and I thought it might be a place to start our discussion. I thought, ''Ah, this will be great.''

After 10 or 15 minutes of working in pairs, we all gathered in the meeting area with me in a chair and the children distributed between the couch and some oversized pillows, all facing me. Lisa was moving around, as if she was so excited that she couldn't wait to share.

Teacher: I'm going to ask Lisa to tell us what she has in her hand.
Lisa: Well, you said that it was 5 hot lunches and 1 milk so we took a red one for 1 milk and we took 5 green ones for the hot lunch.

Lisa proudly held up her 6 unifix cubes. I noticed that all of the other groups had trains of 6 as well, but I really wanted them to be thinking in terms of 12 kids. Where were the cold lunches? I asked if anyone had anything to add to what Lisa had said, and I noticed out of the corner of my eye that Seth was adding more cubes to his train. I wanted the class to explore why, but at the same time I also noticed that the children were becoming fidgety and distracted. I quickly realized that it was a problem that they were all facing me and not each other; this arrangement was not conducive to listening to each other. I stopped the discussion for a moment as we moved the pillows and got into a circle, and then we continued.

Teacher: Seth has something to add.
Seth: I know there was 5 hot lunch and 1 milk and I counted everyone else as a cold lunch and came out with 12.
Teacher: Seth, how did you know how many to choose for cold lunch? I only told you that there were 5 hot lunches and 1 milk.
Seth: 'Cause I added on from 6.
Teacher: Could you show us how you did that so we understand your thinking?
Seth: (using his cubes to show as he explained) I started with 5 hot lunches (pointing to the 5 blue cubes) and I added 1 (pointing to the red one) and I came up with 6 and I added 7 more and it came up to 12.

I had noticed his error in calculation but decided that pointing it out at that time would detract from my main goal, which was to have Seth's thinking understood.

Teacher: Could you show us how you knew how many to add? Did you pick that number out of a hat?
Seth: No. I just . . . I just . . . I remembered it was 5 and I added 7.

Teacher: Is there anyone who could help Seth find the words for his
thinking?

There was a long and very definite pause. I rephrased the question and
there was an even longer pause. The long silence was very frustrating for the
kids and me, but I felt that it was important for them to really listen to Seth
and try to follow his thinking. It seemed as though they were sitting passively
and waiting. I was delighted at Seth's participation and would have welcomed
any comments from anyone else who showed some sort of involvement.

I broke the silence and asked Seth to state once more what he did. After
he spoke, Donald raised his hand and, along with convincing Seth that it was
6 and not 7 cubes that he added, he also said, "Because there's 12 kids in the
class. And with one milk and 5 hot lunches, that's 6—and 6 cold lunches
would add up to 12."

I asked Donald if he could show me that with the cubes and he said,
"No." I knew that we had been sitting for a long time and I was really pushing the attention span of many of the children. In addition, I knew that many
of the children might not be following what was happening. For these reasons,
I wanted a concrete representation with the cubes to help them understand this
thinking.

After several more failed attempts at questioning and a very long silence
that was broken only by a plea for some fresh air, we took a break. Still, I
had this gut feeling that we were at an important place and we needed to move
through it instead of passing over it. Looking back, I can see that it was important for the children to finish this process so that they could begin to understand Seth's thinking, but also so that they would have experienced a model
for the process I wanted to develop—listening to other people's ideas and trying to compare and contrast them with their own ideas. As I reflected quickly
during our short break, I decided to give it one more try and move on.

Teacher: We still have a problem. I want to hear—I want Seth's thinking to be understood (although by then I was the only one who
did).

Seth once again obliged me and explained, although now he was able to
add to his insights that "6 more add up to 12; 6 and 6 is 12; 6 people are
having cold lunch and 5 people are having hot lunch and 1 person is having
milk." After a few more explanations that 6 and 6 is 12, I decided that no
matter how important I thought it was, it wasn't going anywhere. So with a
promise of rest for their tired brains after one more question, I asked them
what the lunch count would look like if all I knew was that 4 people had hot
lunch and 4 people had milk. I noticed that several groups of kids had made
trains of 12 and were using these trains to figure out the question, but I de-

cided not to pursue this for very long because the children were exhausted and my curiosity was satisfied. Many of the children had picked up on the idea that to answer the question, they needed to use 12 cubes, one for each member of the class.

My insights about that day came from thinking about the experience and writing about it in a format that other math teachers would have to read. For writing class that week I wrote:

> Amidst all of the silence, I guess thinking and listening were happening. I could see from the way that they approached the next problem that the discussion had had an effect on that approach. To help me know where to go next, I look for the questions that I have after this experience. What was it that did change? If their thinking changed, what can I do to help them to learn to verbalize it? Was it really worth waiting through the silences and not giving up? I'm not sure. At the end of the 55 minutes of math that day, my second graders informed me that their brains hurt! I told them that was because they used them so much.

THE FRUSTRATION BUILDS

As time went on, I found myself feeling more and more frustrated. I used my writing to vent and I hoped that I wouldn't feel embarrassed when others read about what was happening in my classroom and how hard a time I was having. When I brought this to class, I was relieved and encouraged to find out that many other teachers had similar feelings of frustration.

> I feel so discouraged. I've been looking and looking for signs of a child who has learned something that I wanted her or him to learn, but I haven't seen any. I am so frustrated that lately I've just wanted math to go away! However, I put math in a prominent and unavoidable place in my daily schedule this year so that I couldn't slip past it. So now, there it is. Every day. Waiting to taunt me.
>
> I've tried to create activities that were engaging and meaningful, but the children seem inattentive during discussions and my questions often are answered with silence. I've tried to use resource books to set up activities that are "proven" in order to stimulate thinking and talking, but nothing happens except that I get even more frustrated. So I try to listen to the kids for a direction to go in, but I guess I don't know what I'm hearing yet because that doesn't help me either.

I wrote that after one Friday in September. We had finished our activity very quickly, so I let the kids have some time to explore the manipulatives in our math tubs (I call this tub time): unifix cubes, pattern blocks, junk boxes, geoboards, unifix pattern cards, mosaic frames, and balances. The children quickly became involved in a variety of self-directed activities. Some were building with the unifix cubes, others with pattern blocks. Two boys were busy connecting every geoboard we had to see how big a board they could make. Several children were making long trains of unifix cubes. Throughout the room, I heard excited comments such as, "Wow! Look at this," and, "Ms. Schweitzer, come here. I gotta show you this." "Look at what I did!" I quickly realized that this was perhaps the most interested and invested that the kids had been so far this year. So I thought to myself, "Maybe I should let them explore more. Maybe I'm pushing them too much because I want results that I can write about."

I thought a lot about that activity as I planned for math on Monday. I looked and looked at what occurred on Friday, knowing that an answer had to be there somewhere, but I still couldn't find it. I finally latched on to the unifix cubes. We had done an activity with them the week before and the children were very interested in playing with them, so it seemed like there must be something interesting we could do with them. I decided that on Monday, we would do a structured exploration of the unifix cubes.

Monday arrived and I told the class that they would have 10 minutes to build with the cubes. My plan was for the children to build something other than a train, estimate how many cubes they used, and then count them. We brainstormed different ways to build with them and, after we finished, they all wanted to know if they could make very long trains. I was pulled in opposite directions. Do I go with *my* activity or do I go with what interests *them*? I wanted them to explore things other than trains, but their agenda was long trains. I was confused about how much "playing" to let them do. I compromised by saying that they could have a train as *part* of their structure.

Although I had planned to have each group estimate and then count how many unifix cubes they used, regardless of my instructions only one group built something other than a train. (I guess it's easy to see whose agenda prevailed.) So we did the estimating and counting with that group's buildings, but I had lost the children. It was easy for me to tell when I had lost them because their behavior was so drastically different when they were invested. As soon as I had to start dealing with behavior issues, I knew they were gone.

"Okay," I told myself, feeling too frustrated to fight it any longer, "Let them make the train!" I ended math by telling them that tomorrow they would make the longest train they could, but that they had to figure out a way to make it so that it would be easier to count. We discussed the counting activity that began our year—counting every book in the class. The children remembered that this had been a very confusing task because it was hard to keep track of the counting, so I asked them to think about a way to build the train so that it would be easier to count.

As I look back on how the activity went the next day, I think of the contrast between their involvement during the train construction and their involvement in the group meetings before and after the construction. I also think of my level of frustration and anxiety. I thought that if we were going to make the train, the least we could do was to use it to learn about different ways of counting.

I had planned to "lead" the discussion toward counting by 5s or preferably 10s. To my dismay, with all the different ways I asked the questions, they still wanted to count only by 1s. At one point Lisa said, "We could count by 5s."

"What would that look like?" I asked.

She counted, "5, 10, 15, 20, 25, 30," and as she counted, she pointed to one block at a time. When she got to 30, I held up the stack of 6 blocks and said, "So is this 30 blocks?"

"If you count by 5s it is."

At that point, the class chimed in that we should just count by 1s because anything else was too hard. I rephrased the question, "Can you show me what it would look like to count these by 5s?" but the moment had passed and they were getting restless.

I, on the other hand, was just becoming more frustrated. I couldn't seem to ask the right questions, and when I asked what I thought were the right ones, I didn't get any responses. My discussions were falling flat on their face, and when I tried to push it, all I ended up with was behavior problems.

The discussion had ended and it was time to move on to what the children all really wanted to do—build the longest unifix train they could. As they built the train, I saw the same level of involvement that I had seen during their tub explorations the previous week. They were excited, running up and down the hall to check the progress at both ends. I kept hearing exclamations of, "Wow! Look how long it is." I didn't want the train to be finished because I had no idea what to ask them or where to go from there. I had even offered to trade classes with Susan, who passed by and said, "This looks interesting. Do you know where you are going with it?" That was the last question I wanted to hear because I didn't know. Eventually the children added the last cube and we had to do something. We got together and I asked how they could count them. They again insisted, "By 1s!" They decided to organize it so that some children began counting at one end and some at the other. I hoped that this would fall apart and they would be forced to come up with another way to count.

It did fall apart for many of them. Some were bored because they weren't the ones counting, some were just confused, and some were frustrated because the numbers they were dealing with were becoming too large for them. I tried to jump at the opportunity I saw, and I called the class together for another meeting. We talked about what was happening and then I asked, "How could we count them so that we could all count at once and everybody had something to do?" John suggested that two people could count and when they got tired two other people could count. AHHHHHHH! I was still trying to steer them toward making groups of 10 and then counting by 10s, or breaking the cubes into different smaller groups to count and then adding them back together to get the total. I thought I must not have been asking the right questions because they weren't following where I wanted to lead. I mustered all of the patience and positive energy I had left and said, "That's one way. Is there another way we could do it so that everyone is counting?"

"Oh," John continued, "the rest of the kids could be talking or building with pattern blocks while they wait."

Lisa offered, "One person could point, one person could keep track of the number, and everyone else stand by the wall and count along." John made his suggestion again, and Donald added that it was too hard to put the numbers together when you counted in two parts. He had tried it that way the day before when he counted someone else's train.

I decided to try a different tack. "Where would be a good place for those two children to stop so that it wouldn't be hard to put the numbers together?"

"How about 100?" offered John. The children decided that this sounded reasonable and their interest convinced me that this was a workable strategy, so I restated his idea, added a few organizational tips such as using small tubs to count into, and the children broke up into partners to count 100 unifix cubes per group. When each pair had filled a tub with 100 cubes, we got back together. We decided to use tally marks to keep track of how many tubs the children had filled. The class counted unifix cubes for three days, and then counted up the tally marks. They were delighted to discover that they had used 2,170 unifix cubes to build the train that stretched from one end of the hall to the other.

My reflections that week included the following:

> Looking back, I can begin to see a direction, but that doesn't really make me feel less frustrated, because it's only a glimpse of a direction, and my experiences this week have led me to believe that just because I can see a direction and I try to lead us there, doesn't mean that the children will follow me there. I can't seem to shake that feeling of frustration I experience when over and over my questions are answered by silence. Where is all of that insightful dialogue that is supposed to be happening, anyway?

I spent many hours during those weeks pondering—and fretting and worrying and anguishing—about my math program. The questions came back to me over and over and remained unanswered: "Where am I going?" "Are the children really learning anything?" "Do these activities have any value?" On some days, the answers seemed crystal clear and were overwhelmingly positive, and on others they led only to more questions.

THE GIFT

Once again, I was trying to figure out what to do next and I remembered our unfinished discussion about counting by 5s. I decided to go back and explore Lisa's confusion about this since I had responded to her by pointing out the contradiction, "Are there 30 cubes there?" and the discussion had changed direction before we had a chance to pursue it. Although I knew that revisiting it could be important, I still didn't have a context for our work. I felt like I was grabbing one activity here and another there, and this was adding to my frustration.

Unsure of where the lesson might go, I began math on that Wednesday holding a stack of 6 unifix cubes.

> *Teacher:* Last week Lisa showed us how she counted these by 5s. Lisa, would you show us that again?
> *Lisa:* (Again, she points to one cube at a time) 5, 10, 15, 20, 25, 30.
> *Teacher:* This is where I got confused last time. Are there 30 cubes here?

Several children chimed in emphatically, "No!"

> *Teacher:* So when you guys were telling me the different ways you could count the unifix [cubes], you said you could count them by 5s.

All of a sudden there was a flurry of responses. "Yeah." "Yup." "Right." And a chorus of "5, 10, 15, 20, . . . "

> *Teacher:* So (pointing to the unifix cubes) how can I count them by 5s?

The class appeared stumped, but for once I actually felt like I knew where I was going, at least for the moment. I wanted them to begin thinking about what it meant to count by 5s.

> *Teacher:* Why doesn't this way work? (I repeat the way that was originally shown.)
> *Abby* (and others): Because there aren't 30 there.
> *Teacher:* But I counted by 5s.
> *Donald:* You can't just point to that one and say "5."
> *Teacher:* What do you mean?

The children told me there had to be more blocks.

Teacher: Oh (as I reach for the tub of cubes), so can I count like this? (I begin to grab random anounts of unifix cubes by the handfuls and recite) 5, 10, 15, 20.

"No," they replied in voices that let me know that they thought I was being perfectly silly.

Teacher: So how could I count these by 5s? (No one offers a suggestion, so I go on.) You told me that I couldn't count by 5s like this (I demonstrate one way) or like this (I demonstrate the other way), so I'm going to ask you how I can count them by 5s.

I divided the children up into pairs and gave each pair a small tub of unifix cubes. They worked on how to organize their blocks so that they could count by 5s. The children came up with some interesting ideas and observations, and by the end of the class they had told me that to count by 5s, I had to know that there were 5 things in a group to count. I thought that this was a very successful lesson and I felt kind of proud.

That evening during the writing class, I was given a gift; actually it was two gifts in one. I got back some of my writing in which I had discussed two or three counting activities that we had done, including Lisa's original confusion about counting by 5s. And there it was, a suggestion from Deborah Schifter, our instructor, for an activity! After all this time, waiting to be told what to do, I was finally given a suggestion. She had read my earlier writings and said:

I'm particularly struck by your student's discussion of counting by 5s. I wonder if you're asking them to do something they're not yet close to understanding. Perhaps they don't have a sense of how to count things by groups. What if you worked on counting the number of shoes in the room, or something like that? Or what if you had stations where there are different numbers of objects to count (since they still seem to be engaged by counting)?

I was so excited. I had been hoping that at some point someone would just once "tell" me what to do. I kept my excitement in check, however, because I remembered my earlier experiences with the resource books and how disappointed I was with those activities that someone had "told" me. Would this be different?

The next day I saw Susan and said excitedly, "Deborah gave me an idea!"

"Oh," she replied in that all-too-familiar SummerMath tone that implied that there was something more here that I should be questioning and thinking about.

"Yes, after she read what was happening in my classroom." Aha, something fuzzy was beginning to clear up in my head. I wasn't sure quite yet what it was, but it had something to do with Deborah coming up with a suggestion *after* she read my paper. Hmmm. The idea quickly filed itself somewhere in my brain for another time.

We did an activity that day that involved three stations. Table A had eight plastic four-legged, tailed animals, and they had to count the legs and tails. Table B had dominoes, and they had to count the squares. Table C had pattern blocks, three of each color. The counting was animated and almost all of the children were involved. The discussion brought out a lot of thinking about how to count groups and when you could and couldn't count by 2s or 5s.

I couldn't wait to tell Susan about it. I began to tell her what happened and to explain that I was sure that it was because of the origin of the activity. As I wondered out loud, "Why wouldn't those instructors give us any ideas over the summer if this one worked so well?" I began to answer my own question. That was the second part of the gift. As my thinking unfolded, I realized that the reason that the resource books weren't as helpful as I thought they would be, and the reason that instructors were hesitant to offer ideas for activities in the abstract, and the reason that this activity worked so well, were all the same reason. Marilyn Burns and the SummerMath Institute instructors didn't know my kids and didn't know what kinds of thinking were happening in my room. Deborah's suggestion was based on my observations of my students and their thinking. She could suggest something that worked because she had a sense of where the kids were and what had been happening in the classroom. It was a suggestion rooted in a real situation, not an abstract activity.

I then was able to gain a larger perspective on what was going on in my program. It wasn't until I was given the gift that I began to realize what my frustration was. The lessons that I had done, whether from the books or not, felt isolated and out of context, and I kept feeling like I didn't know where I was headed. All of a sudden it became clear that what we were "doing" in math was thinking about ways of counting and what it actually means to skip count. The kids had been discovering how to apply in meaningful and useful ways those rhythmic patterns of skip counting that they had memorized.

THINGS CHANGE

Things proceeded smoothly during the next four weeks as we embarked on a study of measurement. I wanted to include the story of these weeks as part of this narrative, since they represented a big change for me. At the end of the unit I felt excited and yet still uneasy. I knew things had been different, yet I couldn't identify why.

But writing this narrative has forced me to look at my teaching, and to keep looking until I find some clarity appearing out of the mass of confusion. It has taken three more months of writing, rewriting, and talking with colleagues to figure out what it was that was really different during those weeks. The fog is beginning to lift.

I can now see, in retrospect, that things I had learned from my experiences with counting were beginning to affect what I did as I taught math. I had identified my frustration with resource books and was learning to recognize cues for direction from the children. I was beginning to understand that another large piece of my frustration came from feeling that my math curriculum was made up of unconnected lessons. I did not know it when I began our lessons on measurement, but I was ready for a focus—a unit of study that we could stay with for a while.

After a week of activities that related to measurement, I developed an inkling that we were going to be "doing" measurement. I felt excited and nervous to be purposefully headed somewhere, and comforted because I knew that it was a valid topic to be exploring.

As the weeks continued I was able to find a rhythm to my planning and each activity seemed to flow into the next. I learned not only to listen for the children's questions, but to recognize that learning was happening in these activities. That gave me the confidence to move on. I was also able to shift my agenda when a discussion led us in a different direction.

For example, one day the class was working with some measurement riddles I had written. (I am blue. I am 4 inches on each side. What am I?) The children explored the riddles with curiosity and enthusiasm. I was excited to hear the observations and questions that were coming out of their work. Imagine my surprise when the children began to find many answers to each riddle. As I was listening to the children talk during our class discussion, in my head I was planning to make the subject of the next day's math activity something about how to clarify the riddles by adding more attributes. Their discussion grabbed my attention as I began to hear a very different agenda emerge. The children were discussing whether in fact a curved abalone shell was 8½ inches long. There were some definite disagreements. John argued that it wasn't exactly 8½ and showed us that. Trevor conceded but said that it was close enough because it was hard to measure. The shell bent around but the ruler was straight. "Oh, I can be of some help here," I thought. I said out loud, "We can measure it with this tool. It's called a tape measure and it bends," and I took out a tape measure. I demonstrated on the shell how to use it. "When we measure the shell with this, it's about 10 inches," I reported.

"But it's still an answer to the riddle," Karl objected, "because when you measure with the ruler, it's 8½ inches." I assumed Karl was just confused about the inaccuracy caused by using a straight ruler to measure a curved object; but when I followed up on this, I realized that Karl and several other children were telling me that the inches on this new tool might not be the same as the inches on our ruler.

We explored this issue for the next few days and the children's agenda continued to lead us along the way. During these days I was fascinated by the math that was happening and I felt proud that I had picked up on this confusion.

One day after school, I was telling Susan about what had happened during math. I had learned how important it was to share ideas with a colleague when I had questions about what to do. I wanted to figure out how to present my question for our next math lesson so that I could find out what each of the children was thinking about inches and whether they were always the same length. Susan listened patiently as I threw out idea after idea, and she helped me to imagine what kind of response each question would elicit. I finally settled on a question for the children to answer in their journals. Once again I felt very satisfied with what we would be doing and with how I came to the decision.

In trying to make sense of my changes, I needed to continue to look closely at what happened during those weeks. My program felt connected and focused, and there was continuity between the activities. I felt good that the curriculum had followed the children's questions, and yet we still covered some very important concepts. Things had been different and I was working to identify why.

MOVING ON

There is something so surprising about this whole process of evolution; sometimes, my own actions even surprise me. I sat tonight as I often do before I get ready to write, and I reflected in my math journal. I thought about today's activity.

I had created a word problem involving measurement. I wanted to encourage the children's reflection and I wanted them to record their thinking, so I asked them to glue the word problem into their math journals and to solve it right in their journals. This plan sounded good to me after I finished crafting it, and it met all the criteria I had for that day's lesson. However, as I watched my math class unfold before my eyes, I realized that I had another activity that didn't turn out the way I had planned. Some children were working hard, talking and thinking with their partners, but other children were having difficulties working together, and a few were wandering around the room not doing math at all.

What surprised me was not that this lesson wasn't going to be a complete success story, or that there were things that the class needed to work on, but that I didn't feel that combination of frenzy, frustration, and hopelessness that

I felt five or six weeks earlier. By using my journal as a tool, I was able to figure out that if that many children were not on task, there was something wrong with either the structure or the content of the activity and I needed to re-examine both aspects of what we had done before I decided what to do next.

Don't get me wrong. *All* is not calm and thoughtful. As I sat in the middle of the classroom watching half of my class roam around, not communicating with their partners, I did not feel reflective. I felt frustrated and let down and like I'd failed to find the answer. Again I talked to the children about how "I'll know you are working with your partner because I'll see . . . " and they finished my sentence, "us talking to our partner" in a drony sort of voice, as if to say that they'd heard it all before. "I've got a lot of thinking to do," I thought. At that moment, however, I was just scrambling and searching through my brain to try to find the motivational cue to get them back on task.

But that night, I wrote in my journal:

> Tonight, I knew that the answers lay in my reflection, not in a book or in a manual. . . . Create an activity that has a task for each child and see how that works out. It sounds good in theory, but the only way I'll know is to try it and to watch how it works.

CONCLUSION

Trying to make sense out of all of this is still very difficult. I entered into the SummerMath for Teachers Program looking for some easy answers—a few recipes and a couple of lists. As you have read, I didn't find them, but I did find things that were much more valuable.

One of the most striking things that I have learned about math education is that, at least for the time being, there isn't a source that has the answers neatly prepackaged for me. A year ago I was in search of the perfect resource book to tell me what to do. I looked for answers from someplace else. Now, instead, I think, "What are my students thinking about? What interests second graders? What concepts are they ready to explore?" and even, "What do these children need to learn in second grade?" Instead of looking for the authorities who "know it all" to tell me the answers, I now look to well-trained, experienced teachers to help me interpret what is happening and use their experience to offer suggestions.

I have had a few revelations about the direction of my curriculum during this time. It was a big leap to realize that I didn't need to present the curriculum in the order it's always done in second grade. I remember sitting in my writing class one night and saying to my small group, "You mean I don't have to teach adding, *then* subtracting, *then* trading?" At some point, after I decided that the direction of the curriculum had to come from the children, I also realized that it was okay for me to say, "Ah, this is what they are ready to do now. I can present a challenge to them, or introduce a topic, and look for their questions within that area, for there will surely be some."

The SummerMath for Teachers Mathematics Process Writing Project (the writing class to which I've referred) has played an important role in my course of change. The class gave me a reason to write about what was happening in my classroom, and the writing had to be clear and understandable because other teachers were going to read it. Part of the way through the class, I realized that writing about my frustrations caused me to reflect on what had happened, and even to reflect on earlier reflections. This was part of what was making me feel different about these frustrations.

Meeting with a group of teachers each week helped me not only by giving me feedback on my writing, but with the math that was happening in my classroom, as well. It also gave me a chance to read and hear about what was going on in other classrooms. Developing this habit of reflecting and sharing has been a pivotal part of my change. It has struck me several times that these are pieces that often are missing from teacher education programs and from our daily professional lives, and for me these were pieces that were essential.

I also have realized that I have a lot of work still ahead of me. If there had been easy answers, I would have gotten them and been done with it, but now every question raises a new question, and often even the answers raise questions. I just hope I've learned enough to figure out how to find the answers, and what to do with them once I've found them.

REFERENCES

Burns, M. (1992). *About teaching mathematics.* New York: Math Solution Publications.

Burns, M., & Tank, B. (1988). *A collection of math lessons from grades 1–3.* New York: Math Solution Publications.

Schifter, D. (Ed.). (1996). *What's happening in math class?, Volume 1: Envisioning new practices through teacher narratives.* New York: Teachers College Press.

UNDERSTANDING TEACHING / TEACHING FOR UNDERSTANDING

Anne Marie O'Reilly

This is about understanding. It is about what I have come to understand about teaching. It is about what I have to come to know about teaching for understanding. I have been astounded by how difficult it is to teach this way, and I am only beginning to identify and confront some of the issues that are part of a mathematics pedagogy where teaching, learning, and understanding are so dependent on one another.

As part of the writing project that produced this narrative, I have reflected on the teaching and learning of mathematics that took place in my classroom for the first three months of school. I thought that my writing would result in an accumulation of vignettes that later would form the core of a larger project about the mathematics that took place in my classroom. What I produced, instead, was a far more powerful contribution to my evolution as a teacher. Aided by notes that I struggled to jot down during math lessons, I captured my teaching and my students' learning in fuzzy recollections at the end of the day. They provided me with a vehicle for reflection and understanding, days and, more important, weeks after the teaching and learning took place. What I could not understand at the moment, I began to understand and draw lessons from weeks later.

I am only beginning to realize what it means to teach for understanding. My struggles, as I learn how to teach this way, share many parallels with my students' struggles to learn mathematics. The first three months of my teaching were, in large part, an accumulation of dilemmas. My enthusiasm and clear vision of what teaching mathematics could be, should be, collided head-on with reality. More often than not, my teaching left me with a gnawing, uneasy sense that things were not going as they should. I was reminded of the unsuccessful car salesman who was saying all the right things, but no one was buying his cars. I was trying so hard to offer my students problems and activities that would engage them in meaningful discourse; but more often than not, I found myself wading through confusion, either my own or theirs.

I had a sense that in order to bridge the gap between my visions and my practice, I needed to identify what I brought to my teaching—what I understood and what I still needed to know. In doing so, I clarified the foundations of my ideas about teaching, children, and learning. I also confronted the shortcomings of my knowledge of mathematics.

WHERE I'VE BEEN (OTHER PEOPLE'S CLASSROOMS)

Long before I became a teacher, I suspected that there was more to learning mathematics than the computation and drill that I had enjoyed as a student. I had never been intimidated by math. I had always been successful with math and enjoyed it, until I hit trigonometry in high school. That was when my success and progress stopped. It was like slamming into a brick wall. First semester of freshman year of college officially brought my career as a student of mathematics to an end. That was when calculus convinced me that the wall was insurmountable. I felt frustrated and bewildered. How could I be such a dismal failure at something I used to love?

Twenty years later, when I returned to college to fulfill requirements for postbaccalaureate teacher certification, I was reminded of that frustration. I did not want my students to meet with failure because they hadn't encountered the opportunities they needed in order to succeed. So I set myself the task of finding out just what it takes to do the job right. Two years later, teaching certificate in hand, I felt ill at ease about knowing what it takes to teach many things. I was afraid that my students' learning would be limited by how well I could transmit everything they needed to know. I considered that to be an overwhelming responsibility. I felt inadequate from two conflicting perspectives. On the one hand, I felt that I had been inadequately programmed to function in the role of a manager, someone who ensures smooth transitions and efficient management of children and materials. On the other hand, I believed that teachers needed to be so much more than that. I believed that teachers must be critical thinkers, informed decision makers, and risk takers. My teacher education had fallen miserably short on both counts. At the very least, my knowledge of who children are and how they learn seemed frightfully inadequate. That was reason enough for me to choose to put aside the training that had qualified me for teacher certification and set out to acquire the knowledge that, it seemed to me, teaching required.

The following year, I chose not to look for a teaching position. Instead, I worked as an instructional aide in a second-grade classroom and continued my education informally. The responsibilities associated with my job led me to concentrate on issues directly related to how children learn about language. I discovered the ideas of people like Donald Graves, Don Holdaway, Frank Smith, Nancy Atwell, and Lucy Calkins, and realized that they held meaning for teaching in a much broader sense. Their research and thinking about children held true across subjects and content areas. I began to adopt as my own the idea that children must be in charge of their own learning. I no longer viewed teaching with a sense of awe. I learned to have faith in the act of learning. That removed a lot of mystery from the act of teaching.

I also made some big discoveries about teaching mathematics in particular. I attended a series of workshops conducted by Catherine Twomey Fosnot, a SummerMath for Teachers staff member. I got a tantalizing introduction to how it feels to be thrown into mathematical confusion over something as apparently simple as dividing one fraction by another. I discovered the meaning behind the operations I had memorized and forgotten many years ago. I experienced what it feels like when math makes sense. I had created my own understanding. If understanding meant more than being able to follow someone else's explanation, it naturally followed that my success as a teacher could not be measured by my ability to explain what I understood to my students.

I came away from those workshops feeling excited and empowered. The key to my success as a teacher of mathematics would not come from my ability to write behavioral objectives, follow a teacher's manual, or guide my students through a series of workbook pages. The key to my success would be my understanding of how children learn.

The following year, I returned to college to earn a masters degree in elementary education. I read John Dewey, Jean Piaget, Maxine Greene, Herbert Ginsburg, and others. I had the opportunity to consider the importance of teachers as thoughtful decision makers. I began to develop a sense of what it means to teach for conceptual understanding. I was fascinated and impressed by Herbert Ginsburg's ability to analyze children's mathematical thinking. While I thought I had made real progress in my understanding of children and learning, I knew I could go no further until I took the next step. I needed to teach in my own classroom and connect my ideas with reality.

The following September, masters degree in hand, I was substitute teaching; not the stuff of inspiration or professional satisfaction, but the ticket to a position as a long-term substitute in a sixth-grade class. The final quarter of the school year, from April to June, was mine.

I jumped right in where the regular classroom teacher had left off, "ratios and proportions," and no book for me! I consulted a variety of resources, including John A. Van De Walle's *Elementary School Mathematics: Teaching Developmentally* (1990). I provided interesting problems and activities that I believed would enable my students to come to their own understandings of ratio and proportion. I provided a variety of manipulatives to help my students solve the problems. I fell flat on my face. Nobody was having any fun. My students wanted no part of manipulatives or working together to solve problems.

I felt like a puzzle with some of the pieces missing. I had a vision. I possessed at least an elementary understanding of the theories and ideas that gave rise to and nurtured that vision. Until I found at least some of the missing pieces, I would not be able to put the vision into practice.

My thoughts returned to SummerMath for Teachers. I knew that I needed more direct experiences with the ways in which learning and mathematics connect. I figured that spending every waking hour for two weeks in thought and conversation about learning and teaching mathematics could only help. I was right. After two weeks of discovery and reflection, I knew I had found one of those missing pieces. I realized that my teaching decisions had been based on a limited understanding of learning and on simplistic ideas about elementary mathematics. My understanding of learning was limited largely to the ideas that had been transmitted to me through reading and discussions with other teachers with the same limitations.

As I struggled with mathematics during those two weeks, I remember thinking, "So this is what Piaget meant. This is what it feels like when your understanding comes up short and you struggle to make sense." Sometimes the understanding that I struggled so hard to reach would vaporize, like a ghost. Just as it was about to come into my grasp, it would waver, then suddenly disappear. The frustration was worth it. I knew what it meant to learn. I knew what it meant to understand.

While living the role of teacher-as-student, I also began to identify some of the real "stuff" of mathematics. I gained new respect for multiplication when I tried to figure out the number of possible combinations for arranging five books on a shelf. I realized that there is a lot more to multiplication than repeated addition. I also knew that I had just scratched the surface in understanding all that multiplication could mean.

My investigations and experiences at SummerMath gave me my first opportunities to identify the "big ideas" that mathematics education should be about. I realized that looking for big ideas is not a simple matter of identifying a series of universally agreed-upon concepts. It is not a job to be tackled by one person in isolation. It is an ongoing process that can be undertaken only in a professional community, committed to a serious dialogue that acknowledges the complexity of those concepts. I had begun to identify some of the real "stuff" of mathematics. I had taken some significant steps in identifying the important ideas that my students should confront and explore.

I came away from those two weeks in July with a deeper, more personal understanding of learning and a deeper respect for the mathematics that my students needed to learn. Toward the middle of August, I was hired for my first full-time teaching position. After spending three years in various capacities in other teachers' classrooms, I would finally have a classroom of my own. This would be my first real chance to put my vision into practice. I was aware that I was assigning myself a difficult task. There would be no textbooks to rely on. My students would supply what they understood about mathematics. I would supply what I understood about mathematics and children and teaching. I felt ready.

WHERE I AM (A CLASS OF MY OWN)

I was hired to teach sixth grade in the rural community in which I live, and where I had worked part-time as an aide and a substitute teacher. There are 3 sixth-grade classrooms of 24 students each. In the past that meant swapping students for math instruction to form three homogeneous groups. This year that plan was modified so that only the highest achievers, based on the recommendations of the fifth-grade teachers, are separated for math instruction. The remaining students are divided into two heterogeneous groups. I teach one of the latter. Each of the three classrooms operates from what I perceive to be distinctly different ideas about children and learning and mathematics. The high achievers receive traditional, textbook-driven instruction that emphasizes accuracy in computation. The other heterogeneous group receives textbook-based instruction combined with an attempt to teach logical thinking and problem solving through structured, teacher-directed activities. I started the year with the clear understanding that my students' backgrounds in mathematics had been overwhelmingly traditional, textbook-driven, and teacher-centered.

My students are the beneficiaries of my attempts to relate the skills and concepts outlined in the school district's curriculum to my understanding of mathematics, children, and learning. I am discovering what that means for me as I try to live up to my expectations for myself, as I take on the role of teacher as practitioner, researcher, decision maker. I believe that children learn by applying what they already know to new ideas and problems that challenge them to stretch their existing understandings and uncover their misunderstandings.

While learning in my classroom centers on children, it relies heavily on my ability to come to terms with the mathematics that I present to my students. It also relies heavily on my ability to translate my students' thoughts so that I can identify what they understand and what they misunderstand. Decision making, reflection, and the ability to face my own confusion with honesty and resolve are at the center of my mathematics instruction.

As I prepared to meet my sixth-grade class, I wrote myself the following message: "It will be important for me to listen, listen, listen." The two weeks I had spent at SummerMath had been filled with the sort of thoughtful, active listening that I had previously experienced when receiving and responding to students' writing or when I gathered with students to share our interpretations of a piece of literature. Over the course of those two weeks, I often had been astounded by how much I learned from listening to and reflecting on the ideas of other people as we worked together to bring meaning to mathematics. I looked forward to the exchanges of ideas that would take place in my classroom.

Early on in the school year, I once again was faced with the sense that my practice was falling short of my vision. The exchanges that took place in my classroom often left me feeling confused, at a loss, sorry I'd asked. I found myself groping to make connections between my students' lines of thinking and my own. I came away from many of those exchanges feeling I had missed the point. This time, however, I was committed to analyzing my teaching decisions and my students' reactions to those decisions on a daily basis. Most often my writing took the form of a running narrative of my struggles, and often it was difficult for me to gain meaning from the lessons I was recording. It wasn't until I went back to reflect on my reactions to those lessons, rather than on the narratives of the lessons themselves, that I was able to confront the major cause of the conflict between my practice and my principles. It wasn't until I realized what prevented me from listening that I was able to look back at those lessons and begin to understand what my students were thinking and just how much I had to learn about mathematics.

A PROBLEM

The following lesson is a case in point. It is just one of a series of lessons that taught me just how complicated fractions can be.

I was planning to introduce a series of activities, adapted from Marilyn Burns's book *About Teaching Mathematics* (1992). It was my hope that these activities would help my students develop their understanding of fractional parts. They would work in pairs to divide geoboards first into halves, then fourths, eighths, and sixteenths, in as many ways as they could find. They would then record each way they found on geodot paper.

The introductory activities, in which the students divide the board in half, are intended to provide them with an opportunity to become familiar with the materials and to provide their teacher with some information about what they already know about fractions.

They used the geoboards to explore different ways of dividing the boards into halves. Horizontal, vertical, and diagonal lines were suggested first. Tim suggested a method using zig-zag lines (see Figure 2.1).

He drew his model on the board, and there was general agreement that both pieces were equal. The class had no problem telling me how to write the

FIGURE 2.1. Tim's way of dividing the geoboard into halves

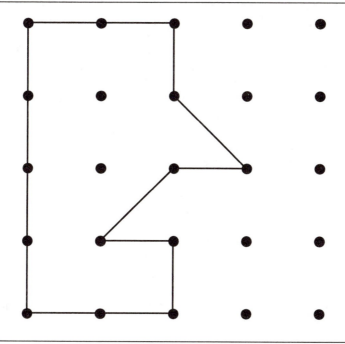

fraction for one-half on the board—"½." Then I asked my students what the top and bottom numbers in that fraction stood for. I was not prepared for David's answer.

1 thing

— cut into

2 equal pieces

David made it clear, as he drew the horizontal bar in the air with his finger, that the line took the place of the words "cut into."

I had done my homework. I had consulted what I considered to be a reliable resource for helping me to understand the mathematics involved in what I was teaching (John A. Van De Walle's *Elementary School Mathematics: Teaching Developmentally*). What I wanted to hear was something to the effect that the top number tells how many things we have and the bottom number tells what fractional part is being counted. I was stunned and at a loss as to how I should challenge David to help him say what I wanted to hear. I looked to his classmates to offer a challenge and asked if anyone else wanted to give an explanation.

Tim offered the following: "One-half means 1 out of 2 equal things."

Now we were getting somewhere. I thought we were back on track, asked for further suggestions, and breathed a sigh of relief when there were none. When I asked for reactions to the two explanations, I was met with a fairly even split in opinion. Some agreed with David's ideas. Others agreed with Tim's. Our 45-minute math period was drawing to a close. For homework, I asked everyone to write to me about what they thought of the two explanations.

To my dismay, most people agreed with David. Some students wrote that they thought Tim's explanation was confusing. Even Tim agreed with David's ideas.

What was my reaction? In my reflections about the lesson, I wrote: "These students have been working with fractions since first grade. They are familiar with standard symbolic form. Some of them, however, are having trouble connecting concepts to the symbolism."

I decided to put the geoboards aside for a while and have the students try some activities with fraction strips. I justified my decision with the comment, "Most of them are unfamiliar with geoboards. I don't want their lack of familiarity with the materials to interfere with their need to see, quickly and graphically, a variety of part-to-whole relationships."

UNDERSTANDING

What was going on here? What do I understand about my teaching in this lesson now, that I could not grasp at the time?

My own struggles with the mathematics and my reliance on the explanation in the Van De Walle text limited my ability to listen to and understand David's thinking. I could see only what was wrong in his ideas. I could not see that his explanation worked for how the symbol "½" represented Tim's drawing. The next question could have been, "Will it always work?"

Instead, I went searching for a more acceptable idea, one that was more in line with what I wanted to hear. I didn't reject David's idea immediately. I put it out for consideration next to Tim's in the hopes that it would be rejected by the class and David, too. When I couldn't get the class to buy into Tim's explanation, which was more comfortable for me, I went in search of the magic activity that would help my students see what I wanted them to see.

I was not able to understand the validity in David's explanation even when confronted with my own faulty thinking by Deborah Schifter, Summer-Math director. When I shared my written account of this lesson with her at the time, she wrote in response to David's idea, "Interesting. It works for unit fractions, but breaks down for others. Or does it? What would [David] say about ⅔?" In response to my decision to put the geoboards aside and move on to fraction strips, she wrote, "Why? What happened to David's idea?"

At the time, I couldn't respond to Deborah's comments. It was only after I had acknowledged my difficulties in unraveling the mathematics I was trying to teach, only after I recognized what I had been expressing in my reflections about my teaching, that I suddenly began to identify instances where my limitations were getting in the way of my listening and teaching for understanding.

In retrospect, I think I somehow slipped back into a habit of thinking about teaching that had its roots in my days as a student and was reinforced in the preservice courses and experiences that earned me my teacher certification: Teachers are keepers and transmitters of the truth. All that I had come to understand about children and teaching and learning was still susceptible to the influence of the powerful model I had experienced as a child, a model that is often reinforced in the surroundings in which I teach. While I never would have accused myself of leading my students to the truth, I had begun to operate under the assumption that we would somehow be in agreement as to just what the truths were in mathematics. The more I struggle with the mathematics that I teach, the less I search for universal truths.

I am just beginning to understand how children learn and how that translates into how teachers teach. I have a lot to learn. The more I struggle, the more I will understand. I understand that my vision of teaching and my practice have benefited from my commitment to know about children and learning. It was important for me to seek out the ideas of people like Dewey, Piaget, Calkins, and Ginsburg. But those ideas needed the problems from my practice to take on real meaning for me.

It is often unsettling to be coming to terms with understanding my teaching, and understanding what it is that I teach, all at the same time. I'm con-

vinced that it's worth it. These are the learning opportunities that will enable
my students to travel as far as they want to with mathematics. I have had to
return to my journey, too. I am only beginning to learn the kind of mathematics that teachers need to know. What are the concepts I should be teaching?
How well do I understand them myself? What sorts of connections can I expect from my children when they struggle with these ideas? My ability to
make meaningful decisions about my teaching can be only as good as my ability to assess my students' learning and understanding. My ability to assess my
students' learning and understanding of mathematics relies on my ability to understand and analyze the mathematics that takes place. I have learned to rely
on my students' expertise as we struggle to understand mathematics in my
classroom.

I wonder how we can expect teachers to struggle with the issues that are
so much a part of teaching mathematics for understanding if we don't encourage them to struggle with these same ideas and support them when they do.

REFERENCES

Burns, M. (1992). *About teaching mathematics*. New York: Math Solution Publications.
Van De Walle, J. A. (1990). *Elementary school mathematics: Teaching developmentally*. White Plains, NY: Longman.

$$+ \quad - \quad \times \quad \div$$

LEARNING WHILE DOING: UNDERSTANDING EARLY EFFORTS TO CREATE NEW PRACTICES OF TEACHING AND LEARNING MATHEMATICS FOR UNDERSTANDING

Ruth M. Heaton

In the culture of teaching it is unusual to find practitioners willing to discuss how confused and frustrated they feel about their work.[1] The openness
and honesty with which Karen Schweitzer and Anne Marie O'Reilly write
about what they did and did not understand, their unsparing accounts of the
false starts and self-doubt that attended their initial efforts to teach mathematics in ways aligned with the current reforms, offer us invaluable insight into
that process. Since such exposure, however vital it is to the prospects for successful reform, places these teachers in a vulnerable position, Schweitzer and
O'Reilly are to be commended for having broken the silence.

When teachers dare to pose problems from their practice, one of two
things usually happens. The first, and less damaging, tendency is for others to

want to solve their problems for them, to rush to their aid with the perfect activity, manipulative, or idea: The difficulties seem obvious; the solutions, simple. The second tendency, the one rightly feared most by teachers, is that they are judged incompetent. On the evidence of their thoughtful reflections and the small but growing number of accounts of other teachers trying to make comparable changes, it seems not only inaccurate but presumptuous to judge either Schweitzer or O'Reilly incompetent (Ball & Rundquist, 1993; Featherstone, Pfeiffer, & Smith, 1993; Heaton, 1994; Heaton & Lampert, 1993; Schifter & Fosnot, 1993).

What their narratives do evidence, instead, is the necessity to stop and examine the complexities of the questions they ask, the problems they face, and especially the difficulties inherent in the sort of teaching they aim to do. Schweitzer's and O'Reilly's personal accounts provide an opportunity to look at the work of two competent and responsible teachers fundamentally transforming their mathematics instruction. What is the nature of the practice they are trying to develop and why is learning to enact it so challenging?

The problems faced by these two teachers do not arise from naive conceptions of teaching mathematics for understanding. Thanks to their participation in SummerMath for Teachers, they began their efforts to teach mathematics in new ways with well-developed images of the kind of practice they wanted for themselves. The frustrations they experienced arose in the gap between those images and the realities of their attempts to enact them.

But these frustrations may have been exacerbated by their looking for relief—a way out of their difficulties—in the wrong places. Their past experiences in teacher education had led them to expect that somewhere "out there" there were rules, guidelines, and instructions for practice; activities "that work"; and books that would tell them what they needed to know. Although such resources have their uses, at this point in the teachers' development their attempts to import answers from outside their classrooms distracted them from looking inside. Schweitzer and O'Reilly would have to start learning from their students. This essay looks at two aspects of the process by which they reconstructed their mathematics instructional practice.

ENGAGING STUDENTS IN MATHEMATICAL DISCUSSION

Schweitzer and O'Reilly view learning as a social, constructive activity. Instead of doing mathematics alone and in silence, they believe their students should work together and talk about ideas. It is the teacher's responsibility to generate opportunities for them to work on problems together in order to make sense of the mathematics.

However, engaging students in discussion is not only a matter of technique, of drawing them into the learning process; it is also a different way— a social way—of knowing mathematics. Constructing knowledge by interacting with others around mathematical ideas is both a *means* of learning mathematics and *an aspect of the very mathematics being learned.* Knowing mathematics includes understanding how to be a member of a community that acknowledges the set of values and norms governing such interactions—participants must learn to conjecture, revise ideas, give and take criticism, offer proof, argue mathematically, and strive for consensus in the context of working on mathematical problems (Hanna, 1989; Lakatos, 1986; Lampert, 1990; Tymoczko, 1986).

Schweitzer's story, especially, allows us to appreciate the difficulty of enacting this aspect of the new mathematics instruction. She wants her students to talk about mathematical ideas, but even when she thinks she has found appropriate questions to ask, she finds that "my questions often are answered with silence. . . . My discussions were falling flat on their face, and when I tried to push it, all I ended up with were behavior problems." She becomes dismayed by her students' lack of involvement, their apparent lack of interest, in what she asks them to do. She is troubled by their bored, frustrated, and confused reactions and wonders if the difficulty rests in the questions she poses, the problems she sets, or her understanding of the mathematics she wants them to learn.

Why is it so difficult to enlist students in discussion of mathematical ideas? How can we understand their silences, their unresponsive behavior, when she invites them to talk?

In fact, these students are responding in quite understandable and predictable ways—as Schweitzer will come to recognize after several years of experience with this kind of practice. In Chapter 3 of this book's companion volume, Jill Bodner Lester (1996) describes being confronted with a similar situation early in the new school year: "I asked how they had arrived at the answer, but there was no response to my question." And a few days later: "There was no sound. There was no movement. I was met with 25 silent, immobile, and expressionless children." However, having worked to create new norms for mathematical discussion with six previous second-grade classes, Lester responds with equanimity rather than panic: "I hadn't really expected any [response], as the question was unfamiliar to them, and they would need time to get used to the kind of question I was asking."

Schweitzer, like Lester, is trying to engage her second graders in a kind of mathematical discourse they have not experienced before. Her students' negative reactions could be indicative of confusion over what they are expected to do. After all, silence and individual work were probably the norm in their previous mathematics classes. Now, suddenly, talk and cooperation are expected.

This first year that Schweitzer is attempting to teach for understanding, she and her students are learning together just what kind of mathematics discussion can take place in a second-grade classroom. The previous summer she participated in a mathematics community composed of adults; now she must create a mathematics community of seven-year-olds. All at once, she must learn about the mathematical notions her young students have, the questions that interest them, and how they express their ideas. And she must learn how to communicate the values, norms, and purposes that guide work in a mathematical community. She must learn to expect and interpret in new ways—even use—such reactions as boredom, frustration, and confusion.

But by the very nature of the practice, she can learn about second-grade mathematical discussion only while *leading* it. This means setting aside the notion that the teacher must always be in control, unfailingly know what decisions to make, and stick to a preconceived script, come what may. This first year, she must allow herself to flounder—in the public arena of her classroom—as she tries to construct, together with her students, a community of mathematical inquirers.

ACQUIRING AND USING MATHEMATICAL KNOWLEDGE

To instruct for understanding, teachers need an appreciation of both (1) the ideas, concepts, connections, and relationships that are important for students to learn; and (2) what their students understand about the mathematical territory. Both elements are necessary if teachers are to help students build on what they already know and then extend that knowledge to the topics mandated by the mathematics curriculum.

At the SummerMath for Teachers Institute, Anne Marie O'Reilly examined and deepened her understanding of fractions by working on problems with colleagues and by observing and analyzing videotapes of children discussing questions about fractions. On her own, she reviewed a teacher education textbook and selected tasks from activity books to bring to her class. However, once in the classroom, she found this preparation insufficient.

One of the difficulties O'Reilly faced is that the mathematics she and her students were trying to understand is very complicated. For example, the definition of numerator and denominator she hoped to hear from her students—"something to the effect that the top number tells how many things we have and the bottom number tells what fractional part is being counted"—represents only one among multiple interpretations of fractional expressions (Behr, Lesh, Post, & Silver, 1983; Hiebert & Behr, 1988). The terrain of rational numbers, of which fractions are a part, is filled with complex ideas, relationships, and connections that are inherently difficult to understand.[2]

But O'Reilly's second difficulty, according to her own account, involved her inability to unravel her students' understandings when these did not match her own. As an example, she tells of one student, David, who suggested that "½" means one (1) thing cut into (—) two (2) pieces and then persuaded most of the class to prefer his interpretation. She wrote:

My own struggles with the mathematics and my reliance on the explanation in the Van De Walle text limited my ability to listen to and understand David's thinking. I could see only what was wrong in his ideas. I could not see that his explanation worked for how the symbol "½" represented Tim's drawing.

What O'Reilly discovered was that a teacher can enter the classroom, armed with what she believes is a deep understanding of mathematics content, only to be thrown by the sense her students make of that content. Suddenly the mathematics she thought she understood comes back at her in unfamiliar shapes. However, if the teacher is responsible for helping students build upon their own mathematical understanding, then, when confronted with unfamiliar ideas, the teacher must do more than look for what is wrong with them—he or she must try to understand how and why they make sense to the students. Sometimes, the teacher must even revise his or her own ideas. In the traditional mathematics classroom, it is the job of the teacher to facilitate students' understandings. In the new mathematics classroom, the influence travels both ways—from teacher to students, yes, but also from students to teacher.

LEARNING FROM EXPERIENCE

As students and teachers together begin to engage with mathematics as active problem solvers and constructors of meaning, they also must learn to reinterpret affective states associated with learning. In particular, they have to realize that, in contrast to traditional ways of being in the classroom, frustration, confusion, or puzzlement are not necessarily indicative of failure. These feelings, too, are part of the process of learning. O'Reilly herself writes that being "thrown into mathematical confusion over something as apparently simple as dividing one fraction by another" was a "tantalizing introduction."

Analogously, as teachers learn to enact a new vision of teaching, their feelings of confusion and frustration must be seen not as indications of failure, but as inevitable and even positive aspects of the process. This is more easily said than done, however, when, as learners in their own classrooms, teachers are so vulnerable, so exposed to the judgment of their students, colleagues, principals, and parents.

Three months into the school year, Schweitzer and O'Reilly have come to expect these challenges and no longer respond with "frenzy and hopelessness." As problems arise in their practice, they have learned to look not to "experts" to tell them what to do, but to themselves—turning, perhaps, to their own journals—or to other teachers who can "help [them] interpret what is happening and use their experience to offer suggestions," much as Schweitzer sought out her colleague, Susan Smith, or used her peers in the writing course to help her analyze classroom process and plan instructional strategies.

The fact that these two teachers have been willing to write about their frustrations enables us all to learn from their experience. These accounts can provide teachers who work to reform their own mathematics instruction with a context for interpreting their feelings of confusion and frustration. And others who are in position to support those teachers—for example, principals and school administrators—especially in the face of skeptical parents, can better understand the complexities and challenges inherent in the process.

NOTES

1. The author would like to thank Deborah Schifter, Kara Suzuka, Magdalene Lampert, and Deborah Ball for their contributions to the ideas and text presented here.

2. For an understanding of the complexity of fractions from a third-grade mathematics teacher's perspective, see Ball (1993).

REFERENCES

Ball, D. L. (1993). Halves, pieces, and twoths: Constructing representational contexts in teaching fractions. In T. P. Carpenter, E. Fennema, & T. Romberg (Eds.), *Rational numbers: An integration of research* (pp. 157-196). Hillsdale, NJ: Lawrence Erlbaum.

Ball, D. L., & Rundquist, S. (1993). Collaboration as a context for joining teacher learning with learning about teaching. In D. K. Cohen, M. W. McLaughlin, & J. E. Talbert (Eds.), *Teaching for understanding: Challenges for policy and practice* (pp. 13-42). San Francisco: Jossey-Bass.

Behr, M. J., Lesh, R., Post, T. R., & Silver, E. A. (1983). Rational-number concepts. In R. Lesh & M. Landau (Eds.), *Acquisition of mathematics concepts and processes* (pp. 91-126). New York: Academic Press.

Featherstone, H., Pfeiffer, L., & Smith, S. P. (1993). Learning in good company: Report on a pilot study (Research Report 93-2). East Lansing: Michigan State University, National Center for Research on Teacher Learning.

Hanna, G. (1989). More than formal proof. *For the Learning of Mathematics, 9*(1), 20-23.

Heaton, R. M. (1994). Creating and studying a practice of teaching elementary mathematics for understanding. Unpublished doctoral dissertation, Michigan State University, East Lansing.

Heaton, R. M., & Lampert, M. (1993). Learning to hear voices: Inventing a new pedagogy of teacher education. In D. K. Cohen, M. W. McLaughlin, & J. E. Talbert (Eds.), *Teaching for understanding: Challenges for policy and practice* (pp. 43-83). San Francisco: Jossey-Bass.

Hiebert, J., & Behr, M. (Eds.). (1988). *Number concepts and operations in the middle grades*. Hillsdale, NJ: Lawrence Erlbaum.

Lakatos, I. (1986). *Proofs and refutations.* Cambridge: Cambridge University Press.

Lampert, M. (1990). When the problem is not the question and the solution is not the answer: Mathematical knowing and teaching. *American Educational Research Journal, 27*(1), 29–63.

Lester, J. B. (1996). Establishing a community of mathematics learners. In D. Schifter (Ed.), *What's happening in math class?, Volume 1: Envisioning new practices through teacher narratives* (pp. 88–102). New York: Teachers College Press.

Schifter, D., & Fosnot, C. T. (1993). *Reconstructing mathematics education: Stories of teachers meeting the challenge of reform.* New York: Teachers College Press.

Tymoczko, T. (1986). Making room for mathematicians in the philosophy of mathematics. *The Mathematical Intelligencer, 8*(3), 44–50.

CHAPTER 3

As Monitors of Student Learning: Inquiring into Students' Mathematical Conceptions

For the new mathematics pedagogy, monitoring student learning requires a practice of disciplined listening quite different from that called for in traditional mathematics instruction—not, as one perceptive teacher puts it, "listening for specific indicators that a student . . . [is] following *my* line of thinking" (Natowich, 1992, p. 3), but instead listening in order to follow the *student's* line of thinking. If, as Stephen Lerman argues, "interpreting what students know from what they say is far from straightforward," the three narratives that precede his essay—by Janice Szymaszek, Christine Anderson, and Jessica Redman—enact the interpretive principle that, in order to discover the sense in what students say, one must inquire into how they arrived at the thought expressed. Disciplined listening is listening for the mathematical sense in student constructions. By the end of a first year of far-reaching change, Szymaszek, Anderson, and Redman have refashioned their identities as monitors of student learning: In instruction dependent on constant assessment of student understanding, sustained inquiry into student constructions has become the basis of their pedagogical decision making. Lerman's essay explores a number of significant implications that this emphasis on inquiry has for teaching, among them a provocative reconception of what constitutes relevant education research.

Janice Szymaszek and Christine Anderson both teach kindergarten, Szymaszek in a laboratory school at a private college and Anderson in an urban public school; Jessica Redman is a second-grade teacher in a college town.

REFERENCE

Natowich, D. (1992). Learning the art of unteaching. Unpublished paper.

A YEAR OF INQUIRY

Janice M. Szymaszek

As I work with the children in my kindergarten class during this, my year of inquiry, I am redefining my role as a teacher of mathematics. I realize that it is not enough for me to maintain a mathematics program that is child-centered and developmentally appropriate; I also must help children develop fundamental understandings and positive attitudes toward learning mathematics. To do this, I must know more about the children's thinking: How have their basic understandings developed in the years leading to kindergarten? What are the concepts they are developing during the kindergarten year?

PRESCHOOLERS' KNOWLEDGE OF NUMBERS

Children in preschool already know a lot about numbers and are trying to create systems for using them. A colleague of mine teaches the youngest of the preschool classes, the three- to four-year-olds. Recently, she shared these two stories with me.

Derek, a four-year-old, was trying to figure out if there was enough room for him to enter an activity intended for a given number of children.

"There's four boys and one girl," he said.

The teacher held up four fingers on one hand and one finger on the other hand, and restated his observation, "So, four boys (gesturing with the hand showing four fingers) and one girl (gesturing with the other hand). I wonder how many kids that makes altogether?"

Derek was bothered by this representation. "No," he said, "not like that. One-four is 14. It's four boys and one girl like this (showing all on one hand). That's five!"

The teacher wondered, "So, what's one and two (gesturing as before, with one finger on one hand, and two on the other)?"

Without hesitation, Derek offered, "Twelve!"

Another example of preschoolers' sense of numbers occurred as the group was trying to count how many children were present that day. The teacher invited them to join her as she began to count: "One, two, three, four," but she was interrupted. "No, no. I'm not four. I'm three." Then again when they got to the seventh child, "Seven, eight." "Nope. My brother's seven, I'm three." From the other side of the circle came disagreement, "No, I'm three. . . . "

These examples from preschool are instructive and illuminating. How do children work through such confusion as they untangle the multiple meanings numbers have? How do they learn to "call up" the appropriate meaning, based on the context of its use (for example, when three means "how many" and when three means "how old")? The stories also suggest remarkable growth in the two years between preschool and kindergarten. In this narrative I have included many stories, taken from my class, that will show that, by the time children reach kindergarten, they have made sense of these ambiguities and are already confronting new challenges.

What is my role as a kindergarten teacher who is trying to help children develop further such mathematical understanding?

MY ROLE

My role has become listening for, and identifying, the mathematics involved in the concepts children are constructing, and finding ways to connect it to what they are trying to do. Through interviews, observations, and conversations I have had with them, the children are teaching me a lot about how they think about numbers and mathematics. I'm learning how to support and challenge their thinking, stimulate their interests, and inspire them to stretch their understanding to make new discoveries. Sometimes I meet with success, and sometimes I fail. I've learned what not to do as often as I've found something that works. The journey has been both glorious and bewildering.

The bewildering moments happen most often when I'm faced with something unexpected: children's comments that let me know that I have misunderstood their thinking or that I have not considered some aspect of their work. Of course, expecting the unexpected is one "given" of teaching children in kindergarten. They do not always follow a line of logic I would predict. They can often say the words that lead me to assume I know how they're thinking, but there are often different ideas lying beneath the surface of their words. On the other hand, they know more, in some cases, than they can put into words. Every time I have one of these bewildering moments, I am forced to reflect on and to analyze how the problem looks from the perspective of a five- or six-year-old.

JENNY

In December, I interviewed Jenny, age five-and-a-half, to find out how she was thinking about numbers and counting. The interview focused on four areas: rote counting, counting objects, number recognition, and problem solving. I began by asking Jenny to count.

She counted, "One, two, free [three], . . . [to] . . . twelf, furteen [thirteen], furteen [fourteen], fifteen, sixteen, seventeen, eighteen," then stopped.

She counted again, this time stopping after "furteen [thirteen], furteen [fourteen]." "I don't know why I do that," she said, "I say a same fing [the same thing] two times. I just do it yike yat [like that]."

In January, I asked Jenny to count again. A colleague, upon hearing Jenny's story, had asked me what happened when she got to the thirties and forties. I decided to find out. This time, when Jenny got to thirteen, she rolled up her tongue and thrust it forward, attempting to make the "th" sound, said "thhha-urteen, furteen, fifteen, sixteen, seventeen, eighteen, nineteen, twenty . . . [to] . . . twenty-nine, furty, furty-one . . . [to] . . . furty-nine, furty, furty-one . . . [to] . . . fifty."

What does Jenny know about counting? She knows the conventional tags (labels) for the counting sequence. She knows that there is a fixed order to that sequence. She is also aware that within that fixed order, each tag must be distinct and unique. It didn't make sense to her that she had what sounded like the same number to indicate two different places in the sequence. What surprised me most about her understanding was the level of her own consciousness about counting and her ability to express it.

Through our exchange, Jenny taught me an important lesson about listening to what children are trying to do. Often, their product masks the hard work and complexity of their process.

COUNTING RULES

In years past, I thought that counting and numeration were fairly simple cognitive tasks. Now, I'm not so sure. I wonder: How do children learn to count? What do their counting "errors" reveal about their understanding of the number system and how it works? What is interesting to them about counting? How can their understanding be challenged in ways that lead them to make new discoveries about numbers? What powers the children's drive to count and order?

Inspired by the insights gained through my interviews with Jenny, I decided to initiate a whole group discussion about counting. One day, I started with the following message to my class, called "Group J":

February 5, 1991

Dear Group J,

I've been thinking . . .
We count pennies in the penny jar.
We count kids in Group J.
We count days on our weather chart.

We count a lot!
How did you learn to count?

Love,
Ms. Szymaszek

Katie said, "I used to count like this, '1, 5, 6, 4,' until my mom and dad taught me how." Many of the children liked the now-apparent absurdity of their former counting technique, and they related similar tales. When I asked them what they thought was wrong with that counting, several children said, "You can't skip any numbers!" Adam, age six, reminded the group, "Except when you dial." A brief discussion followed. Children described telephone number sequences as different from counting sequences because they didn't go "1, 2, 3 . . . ." Carl added, "But sometimes it does. My telephone number goes 586-4517. The four, five goes right!"

These comments provided another lesson for me. I'd never considered the confusion with which children must grapple to resolve the conflict between these two well-known, but very different, number sequences. I wondered how many other such ambiguities were resting beneath the surface of the children's understanding.

Despite this new insight, I remember leaving that discussion feeling somewhat disappointed. I had hoped for more. I was frustrated at not having the right questions to probe their understanding. When the meeting ended, I had a moment to reflect—and some ideas occurred to me. I thought about what the children would do if I proposed new ways of counting. What if I skipped numbers? What if I didn't count in the order they expected? By having them describe why my new ways of counting were incorrect, I hoped they would be clearer about what counting was. I quickly jotted my ideas into my notebook, so I could come back to them.

Despite my frustration, I felt that for the children, I had put counting, an activity often taken for granted, on the table for scrutiny. Counting became something to talk about, not just something to do.

A few days later, I tried my nonexamples. The message for that day read:

February 7, 1991

Dear Group J,

I was thinking . . .
When you count out loud, you say,
"———, ———, ———, ———, ———, ———, ———,
———, ———, ———." When you count things, you say,
"———, ———, ———, ———, ———, ———,———,

_____, _____, _____.'' Why can't you say, "One, one, one, one, one, one, one, one, one, one,'' when you count things?

Love,
Ms. Szymaszek

After reading the message and filling in the blanks with the number words from one to ten, we got to the question at hand.

Me: Why is it that you can't count these [seven unifix cubes] like this: one, one, one, one, one, one, one?

No response, so I asked again.

Me: Why can't I say that? This (holding up the first cube) is one, isn't it? And this (holding up the second cube) is one . . .
Unison: No. It's two!
Me: Look at it! It's one. I have one in my hand. (Giggles)
Paul: No, it's two. You have one in your hand, but it's two. That's how it is when you count.
Me: So if I have one thing in my hand, it's one, right?
Nancy: No, it's two because you already said one for the first one!
Me: Okay, so let's count these cubes to find out how many are really here. I have another question I want to ask you.

We counted, "1, 2, 3, 4, 5, 6, 7.''

Me: How many are there?
Unison: Seven
Me: What if I counted them like this: 1, 5, 4, 6, 2, 3, 7?
Joe: No, you're skipping so many!
Me: But I got seven!
Laura: You just said seven for the last one.
Joe: You counted a different way.
Me: What's wrong with that?
Abbie: That's not another way to count; but there is another way to count to seven—in another language.
Joe: It doesn't make a difference. That would just be Spanish or something.

Bringing the discussion back to my original question, I counted "1, 5, 4, 6, 2, 3, 7" and asked, "Why does that bother you so much?"

Carl: No, you can't count like that. That's like a telephone number (recalling Adam's comment from the other day, I believe). You skipped numbers!

Sarah: She didn't skip any, she just mixed it up. (No one attends to her comment.)

Me: On Tuesday, you told me that the important thing about counting is not to skip any numbers. Now you're saying that there's another thing to remember about counting.

Sam: You can't just go "5, 6, 7, 9, 10, 100, 12" (touching one cube for each number). You have to go 1, 2, 3, 4, 5, 6, 7.

Joe: Yeah, you skipped.

Me: I didn't skip any. I'll show you. (I write each number on an index card, put the numbers in order, and then mix them up, using each one.)

Joe: But that doesn't make any sense. They're out of order.

Me: So, what you're saying is that now I have to remember not to skip any numbers and they have to go in a certain order?

Katie: But you could count by 10s!

This indicated, I think, a misconception about "skip counting," which was really confusing, because when you count by 10s, it *seems* that you've "skipped" 1–9. When you say "ten," you've made only one count. What an apparent contradiction!

At this point, I thought our discussion was over, so I put the cubes away and was ready to move on. Just to be sure, I asked, "Is there anything else you want to say about counting?"

Jenny: You could count backwards.

Joe: Yeah. It doesn't make a difference.

I took back some cubes. This time there were 12 altogether. I asked, "Count backwards—so, what should we start with?"

Joe: Ten.

We counted "10, 9, 8, 7, 6, 5, 4, 3, 2, 1" and there were two left over. A few children counted the next one as zero, and the others were either totally surprised or not interested.

Me: What's this (holding up the last cube)?

Anthony: Negative one.

Katie: Negative one.

Carl: Nine.

Lena: One hundred!

Anthony: Negative one means you (pause) because counting doesn't
ever start or end. You start from uh . . . uh . . . minus are half left
of the number system. One is not the only start. Numbers have no
end and no start.

He lost most of his classmates, but I nodded, knowing I'd get back to him
at another time, and we tried the backwards count again. I wanted them to be
as bothered as I was about their calling something zero. I thought that the error of not starting at the right place was as obvious to them as it was to me,
so I asked, "What was the problem? Let's try it again." Sarah suggested starting with 11. This time, I stopped when we got to zero.

Me: This (holding up the cube) is not zero. This is something, and
zero is nothing. You can't convince me that this is zero.

Sam: It's BLAST-OFF!

Obviously, enough for this day!

Probing their understanding with direct questions, I had hoped to gain insights into children's rules for counting. To some extent, I learned what I was
after; however, I was not completely satisfied with how things went. Kindergarten children learn by doing, not just discussing! I learned about their rules
for counting, but did they? For me, identifying the issues was a necessary first
step, but I thought the children would have had an easier time making generalizations about the counting process. Perhaps my efforts were misplaced.

As my process of inquiry evolves into a plan of action, I want the children in my class to "put counting on the table" for themselves as the result
of some problem-solving experience that makes them examine what they know
about counting. The process, then, would be learner-driven, with the teacher
"leading from behind" (Newman, 1989).

USING THE DAILY NUMBER CHART

One feature of my math program that seems to promote such learner-
driven inquiry about numbers, counting, and the number system comes from
our daily recording of how many days we've been in school.

Each day, we put a penny in our penny jar and write the corresponding
number on a grid. As the number of days increases and the numbers are recorded, the children start to notice patterns in the repeated elements: "All the
1s are here, the 2s are here," or "It goes 1, 2, 3, 4, 5, 6, 7, 8, 9, 0, and
then 1, 2, 3, 4, 5, 6, 7, 8, 9, 0, again and again." They were intrigued by
the notion of twin digits (11, 22, 33, and so on) and were very interested in

the triple digit 111. Paul even went on to generate the triple digit numbers to one thousand!

What's the point of all this? I believe it gives children the opportunity to ponder, speculate, and develop an analytical perspective about numbers. Consider the following discussion that I recently overheard:

Dennis: 124 isn't counting by 5s.

Nancy: Yesterday, 123; today, 124; tomorrow, 125. It's sort of like counting, but the same ones are in the middle, and the counting is at the end, see? 1, 2, 1; 1, 2, 2; 1, 2, 3; 1, 2, 4; 1, 2, 5 . . .

John: Hey, on 123, it went 1, 2, 3!

Sarah: It's different from the beginning, though, because the numbers in 123 are all in the same box.

Anthony: The first ones [first row on the chart] are all only one [digit], then comes two [digits], then we get to three [digits] in each box. When it's more [meaning when the number gets bigger], it keeps getting more numbers. I wonder how much [meaning how many digits] will be in the ten thousands.

The pennies in the penny jar offer similar daily encounters with numbers, but here the children explore number quantities. Questions about fair sharing lead to ongoing work with taking numbers apart and putting them back together. For example, when we wanted to find out if we had enough pennies for each of us to get two, we dealt out the pennies from our penny jar, giving one to each child.

When we had 117 pennies, I asked how many each person would get. Joe responded, "It wouldn't be fair, yet. Not everybody will get six, yet." When I asked him why he started there, he said, "I knew that when we had 100 all the kids had five, so when we get another 20, we'll all get six. But we have three more to go until we get the next 20." Sarah chimed in, "On the chart, you have to wait two [rows] to be able to have everybody get one!" She noticed that the quantities that could be divided equally among the group followed a pattern on the number chart: not 10, but 20; not 30, but 40; not 50, but 60, and so on. I'm not sure if she understood that the number represented by "waiting two rows" was the same as the number of children in the class, and that's why her theory worked; but hers was a workable theory nonetheless.

COUNTING "ONE HUNDRED"

Keeping track of the number of days we've been in school builds toward the celebration of our hundredth day. On that day, I wanted to give the children a chance to see what 100 looked like. One hundred is a wonderful number for kindergartners to explore. For some, it's the limit of their rote counting. For others, it's the biggest number they can think of. For most, it is a quantity that they have rarely encountered or examined. I wanted to provide a structure for my students to experience counting with a number that big.

Each child brought a collection of items from home (things like macaroni, beans, washers, and pennies) to glue onto a line that I drew on a large mural paper. To help children keep track of the number they "were on," I established check-in points. After gluing 10 objects, the child would call me over to his or her line to record the next "10." The only numbers written on each child's line were 10, 20, 30, 40, 50, 60, 70, 80, 90, and 100.

Because each item in each collection was touching the item that came before it on the line, and because from collection to collection the items varied in size, some children's collections covered only a yard and some continued up to and onto the ceiling! As the children were working on gluing their items to their lines, they practiced counting, counting on (it was easier to start from 39, for example, than to go back to 1!), and thinking in terms of 10s.

John was puzzled by the differing lengths of people's lines, despite the number they were on. "Wait a minute, that's 30 and it's way up there, but that's 50 and it only goes that far!" He was articulating the principle of conservation of number; that is, that quantity is determined by the number of objects in the collection, not by the (perception of the) length of the collection. Obviously, John was close enough to understanding this phenomenon that he was bothered by what he noticed. Some children never recognized the problem. It was not within what Vygotsky (1962/1984) calls their "zone of proximal development" (which he defines as "the discrepency between a child's actual mental age and the level he reaches in solving problems with assistance" [p. 103]). For others, the explanation was so obvious that they were not puzzled at all. Sarah's comment expressed their perspective: "Those macaroni noodles are longer than the rice, so that hundred just looks bigger. They're still the same!" This is the kind of range that is common in kindergarten.

Since the murals were left on display, the children continued to talk a lot about one hundred and about the variation in height of the collections. One day at snack time, I joined a group of six children, and as I sat down I read the sign that was next to the murals: "How much is 100?"

"Fifty and fifty," said Ken.

"Ten groups of ten," said Laura.

"What do you mean?" I asked.

Laura responded, "When I counted my shells, I counted ten groups of ten."

I continued to probe, "What does that have to do with one hundred?" Laura explained how she took her shells and when she made 10 groups of 10, she had 100. (She still didn't say where she got the idea to stop at 10 groups of 10, but there was something about the way she explained it that made me think her parents or older brother had suggested it. By this time, most of the other children at the table were involved in our discussion.)

From the other end of the table, Nancy said, "See?" She walked over to her collection and moved her finger from number to number: "1, 2, 3, 4, 5, 6, 7, 8, 9, 10."

I wanted to push her thinking. "But when you said one, your finger was on the number ten, and when you said two, your finger was on the number twenty. I don't get it!"

"I think I know what she means. I can explain it," interjected Laura as she joined Nancy at the mural. "From there to there is ten."

Nancy responded, "Yeah, here's a line of ten, here's a line of ten, here's a line of ten, . . . "

Ken commented, "It's like multiplying!"

I wondered if he truly did grasp the fundamental understanding of multiplication that his comment implied, so I asked him what he meant. He didn't respond. I went back to Laura's and Nancy's explanations. They seemed so convinced and so clear in their joint statement that I was sure they really understood the idea behind their words. In fact, it seemed to me that Laura grasped the concept right then and there, in a way she had never understood it before. I wanted one last chance to check in and have them apply their new understanding. "Oh, so, 10 groups of 10 are 100. I wonder what 5 groups of 10 would be?" Ken began counting on his fingers, mouthing something (numbers?) to himself. But Laura responded quickly, "I don't know what it would be, but I know it would probably be much bigger than 100!!!!"

I was so surprised that I had been so misled about her understanding. I expected her to respond with certainty, which she did; but I also expected that she knew that five 10s would be much less than 100 (which she was calling ten 10s). I wondered where I went wrong in following her understanding. I wanted to try again.

The next day, I sat with the same children, pursued the same line of thinking, and asked the same question.

Me: How much is 100?
Laura: Ten groups of ten.
Sam: Fifty plus fifty.
Me: Laura, why did you say 10 groups of 10? Could it be 11 groups of 10?

Laura looked as if she was going to say she didn't know, but got interrupted by Sam.

Sam: It would make a higher number. That's 111. No, 110. Yeah, 110.
Me: So what makes you think about 100 as 10 groups of 10?
Laura: Ten piles of ten.
Ken: Count 10 ten times, you get 100.
Nancy: Ten 10s are 20.
Ken: No, that's when you count ten TWO times.
Nancy: Oh, yeah.

Nancy, Laura, and Katie moved to the mural with Nancy's collection on it and repeated a version of yesterday's 10-lines-of-10, saying "one," when they got to 10, "two," when they got to 20, and so on.

Me: Sam, you said 100 was 50 plus 50. What did you mean?
Sam: I know my pluses.
Me: What are pluses?
Sam: It means you get a higher number. See? Ten plus ten is 20, so we're right!
Me: So the opposite of plus is what?
Sam: Times, and times takes away things.
Paul: Five 10s of 5 makes up the 50.

Often, during such interactions with the children in my class, I cannot keep up with all the ideas that surface, but, if I'm lucky, I can catch a few that will inform my work this year with these individuals and with the whole group. Some of the ideas I cannot handle in the current year, either because I am ill-equipped to interpret them, or because they seem too idiosyncratic, at this time, to warrant further probing. I record them in my notes and save them for summer reflection.

For now, I'm concentrating on the ones that will further my understanding of how children think about the mathematical concepts that are more universally accessible to kindergarten children. While it is true that the range of possibilities is interesting and informative, I want to focus on those concepts that are typically most interesting and powerful.

COUNTING: PLANNED LESSONS

Spontaneous, informal discussions with children can be quite enlightening, but they cannot match the deeper mathematical understanding that children develop from working with problems that challenge their current understanding and force them to re-examine, reflect, and revise their thinking.

The "Number of Legs" problems were inspired by a colleague who had suggested the first problem of the series when she told me about her experience with having her second-grade students figure out (without looking) how many legs were under the table where they were sitting. I was intrigued. I wondered what kindergartners would do with the same problem. I liked the interesting possibilities that the problem offered for working with counting.

The children were to find out how many legs, then how many heads, then how many eyes, then how many noses, and finally how many fingers there were at their table. (Tables had either five, six, or eight children at them.) They could look under the table or do whatever they needed to in order to solve the problem. The problem of finding out how many fingers was a special challenge, and there was great creativity in solving it. Anthony actually tried to count each person's fingers and got quite frustrated. Joanne used her own fingers and recounted them as many times as she needed. She counted all her fingers once, and said, "That's for Adam." Then she went on, "These are for Elena. One, two." "One?" I interrupted. "Not one," she said, "I have to start with a new number. It's 11, 12 . . . [to] . . . 20. Now for Max: 21, 22 . . . [to] . . . 30." Joanne continued for each person at the table. For her, it was a "counting-on problem." John counted by 10s: "10, 20, 30, 40, 50, 60, 70, 80. That was easy!"

Having given them a chance, in the previous problem, to count things "at hand," I wanted them to extend their thinking to quantities that were represented pictorially. "Today, you will count the number of legs you have in your family. Include people and animals." Following a discussion about whether or not to include grandparents, pets that had died, or a divorced parent, they began drawing their pictures to represent the number of legs.

As we gathered to share our results, we made a chart to show, for each child's family, how many legs in total were made by how many people and how many animals. (We agreed not to count fish because they didn't contribute to the leg total, but another time this might present an interesting problem.) By wonderful coincidence, Nancy's results were below Lena's.

| Lena | 12 legs | 4 people | 1 animal |
| Nancy | 12 legs | 3 people | 2 animals |

"How can that be?" I asked. "They both have 12 legs!" Because the day ended here, the children didn't have a chance to respond, but I was excited about the direction our work was heading.

The next day, we brought out the chart again and looked for different ways someone could "get to" the same total. I gave them a new problem about a pretend family that had 12 legs. "How could they have made 12 with people and animals?" Sam asked if there could be all people and no animals or if there could be all animals and no people. I decided to make those possibilities legitimate, too. I modeled another one of their suggestions by drawing it according to a new format. For this lesson, instead of giving them a blank paper, on which it was difficult for some to organize their work, I labeled the papers with a space for representing people's legs, a space for representing animals with four legs, and a space for representing animals with two legs. I hoped this would provide a useful, and yet not limiting, structure, and that it would also help us compare results when we looked at them all together.

Jenny's drawing (Figure 3.1) was typical of many children's work and shows the most common combination: four people and one animal with four legs.

It is interesting to note the order in which she proceeded, as indicated by her numerals. She started with two people and got to four legs. Then, she made an animal with four legs and got to eight, by counting on. Finally, she added two more people and got to the total, 12.

I wondered what this indicated about her interpretation of the problem and about her sense of numbers. Did she want to include both people and animals? Did she think that two people would be as many people as she could have, and that one animal with four legs would get her to 12? Or was she going along by trial and error, without a bigger plan? Because I didn't ask her during her work, I could not know for sure.

John, and four or five other children, were inspired to find several solutions to the problem. Three of John's attempts are shown in Figure 3.2.

A challenging aspect of this problem, for John, as well as the whole

FIGURE 3.1. Jenny's Combination

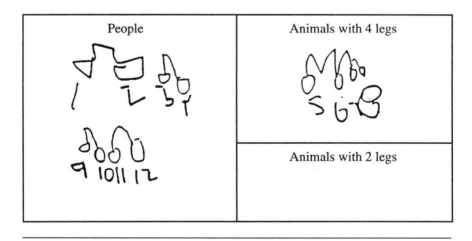

FIGURE 3.2. John's Combinations

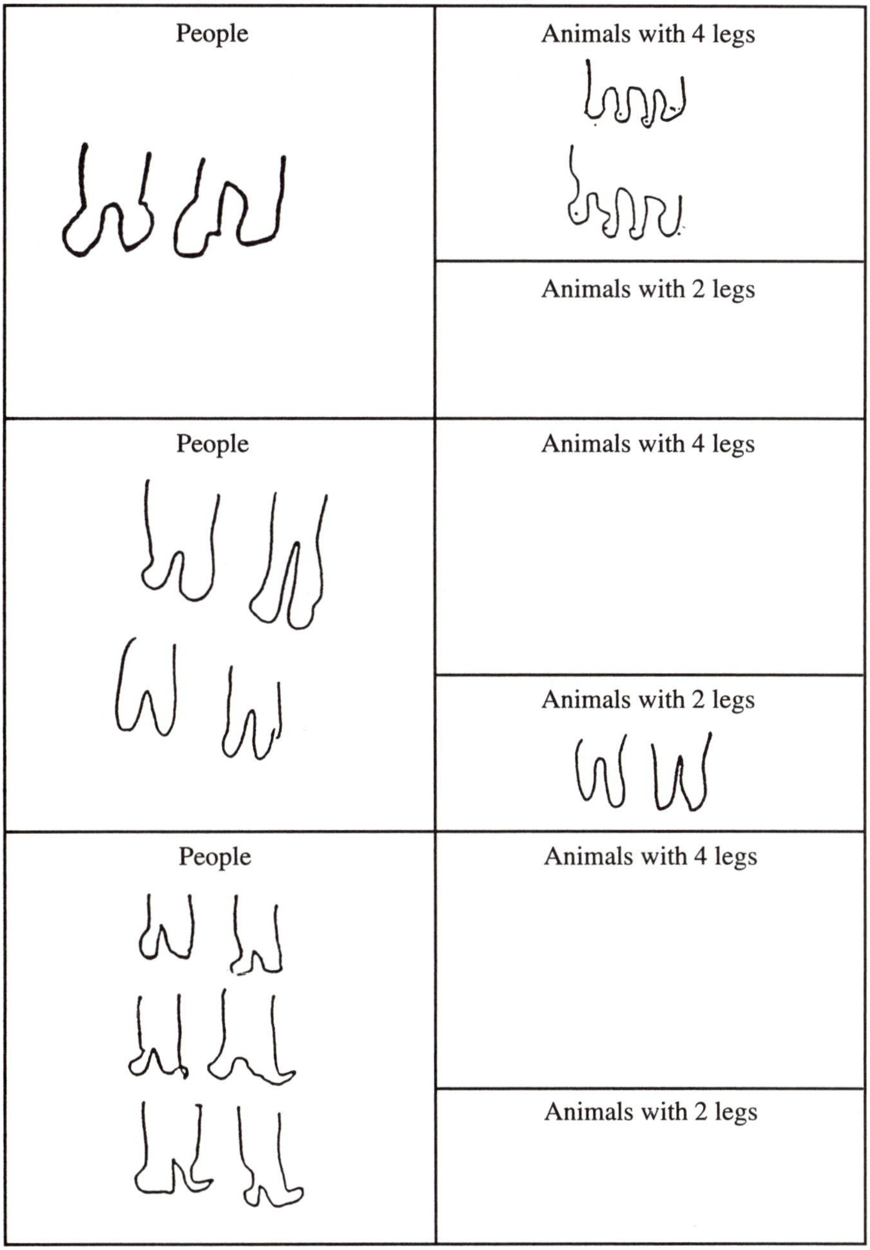

People	Animals with 4 legs
	Animals with 2 legs
People	Animals with 4 legs
	Animals with 2 legs
People	Animals with 4 legs
	Animals with 2 legs

group when we shared results, was that it involved the children's ability to think flexibly about a number quantity. Invariance of number (for example, that 5 could be 2 and 3 and that 5 could also be 1 and 4) is an important milestone in children's logical-mathematical thinking. The "Twelve Legs Problem" made children confront this idea, and many worked with it effectively in this situation.

ENDING AT THE BEGINNING: REFLECTIONS

At the beginning of this narrative, I stated that this year has been both glorious and bewildering. It has been bewildering in the unpredictable, unexpected ways in which kindergarten children think; but that also has been its glory. Despite the developmental constraints on their thinking, kindergarten children can do so much! I celebrate their persistence and determination to make sense of all that is around them. They invent their own rules and systems, and test out the validity of those systems. My role as "teacher" is to "lead from behind" by identifying the mathematics involved, responding to what the children are trying to do, and inspiring their thinking.

For me, "leading from behind" is a powerful model for teaching because it acknowledges that the learner is in control of the learning process; but it also insists that the teacher plays a key role in shaping the learner's experience. It challenges the teacher to be a careful observer of children and to know how to interpret what she sees. This demands that the teacher know the children and the content well enough to make meaningful connections between them when the time is right.

ACKNOWLEDGMENTS

I owe special thanks to the many friends who read the drafts of this narrative and offered support and advice. Their contributions and insights have been significant for this work. Thanks to Nancy Hendry and Bobbie Miller, my writing partners, and to Deborah Schifter and other participants in this project. Thanks also to those outside of this project: Charlie Parham, Margaret Phinney, Marie Hershkowitz, Kelly Nerbonne, Shauneen Kroll, and my husband and colleague, Scott Messinger.

REFERENCES

Newman, J. (1989). *Leading from behind in a whole language classroom* (Reading Around Series, No. 4). Carlton, Victoria: Australian Reading Association.
Vygotsky, L. (1984). *Thought and language*. Cambridge, MA: M.I.T. Press. (Original work published 1962)

+   −   ×   ÷

SHAPING UP

Christine D. Anderson

The bell rings. Many anxious and excited four- and five-year-old children enter kindergarten for the first time. Butterflies flutter in some tummies and tears well up in some eyes. Whatever the emotions, children, parents, and teachers are all eager to begin a new and exciting school year.

The school in which I teach is located in an economically deprived area of a financially strapped city in western Massachusetts. In order to attract many different ethnic and racial groups to the school, we offer a variety of programs: a schoolwide Chapter I program, a magnet reading program, a Chapter 636 multicultural program, and a before- and after-school, extended-day program.

Because of all of the programs available at this school, we are able to attract a variety of students, achieving a racial makeup that is reflective of the public school population in general—76% minority, mostly Spanish speaking, and 24% Anglo.

As is the case in most other schools, the month of September includes pretesting for our kindergarten children. From these tests, as well as classroom performance and teacher observation, we determine which children will be targeted for which program. The children who appear to have had less exposure to some of life's early educational experiences usually become Chapter I target children. This is where my role as a Chapter I kindergarten teacher begins.

I spend my day working in two full-day kindergarten classes, each with 25 students. In both classes, I work with small groups of children, usually five or six at a time, to reinforce the concepts that the classroom teacher is working on.

In the fall of each year my groups usually work on such things as color recognition, shape identification, counting, recognizing their own names, identifying letters of the alphabet, and sorting and classifying objects. It is in the area of shape identification that I've decided to share with you some of our discoveries this year.

As you follow along with our discussions, you'll become familiar with the particular group of children on whom I've decided to focus my writing. This heterogeneous group comprises children who come from a variety of ethnic and racial backgrounds. Three of the youngsters, Julio, Rosa, and Juan, are Hispanic; Megan is an Anglo girl with some Irish heritage; and Nikima is an African-American girl.

SHAPES, SHAPES, AND MORE SHAPES

Everywhere we look we see shapes. Since the vast majority of our young children enter school as nonreaders, many of the directions we give them refer to a color or a shape. Therefore, it is vital to "kindergarten survival" to be able to differentiate color from color and shape from shape. Is this an easy task? Not for all children! And when all is said and done, language and vocabulary play an important part in accomplishing this task.

When I taught in the past, I wanted my students to become familiar with the shapes and to be able to identify them using the appropriate names. Naturally, *I* would describe each shape and then we would count the number of sides and corners together. But, as I think back, every time we worked on these shapes, *I* would direct them to count these things. *I* would point out that the rectangle had two long sides and two short sides. *I* would describe the properties of each shape.

This year I made an important decision. I would allow my students to do more of the talking and directing. The more opportunities that students have to speak and explain and describe something, the better able they will be to express their thoughts and ideas. So why not begin with a discussion of the shapes located in many areas throughout our classroom?

The importance of vocabulary has been a topic of discussion in many SummerMath classes. In order to discuss anything, participants need to have a common understanding of the terms being used in the conversation.

The exchange of ideas in a kindergarten classroom is no exception to this rule. In fact, it is right here, at the ground level of a child's formal education, that a common understanding of math terms must begin.

I wanted things to be different this year. I wanted the children to discover what properties each shape had that made it fall into whatever category we were discussing: circle, square, triangle, or rectangle.

I asked myself the following question: "Is it really important to identify these characteristics at this young age?" I feel that any concept that the children are able to understand is important. Providing educational opportunities that encourage children to explore and discover these properties will strengthen their grasp of geometric concepts.

For most of the first four months of this school year, I allowed the things children said about geometric shapes on the preceding day to lead me into the topic of discussion for the following day.

My new approach to teaching, which freed the children to discover the characteristics of geometric shapes on their own, has been so very exciting to me! It was a way of empowering my students to develop a better mathematical understanding of these shapes.

IDENTIFYING SHAPES AND THEIR PARTS

I decided to begin a group discussion by asking the children to compare two shapes. Holding up one yellow triangle and one yellow square I asked, "Are these two objects the same or are they different?"

Juan, who is always willing to jump right in and let us know what he is thinking, said, "One's a box and one's a witch's hat."

Julio, who seems to know the more technical terms for the objects, added, "That one is a triangle and that one is a square."

Teacher: Are a triangle and a square the same shape, Julio, or are they different?
Julio: They're not the same.
Teacher: Well, how are they different?
Julio: The triangle has three corners and the square has four corners.
Megan: This one has three lines and this one has four lines.
Rosa: Or three sides and four sides.

The children all pointed to the appropriate shapes as they commented. I was quite pleased with the way our discussion was progressing. Megan and Rosa were able to identify some properties of these shapes. Even though, in my mind, I questioned whether Juan, Rosa, and Megan knew the names "triangle" and "square," I had a sense that they were seeing the differences in the two objects being discussed.

Then Nikima surprised me with her thoughts.

Nikima: But they're twins.

Egad! Nikima had been quiet up to this point, but I thought from the expression on her face and the occasional nod of her head that she was following right along with the differences that had been noticed.

Teacher: How are they like twins, Nikima?
Nikima: They're both yellow.

I had purposely used two yellow shapes in order to provide a common characteristic. Then, when Nikima noticed the colors were similar, I thought she was totally confused. I hope that my feelings weren't obvious to the children, since Nikima continued, "This is a yellow square and this is a yellow triangle."

After I realized that Nikima's previous body language had not been misinterpreted by me, I labeled the square and the triangle and we listed the special qualities of each. Then to conclude the lesson, I taught them a song about the triangle.

Ring, ring, ring, ting-a-ling,
Ring, ring, ring, ting-a-ling,
Ring, ring, ring, ting-a-ling,
We'll make the triangle sing, ting-a-ling.

I was pleased with the differences the children had noticed about the shapes and with what they had discovered about the properties of each. Therefore, when our group met the next day, I decided to continue their vocabulary development by asking the children to compare a square and a rectangle.

With a red square in one hand and a blue rectangle in the other, I began our group discussion by asking, "How are these two shapes the same, and how are they different?"

Nikima: The red one is a square and the blue one is a triangle.
Teacher: Do you all agree?
Juan: I don't think that one [the rectangle] is a triangle because the Ting-a-Ling song said, "We'll make the triangle sing, ting-a-ling," and it looked like a witch's hat.
Nikima: Right.
Megan: I know! I know! It's a "rec" something.

Julio had been a little distracted by a group working next to our area. However, he seemed to tune in at this point.

Julio: That blue one is a rectangle.
Teacher: So, this red one is a square, you say. And this blue one is called a rectangle. How are they alike?
Rosa: There's four corners (touching the rectangle) and there's four corners (touching the square).
Julio: There's four sides and four sides.
Megan: If you touch the sides, the top and the bottom are the same.

At this point, Megan took the square and the rectangle and put the shapes right next to each other, to show that the measurement of the side of the square was equal to the measurement of the short side of the rectangle.

Rosa: Two squares make a rectangle. See?

Rosa's observation seemed correct in this case. When Megan placed the two shapes near one another, Rosa had noticed this detail immediately.

Juan: Cut the blue in half and you get two squares.

There was a short period of silence before Julio spoke.

Julio: The rectangle has two sides that are very long and two sides that are very short.
Rosa: And the square has all short sides!

The children continually amaze me with their observations. They pointed out that the square and rectangle each had four corners and four sides and that, in this case, the rectangle could be cut in half and the result would be two squares. And Rosa noticed that the square had all short sides! If that wasn't another way of saying "equal sides," I don't know what is.

Both Juan and Rosa have shared some interesting ideas here. Juan was able to notice the relationship between the rectangle and two squares, and Rosa focused in on the lengths of the sides of the square.

A sense of accomplishment was beginning to envelop me. The children seemed to be developing a real understanding of shapes. Perhaps that is why I was quite surprised by a conversation that took place at our next group meeting.

WHAT IS A SIDE?

The children just love to see me walk over to the math center and bring the tubs of pattern blocks back to our work area. Not only do they enjoy exploring and creating with these colorful shapes, but they seem to eagerly anticipate the time when I'll be sharing some questions and ideas with each one of them.

Nikima had created some interesting animals with her shapes.

Nikima: Do you know what this is?
Teacher: It looks like an animal to me.
Nikima: Yes! What one? I'll give you a clue. It says, "Bow wow."

Nikima's eyes were as big as saucers and she was smiling from ear to ear.

As I responded, "A dog," she gave me a big hug and told me how proud she was of me. I guess I made her day! She answered some of my questions about the number of squares that she had used, the shape that she had made the dog's head (a triangle), and so on.

Juan informed me that he made two different kinds of squares. Indeed, he had. He made a solid square using 25 square pieces and a "doughnut square" with a hole in the middle, using only 16 square pieces (see Figure 3.3).

Megan and Julio decided to combine their shapes and re-create Columbus's three ships. This lent itself to comparing which ship had more triangles in it, how many squares were used all together, which ship was the biggest, and so on.

Then, as we discussed a floral design Julio had made, I began to ask some review questions. Julio said something that really got us all thinking.

FIGURE 3.3. Juan's Two Ways To Make a Square

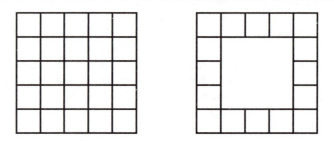

Teacher: Julio, what shape did you use for the center of this flower?
Julio: A square.
Teacher: Tell me some special things about a square.
Julio: It has four corners, the sides are the same, and there are four of
　　them.

The stem of one of his flowers was made by putting two squares together.

Teacher: What shape is this?

I had picked up the two squares.

Julio: A rectangle.
Teacher: Describe a rectangle for me, honey.
Julio: Let's see. (Julio twists his lips and scratches his head.) It has
　　four corners and . . . (Julio started counting the sides) And eight
　　sides.
Teacher: Show me how you counted the sides.
Julio: Like this: 1, 2, 3, 4, 5, 6, 7, 8. (See Figure 3.4(a).)

**FIGURE 3.4. Children Counting Sides of Rectangles Composed of Two
　　Squares**

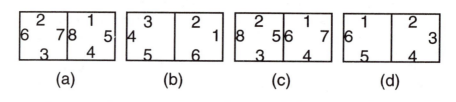

Rosa: I think it has six sides.

Teacher: Count them, honey.

Rosa: 1, 2, 3, 4, 5, 6. (See Figure 3.4(b).)

Teacher: What would happen if I superglued these two sides together? If you couldn't separate them?

Rosa pretended that she couldn't pull the two squares apart and grunted. She loves to tease us and she had such a big smile on her face that she looked like the cat that ate the canary. Then she counted to 6 again.

Teacher: Julio, how many sides are on this rectangle? (I indicate the one that had been superglued.)

Julio: 1, 2, 3, 4, 5, 6, 7, 8. (See Figure 3.4(c).)

Teacher: Would anyone else like to tell us how many sides this rectangle has?

Megan: Probably six or eight.

Teacher: Show me, Meg.

Megan: Like this. 1, 2, 3, 4, 5, 6, or maybe 7, 8. (See Figure 3.4(d).)

She included the two edges in the center.

Juan: I think 6.

Several days earlier, when the children had looked at a rectangle, they counted four sides. But today, when they examined a rectangle composed of two squares, they debated whether it had six or eight sides—they didn't even consider four. They disagreed about whether to count the internal sides of the square, but they were all in agreement that the external sides of the squares should be counted separately as sides of the rectangle. Apparently they couldn't conceive that a length that was a whole side (of a square) could at the same time be half a side (of a rectangle).

I puzzled for several days, reflecting on their idea that a rectangle could have six or eight sides. About a week after this discussion, I decided to use a different approach. Before the class arrived, I took two squares from the tub of pattern blocks and taped them together. To begin the day's activity, I showed the children the taped squares and then two other squares that were placed adjacent to one another. I pointed to the taped squares and asked, "What do we call this shape?"

All the children: A rectangle.

Teacher: And tell me how many sides does this rectangle have?

Rosa: (using her finger to count each side in turn) 1, 2, 3, 4. It has four sides.

Teacher: What do we call this shape? (outlining the two adjacent
   squares in the same manner as before)
Juan: A rectangle.
Teacher: Does anyone disagree?
Children: No.
Teacher: How many sides does this rectangle have?
Julio: (Just as if I rewound a videotape, Julio begins, as he did a week
   earlier, to count eight sides.) 1, 2, 3, 4, 5, 6, 7, 8.

The children were so firm in their convictions, I decided not to challenge
them. The notion that something can be a side and not a side at the same time
is a sophisticated one. It's related to the idea that a single object can be a
whole and a part at the same time. They will have future opportunities to
wrestle with this when they contemplate the fact that *two* shoes make up *one*
pair and that *one whole* shoe is *part* of a pair. Still later they will ponder how
one-half of a foot is at the same time *one-sixth* of a yard.

WHAT MAKES A TRIANGLE A TRIANGLE?

The triangles young children recognize as triangles are usually either isosceles or equilateral, with a horizontal base and a vertex above it. Having been
quite encouraged by their use of vocabulary and descriptions of the properties
of shapes in our previous discussions, I decided to ask the children to compare
three paper triangles that were congruent but were placed on our work table
in different orientations (see Figure 3.5(a)). Our discussion began when I
asked the children, "What do you notice about these papers?"

Rosa: This one (pointing to the red paper) is a triangle.
Teacher: Can you refresh my memory? What is it that makes a shape a
   triangle?
Julio: If it has three corners, it's a triangle.
Teacher: Okay. Thank you for helping me. Let's see if I have this
   right. A triangle has three corners and three sides.
All the children: Yes!
Teacher: So this red piece of paper is a triangle. What else do you no-
   tice?
Juan: This one [the blue paper] isn't a triangle, but it looks like an ice
   cream cone.
Megan: Yeah! It has a point at the bottom.
Rosa: This [the yellow paper] is like the flags on the Whittaker's car.

We had recently read a story in which the Whittaker family decorated
their car on the way to a Halloween party. The decorations included flags that
had pumpkins painted on them.

FIGURE 3.5. Comparing Three Triangles

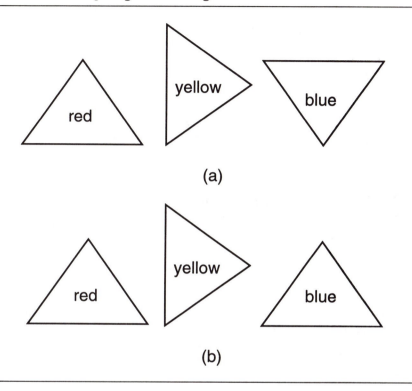

(a)

(b)

Teacher: Yes, I remember seeing those flags.
Megan: See, that one [the yellow paper] has a point in front.

Megan seemed to be noticing that that point was appearing in many places. It was at the bottom of the ice cream cone and in the front of the flag.

Teacher: What else do you notice?

There was a short period of silence, which seemed to cause Juan to get quite fidgety. He kept putting his head on the table. First his left ear would touch the top of the table, then the right. After he did this a few times, he noticed something!

Juan: Hey, turn the ice cream cone around!
Teacher: Like this? (I flip the paper over without changing the position of "the point.")

Juan: No!
Teacher: Juan, you turn the cone the way you want it.

Eagerly, Juan turned the blue paper to the same orientation as the red (see Figure 3.5(b)).
Nikima joined our discussion at this point.

Nikima: Look! They're twins! The red and the blue are twins.
Juan: Two triangles? Yes, two triangles!
Teacher: So, we have two triangles. Do these [the red and blue] papers each have three corners?
Megan and Nikima: Yes.

There was a certain part of me that really wanted to keep questioning them about the yellow paper until the children noticed that it, too, was a triangle. However, I forced myself to overcome this temptation and decided to draw this discussion to a close with our rendition of: "Ring, ring, ring, ting-a-ling." I knew that I'd bring these shapes out again in the not-so-distant future, and maybe the fact that the yellow paper also was a triangle would then be discovered.
As we began to clear off our work space, Megan picked up the three papers and handed them to me.

Megan: Wait! Look! They are all the same.

Quite by accident, Megan had made the discovery.

All the children: What?
Megan: The yellow one is twins with all of them.
Children: Let's see!

Megan had the three papers piled on top of each other and put them back on the table.

Megan: They all have three corners and three sides. They're all triangles.

So by the end of our session, the children did identify the three papers' properties to confirm that they were all triangles.
As an extension of this activity, I planned to have the children make their own shapes. To start, I brought out the geoboards that were stored in the math center. The children's eyes glistened. All but one of this enthusiastic group were on their feet.

"What's that?"
"Can we try it?"
"Oh!"
"Let's see."

They were eager to get their little hands on both the boards and the rubber bands that were used with them.

Geoboards are math tools that are usually square-shaped. They are somewhat like peg boards, but instead of holes, they have fixed pegs sticking out of them.

I knew from past experience that I had to lay down some very specific ground rules. Those useful little rubber bands have a special purpose and I had to make it clear that we would use these items carefully. I demonstrated to the children how I use one hand to stretch the elastic band and the other to hold it down on the peg. I had each one of them copy my movements and complimented them for being so responsible with this activity. I gave them 15 minutes to explore on their own. Then came the assignment.

Each child was given one geoboard and four different colored rubber bands. Without specifying which shapes to make or stipulating that they had to be different, I asked the children to make four shapes using the elastics and the geoboard.

The children were used to working together by now, so they began by sharing their ideas. "Let's all make a big square," said Megan. Each of them made one big square using the exterior pegs on the board. After the children repeatedly asked each other, "Can you do this?" we began to see different creations: large and small, fat and skinny, tall and short shapes. Our discussion then centered on what to call the shape in Figure 3.6.

Rosa: A long nail.
Julio: Is it one of our shapes?
Rosa: (shrugs her shoulders) I don't know.
Teacher: (looking at Julio) Do you think it's one of our shapes?
Julio: It has three corners.
Juan: Three corners? Then it must be a triangle. Look. Stretch it out.

Juan moved the elastic from the second to the third peg on the far right.

Juan: It's the same as before. I just made it fatter on this side.
Teacher: (looking at Rosa and Julio) Do you agree?
Julio: Yes. It's just a long skinny triangle when we started. I didn't
          know a triangle could be so skinny.

The children really seem able to work through their own dilemmas by discussing their ideas with one another and using their previous definitions of the different shapes.

FIGURE 3.6. The Children Called the Triangle "A Long Nail"

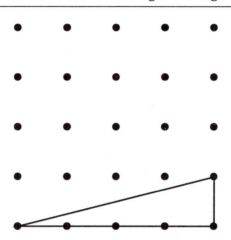

Their conception of what a triangle is has really been expanded! It's no longer just a witch's hat. A triangle can be long and skinny (like a nail), stretched out, or made fatter. Sometimes it's symmetrical, but it can also be lopsided. The ultimate test is that it has three corners.

DRAWING SHAPES

I must admit that I was pleased with what this particular group of children had done with shapes. Next, I wanted the children to draw each shape when the name was given. I realized that although I would be looking for certain properties, the degree of success in making these shapes would depend somewhat on each child's development of fine motor skills. Still, I wanted to have an idea of their ability to create these shapes. Figure 3.7 contains samples of the children's work.

In the upper left-hand corner of each paper is the circle each child made. The square is in the upper right, the triangle in the lower left, and the rectangle in the lower right.

The properties that I was interested in seeing are: circle—round, no flat sides; square—4 corners, 4 sides, equal sides; triangle—3 corners, 3 sides; rectangle—4 corners, 2 short sides, 2 long sides; all shapes—closed.

Julio's was the only circle that seemed to have one flat side and a point where the circle started and ended. The other four samples came very close to being circles.

Except for Rosa's, the triangles were made with square corners. The chil-

FIGURE 3.7. Work Samples: Julio, Rosa, Juan, Megan, Nikima

Julio   Rosa

Juan   Megan

Nikima

dren seemed to have trouble drawing acute angles. This, I believe, is due to the fact that children generally have more difficulty drawing slanted lines. This difficulty is often apparent when children try to form the letters of their own name. However, time and practice usually improve the situation.

In general, for a first attempt, the children did a pretty good job.

Then came a challenge that proved to be very interesting. Having hung up a large piece of construction paper, I said, "Tell me how to make a square."

> *Juan:* Make a line going across the paper like this. (Juan made the line in the air going from left to right. See Figure 3.8(a).)
>
> *Megan:* Now go down from this corner. (She points to the left end of the original line.)

In order to provide a bit of a challenge, I made the second line about twice as long as the first.

> *Megan:* No! No! No! Stop!

Using her hand, she directed me to end the line at a point that would be just about equal in length to the first line (see Figure 3.8(b)).

> *Juan:* Now make one on this side [the right] that is as big as that one (pointing to the line that Megan had directed). (See Figure 3.8(c).)
>
> *Nikima:* Just touch the bottom of this line to the bottom of this line. (See Figure 3.8(d).)
>
> *Teacher:* What did we make?
>
> *All the children:* A square!

FIGURE 3.8. Constructing a Square

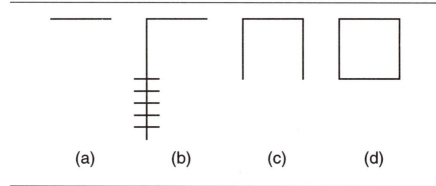

(a)   (b)   (c)   (d)

Their directions for the rectangle were similar, but with two long sides and two short sides.

I was amazed by their point of origin for the triangle.

Nikima: Make a dot. Kick one leg this way [diagonally to the right]. Kick the other leg this way [diagonally to the left].

I drew according to Nikima's directions as shown in Figure 3.9(a). Nikima stared at the lines I had drawn. I began to wonder what she was thinking.

Teacher: Did I do what you wanted me to, Nikima?
Nikima: No.
Teacher: Tell me what needs to be different.
Nikima: I'm not sure. It might work this way.
Julio: Make this line touch the dot and then you get a triangle. (See Figure 3.9(b).)
Teacher: Nikima, what do you think?
Nikima: Okay. Let's see. Yes, it's sideways. It's a sideways triangle.

(Nikima still feels that the correct way to depict a triangle is to have an isosceles or equilateral representation with a vertical line of symmetry.)

I was still curious as to what Nikima's original plan had been, so I asked her to draw a triangle for me. She started with her dot. She "kicked" one leg to the right. She returned to the dot and "kicked" the second leg to the left. Then she connected the two "feet" (see Figure 3.9(c)).

Have you ever tried to describe how to draw a circle? Without a doubt it was the hardest shape to describe how to make.

FIGURE 3.9. Constructing a Triangle

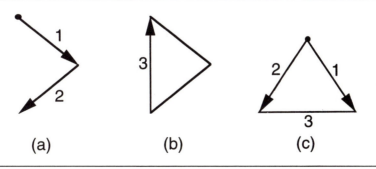

(a)   (b)   (c)

Rosa: Put the pencil on your paper and make it go around.
Julio: Go around like the outside of a penny.
Megan: It's round.

The children all demonstrated their thought by making a circle in the air. Yes, they knew what they wanted to have me do, but it was very hard to put these directions into words.

I decided to carry this task home with me. I asked my own daughter, who is in grade 5, to describe how to draw a circle for a person who has never seen one before. Much to my surprise, she did exactly the same thing that these kindergarten children had done.

"You go around like this," she said, as she formed a circle in the air with her index finger.

From having the children do this task, I learned that they had a definite understanding of what to do to create a given shape. Their vocabulary impressed me. Line, corner, side, and dot were all distinct descriptions of different points of focus. I also learned that a circle is the most difficult shape to explain how to draw. Except for the word "dot," none of the other words could be used to help explain how to create this round shape.

WHAT WAS LEARNED?

One question that I always ask myself is, "What did the children really learn?"

In the past, I had been very satisfied if the children succeeded in looking at a circle, square, triangle, and rectangle and correctly naming each shape. Did we reach that goal this year? We certainly did! In addition to being able to identify these shapes, we went even further. This group of youngsters has a keen awareness of some of the characteristics that are important properties of each shape.

When we work as a group, and when the children work independently, they eagerly point out the special qualities of these shapes to anyone who is willing to listen. If no one is available to lend an ear, I have on several occasions heard my young students describe these properties to themselves and to some dolls or stuffed animals that reside in the classroom.

Progress, as I would expect, has been different for each child.

Nikima still expects a triangle to look like a witch's hat. In another orientation she refers to an isosceles triangle as a "sideways triangle" because it does not have a vertical line of symmetry.

Juan went from calling a triangle a "witch's hat" to recognizing that two triangles that were placed in different positions were actually congruent.

When our discussions began, Megan observed that a triangle had three lines and a square had four lines. At the end of our comparison of three triangles in different orientations, she discovered that all three were triangles. They all had three corners and three sides.

Rosa started off by describing a triangle as three sided, then went on to create a triangle on the geoboard, but was unsure if it was one of the shapes that we had been discussing.

Julio knew from the beginning the names of the triangle and the square and was aware of the number of corners that each of these shapes had. When working with the geoboard he amazed himself by identifying the "long nail" as a triangle because it had three corners.

Each time a triangle, square, or rectangle is the topic of our discussion, the children proudly describe the properties of the shape. They mention the number of corners, the number of sides, the lengths of the sides, and the name of the shape.

The approach that I used with the children this year, when discussing the properties of the four basic shapes, seemed to give them more ownership of the mathematics involved in analyzing these geometric figures.

At the beginning of December, after I had completed this work with the children, I was given an article to read in which I discovered that two Dutch educators had spent years researching and developing a model of geometric thought. Their findings and my results were amazingly similar. According to the article (Crowley, 1987), Pierre Marie van Hiele and Dina van Hiele-Geldof had done extensive research on the type of instruction that children receive.

My new approach to teaching, which allowed the children to discover on their own the characteristics of the shapes, was one that I could not only live with, but one that I couldn't live without. This approach allowed the children to explore more freely, discover more properties, expand their mathematical vocabulary, and increase their understandings.

REFERENCE

Crowley, M. (1987). The van Hiele model of the development of geometric thought. In M. M. Lindquist & A. P. Shulte (Eds.), *Learning and teaching geometry, K-12* (pp. 1-8). Reston, VA: National Council of Teachers of Mathematics.

CONVERSATIONS ABOUT COUNTING

Jessica Dobie Redman

Second graders love to count. If they hear someone else counting, they join right in. They are even happier if the counting is done by 2s, 5s, or 10s.

They count just as they chant. Their voices become rhythmic and chorus-like: "fif-teen, twen-ty, twen-ty-five, thir-ty, . . . " They often move their heads or bodies in rhythm as well.

However, early in the year, as I listened to my class of second graders count, I began to wonder whether they *really* understand counting. Do they see the necessity of one-to-one correspondence? Can they picture how much a number really is? Do they know the order of numbers past 100? They count by 2s and 5s, but are they able to see a pair or a group of 5 as a unit, just as 1 is a unit in counting?

This is my first year teaching second grade, and the differences between these seven-year-olds and the third graders that I taught previously are striking. I wanted to know more about what second graders thought about numbers, about counting, and about mathematics in general. I decided that the best way for me to learn was to watch and listen closely. I did some exploratory activities with the class to form a baseline of understanding. During these lessons I formulated the above questions and more.

WHAT IS COUNTING, ANYWAY?

During the second week of school, I presented unifix cubes to the class and asked them to explore. The only direction I gave was that they record whatever they did in their math notebooks. Many of the children became involved in connecting the cubes to form a long snake across the room. When they ran out of cubes, they looked back at the length of the snake. Carrie exclaimed, "I wonder how many unifix cubes we used! Let's count them!" The other children enthusiastically agreed with Carrie, and several children began counting. Organizing who would count was difficult for them, but finally they decided on Lynn. The next day, during our whole class discussion, I asked Lynn how many cubes the snake had had. "Eleven hundred," she answered. Immediately I thought, "What an adult way to use numbers," but then, since I knew something that sounds like a "right" answer may actually be a misunderstanding, I questioned her further.

Teacher: What do you mean "eleven hundred"? Do you mean it's bigger than one thousand?
Lynn: No, I didn't get to one thousand.
Teacher: Well, what did you count after nine hundred?
Lynn: I didn't get to nine hundred. I just got eleven hundred.

I was confused about how Lynn had counted, but I couldn't think of how to encourage her to explain her counting, so I made a mental note to come back to this and moved the conversation on. This early exchange confirmed for me a need to give the children opportunities to count large numbers—numbers over 100.

I became even more baffled about what my second graders understood about counting as I watched and listened in the following days. Lisa was counting unifix cubes that were connected in a circle surrounding a round table. As she said the numbers, "46, 47, 48, . . . " she slid her finger over the cubes but did not rest it on each cube as she recited a number. Instead, her finger moved continuously over the cubes while she counted in a different rhythm. Lisa's partner watched as she counted, and she didn't speak up as I thought she might: "You're skipping cubes," or "You're counting too fast." When Lisa completed the circle, she looked up and said, "There's 900 unifix cubes here." Her partner looked at her with wide eyes and opened her mouth in awe. Again I waited for a suggestion that Lisa might have miscounted, but none came. I acknowledged to myself that these two girls, Lisa and Alice, did *not* understand that counting included a one-to-one correspondence. Again, I tucked that information into my brain for further reflection.

Several days later, I set up counting stations around the classroom. I wanted the class to have the opportunity to count lots of objects and lots of different kinds of objects. My goal was to learn more about the class by observing how they counted. They had to travel to the various stations and count the objects at each. The objects I used included unifix cubes, playing cards, wooden blocks, and crayons. The children worked at the stations for about 45 minutes. Then we sat down to share our answers. I was discouraged as I listened to the children speak. They offered many different answers for each station, and, worse yet, no one particularly cared that they had different answers! How were we going to talk about counting if the children didn't care about the results?

The evening after that lesson, I sat down and thought it over. It seemed to me then that I had asked the children to overcome too many challenges at one time. They had been required to count higher than many of them felt confident counting. They had been surrounded by many counting stations; perhaps they felt pressured. Then, during our group conversation, I'd asked the children to think about counting in a new way, a critical, analytical way. I'd asked: "Why do you think we have so many different answers? How do you know if you have the right answer? Is there a right answer?" Most of the children were uneasy discussing math this way.

Each of the above math activities helped me to focus more clearly on the important ideas of counting. I began to understand what "counting" really entails and what I expect from a child when I ask him or her to "count." Counting necessitates an understanding of one-to-one correspondence; a child needs to say or think one number while he or she looks or points at one object. Further even, the number attached to an object actually stands for all of the accumulated previous objects. When counting, the number 1 might stand for one object or it might symbolize one group of objects. Skip counting or repetitive addition refers to adding groups by using an abbreviated method. I could see that in order to more fully comprehend counting, my class would need to be pushed to look further. Some of this would come with development. However, deeper, clearer insight comes from wondering and discovering, not just from growing older. With a more clearly defined vision of counting, I could better design lessons to guide the children toward those ideas.

As I sat down to plan further counting activities, I imagined my class of 25 second graders. They are a somewhat homogeneous group in ethnic, racial, and socioeconomic terms: primarily white and middle class, but the similarities end there. The class includes, as most do, learners with a whole range of abilities. I knew that my counting activities needed to challenge each learner. I also predicted that there were some children who appeared to be successful mathematics students who would become very confused with the kinds of things I was going to ask of them.

1, 2, 3, COUNT!

I set up the counting stations again. Most of the children were very eager to return to this activity. They cheered when I announced the plan. This time I reminded the children that it was not necessary to get to every station, and I put fewer objects at each station so the children wouldn't be using numbers they were less familiar with. I wanted the emphasis to be on counting carefully and accurately. And I hoped that at least some of the children would begin getting accurate answers.

After each pair had been to many of the counting stations, I called the class to the area where we gather for whole class discussions. It soon became obvious that instead of everyone having gotten the same counting results, most pairs had very different answers. So the chart looked like this:

unifix cubes—63, 67, 72, 64, 64, 70
crayons—44, 42, 41, 46, 41, 50
cards—51, 48, 33, 50, 49, 49

What did the class think about this? I was anxious to hear their thoughts. I expected some arguing among children who believed that their answers were the right answers. However, I was surprised.

Teacher: Look at this. We have many different counts for each station. Is anyone bothered that we have many different answers?

No one looked bothered. I decided to clarify my question.

Teacher: Raise your hand if you are bothered that we have lots of different numbers of cards.

Still no one gestured or offered a comment. I looked around. Everyone appeared to be involved and interested. No one was sleeping. I looked at the clock and noticed that it was almost time for recess. I wondered to myself, "What do I do now? Do I leave them thinking it's okay to have five different answers?" With the little remaining time, I tried to get a better understanding of what the class was thinking.

> *Teacher:* If you think it's okay to have all these different answers, raise your hand to tell me what you're thinking. (About seven children raised their hands.) Billy, what do you think?
>
> *Billy:* Well, it would be boring if we all got the same answers. Then when you'd ask what we got, we'd all have the same thing.

Lots of voices yelled out agreement. Now I was even more confused about the class' understandings about counting. If they could believe that the same pile of crayons is 44 for one counter and 50 for another, what does that say about their sense of number—how much a number really is? And do they see that a number is the same, whether it represents cubes or horses or pencils? How could I help them to realize that a careful, correct count should yield only one answer?

THE SEARCH FOR A "RIGHT" ANSWER

One amount that the children did seem to feel was constant was the number of children in our class. They were aware there were 25 children, and often while taking attendance I would ask a question like, "There are two people absent. How many kids are here today?" After some thinking, almost everyone in the class was able to come up with the correct answer. So when a colleague suggested I have the class count the number of children in our room, I thought, "That sounds like a problem with *one* right answer!" I knew from our discussion about the counting stations that I needed to present the class with a problem that *needed* a right answer, a problem that wouldn't make sense to them with different answers.

What if we counted the children and then they all got up and moved around? Would we need to recount? At first I thought this activity might be too basic, but I didn't want to overestimate the children's understanding. Several weeks ago, I would not have expected the class to feel comfortable with many different counts for a fixed number of objects.

I explained to the class that we were going to count how many children there were by counting around in a circle until we reached the starting point. Quite easily and quickly each child said the expected number for his or her turn. We had 24 children in the circle. (One child was absent.) Then I asked,

"What if everyone gets up and walks around the room and then comes back and sits down? Will there still be 24 children?"

Some of the children looked at me like that was the craziest question they'd ever heard. Then several began exclaiming, "Yes! There'd still be 24!" One child even said, "Yeah, unless someone walked out of the room!" Everyone laughed. We tried it. Everyone moved around the classroom and came back. We counted our circle just as we had the first time. "See, there's still 24!" several children shouted out.

I thought back to an explanation that Alison had given for many different answers to the counting stations several weeks ago: "If we all count in different ways, like by 2s, 3s, or 5s, we'll all get different answers." Alison's idea had been sitting in the back of my mind waiting for the right moment, and now I saw it. So I asked the class, "Okay, what about if we count the class by 2s? Will there still be 24 children?" Most of the class shouted out their agreement, but I began to sense a few of the children becoming less sure of their response. Alison's forehead was wrinkled, and she looked around at the other children as if to see what they were thinking. Lisa didn't say anything. Instead she looked to her neighbor to see what she was saying.

"Maybe this is worth pursuing," I thought as I observed this. So we tried it. The children next to each other paired up, and we began to count. I soon realized that several of the children really didn't know what counting by 2s sounded like. I helped the class count together, leading with my voice: "1, **2**, 3, **4**, 5, **6**, . . . **24**." I used a louder voice to emphasize the even numbers. I hoped the children would see that we were still counting everybody, but we were *hearing* the even numbers. I also noted that we'd need to come back to skip counting for more experience.

> *Teacher:* 24! We got 24 counting by 2s. Do you think we'd get 24 counting another way?
> *Billy:* Yeah! There's only 24 of us.
> *Mary:* Well, what if we count by 8s? My mom taught me how to count by 8s because she used to be a teacher.
> *Teacher:* What do you think, Mary, if we count by 8s will we still have the same number of kids in the class?
> *Mary:* I don't know. It's hard to count by 8s.
> *Teacher:* What does anyone else think about this?
> *Alison:* I don't know. We'd have to do it to see.

About half the class appeared as confused as Mary and Alison. I think that counting by 8s seemed unimaginable to them. For some of the children, "counting by" is just another fun way to chant. They have not yet realized that "counting by" refers to grouping for more efficient counting. Other children were still shouting out, "Of course we'll still have 24 kids! We're all still here!"

As so often happens, the bell ended our limited time for exploration. Later in the day, as I looked back on this activity, I was able to see that the children could be roughly grouped according to their present understandings of counting, number sense, and number constancy. One group seemed firmly grounded in their understandings. This group of children was aware that 20 objects would be 20 objects no matter how they were counted. These children were also confident undertaking the mechanics of counting (what number comes next? how do numbers form patterns?).

Another group comprised the children who had become easily confused during the day's counting activity—the children who weren't sure how to count by 2s, those who paused and wondered each time the question (will we still have 24 kids?) was posed. It seemed to me that this group did not understand that a group of objects will remain the same number however counted.

Then there were the children with an unstable understanding of number constancy. These children felt quite sure that there were 24 children in the class when they counted by 1s, 2s, and 3s, but were less sure about counting them by 8s. They hadn't had any experience with grouping 8s, so they didn't yet agree that it would have the same effect.

Realizing that there were such different levels of understanding of counting frightened me. How could I present the class with more counting experiences yet keep the more "mature" group challenged? How could I guide the other children to become confident counters? What realistic situation could I use to help the class see that the number of objects remains the same, regardless of the counting method?

COUNTING NOSES (AND FINGERS AND FEET)

Since we'd counted bodies, the next logical step seemed to me to be counting noses, feet, and fingers of all of the people in our class. I also anticipated that this problem would be a convenient step into a discussion about skip counting, because both feet and fingers are more efficiently counted in groups. When I explained this problem to the children, the first response was, "Noses are too easy! Everyone has one nose, and there are 25 kids!" I thought to myself, "Maybe that is clear to the children speaking up, but it may not be clear to everyone." I am beginning to learn to pay more attention to the children who don't say anything than to those who speak most. The children who continued to surprise me were the ones I didn't hear much from during whole class discussions. So this time I didn't worry that perhaps this activity was too easy. I made available a copy of the class list for children who wanted it, and I asked the class to begin working.

I circulated and listened in on some of the conversations. Linda and Mary were using unifix cubes to count the noses in the classroom. Linda called off each name on the class list as Mary placed one cube in a pile. Linda read slowly and kept checking to see that Mary was keeping up with her. I could see that Linda was thinking that this method would work only if there was one cube per person.

The two girls used another mode of representation to record their count on paper. After they had a pile of 25 cubes, Linda picked up the class list and drew a nose next to each name. This was interesting; they were able to use two different representations to solve the problem—cubes to count verbally and drawings to record on paper.

Randy and Diane had chosen a different strategy. Randy was writing numbers next to each name on the list. He began with "1" at the first name and numbered consecutively until he reached "25" at the last name. Then I noticed they had written a second column of numbers, "26" through "50."

Teacher: What have you written here?

Randy: Well, this first list counts for one foot, and this next list counts the other foot.

Diane: See everyone has two feet! So there are 50 feet in our class!
(Her eyes are wide and her voice enthusiastic.)

Diane is usually very soft-spoken. I often wonder whether she is following our class discussions. I was pleased to see her so involved and excited about this activity.

I stopped where Alison and Lynn were working. Alison had demonstrated some confusion about counting during the count-around circle we'd done several days before, and I wondered how she was doing with this activity. Alison was putting a check next to every name on the list. When I asked her to tell me about her strategy, she said, "I counted each person two times when I put a check on, 'cause each person has two feet." Alison nodded her head as she spoke confidently to me. Lynn, her partner, had written "50" on the top of their paper. I moved on, wondering why Alison's understanding seemed so stable today when at other times she'd seemed so confused. I reminded myself to check on her and Lynn again soon.

Sammy was talking quickly to Terrie, who stared off at the wall. I did a quick assessment of the situation. Sammy, a flexible, mature problem solver, had already figured out the solution, and he was trying to tell Terrie about it. Terrie is a young second grader who tends to be a very concrete thinker. She usually chooses unifix cubes for solving problems. Sammy, on the other hand, thinks abstractly and appeared to be working on counting feet in his head. I listened in.

Sammy: See, there's 25 people and 25 + 25 = 50. If you add
    20 + 20, it equals 40. And 5 + 5 = 10. So 25 + 25 = 50.

I looked at Terrie. She squinted her eyes and wrinkled up her nose. She
looked at me for help.

Teacher: Terrie, tell us what you understand about Sammy's way of
    solving this.
Terrie: Nothing. (She wrinkles her nose again and smiles at me.)

At this point, in another situation, I might have urged the child to try to
tell me at least one thing she understood about what her partner had been saying, but I sensed that Terrie was being truthful. I also felt that she was becoming frustrated. So I decided not to press that point.

Teacher: How would you solve this?

I thought it was more important for Terrie to find her own way to solve
this than just to listen to *Sammy's* way of solving it.

Terrie: I'd count everybody's feet.
Teacher: Well, why don't you do that and then compare your answer
    with Sammy's?
Terrie: Okay. (She looks down at the class list.) I'll start with Brenda.

Brenda's name was first on the list so I could see that Terrie was thinking
of a way to organize her counting. Terrie walked up to Brenda, pointed at her
feet and whispered, "One, two." Then she looked at the list and went on to
the next child. A little while later, Terrie came to me, smiling, and said, "I
counted 50 feet!" Sammy, also smiling, looked at her and exclaimed, "I got
50, too!"

What I had hoped would happen, did. Sammy had chosen a strategy that
challenged him to think abstractly and numerically, while Terrie had found a
method that made sense to her. They were still able to function together as
they tried to communicate their ideas and then confer on the answer.

ALIENS' EYES (OR WHAT IS SKIP COUNTING?)

Over the next few weeks, I had begun to feel that the children were becoming more confident counters. They were showing signs of understanding
that there is only one possible answer. They were beginning to organize their
counting in groups, rows, or numbers. When the class came together to dis-

cuss the solution of a problem, we usually agreed upon one answer. If a child or a group had another answer, the class was beginning to search for such logical explanations of the differences as miscounting, losing count, or counting something more than once.

Next I decided to give the class an opportunity to skip count—to count by 2s, 3s, 4s, and 5s. I felt as if they had gained some understanding of counting with 1 as the unit, and now I wanted to introduce them to the use of another number as a unit of counting. Also, I wanted them to begin to see the efficiency of grouping for counting. And I wanted the need for a single answer to be built in. I drew four kinds of aliens on cards: dubloids with 2 eyes; troids with 3 eyes; quatroids with 4 eyes; and pentoids with 5 eyes. I grouped like aliens together to try to encourage the children to use skip counting. The class was asked to find out how many eyes there were in each group. In the packet of dubloids, 2-eyed aliens, there were 13 aliens or 26 eyes. Seven troids (3-eyed aliens) were grouped together for 21 eyes, and 10 quatroids had 40 eyes. The packet of pentoids contained 15 aliens, or 75 eyes. I predicted that the children would probably use skip counting by 2s and 5s but maybe not 3s and 4s. I had observed that they were much more familiar with the former.

The children worked in groups of three, employing various problem-solving techniques. Mike, Missy, and Sammy connected the repetitive addition to the multiplication table that is coincidentally on the back of their notebooks. They called it a "counting chart."

> *Missy:* We added 4 + 4 and it equals 8. So then we saw we had five
> 8s. We looked on the back of our notebooks at this counting chart.
> See, here's five 8s equals 40.

I don't know why Missy and her partners were able to make this connection. My guess is that at least one of them had spent some time looking at the table and formed a good understanding of what it represents. I was amazed that this group was able to apply the use of the table in such an appropriate way. I will be interested in exploring more about their understanding of this in the future.

When I stopped to observe Lily, Brenda, and Randy, I was also somewhat surprised. I had been wondering about the depth of understanding of all three of these children. This group was counting pentoids (5-eyed aliens).

> *Brenda:* 1, 2, 3, . . . 15. There are 15 aliens. (She holds the pile in
> one hand and puts down one picture at a time.)
> *Randy:* Now let's count the eyes. (Randy uses the same dealing technique that Brenda has just used.) 5, 10, 15, . . . 75. There are 75
> eyes! (He looks at his partners as he raises his voice.)

Both Brenda's and Randy's counting had been fluent and confident. I felt sure that each of them understood the size of each unit that had been counted: 1 alien, 5 eyes. However, Lily, the third group member, had been looking away, very distracted by something on her fingers. I wanted to see what she understood about her partners' counting.

Teacher: Lily, can you tell me what Brenda just did?
Lily: Yeah, she counted how many people there are. She got 15.
Teacher: Yes. And what did Randy do?
Lily: He counted how many eyes there are. He got . . . (Lily turns her head and frowns.)
Randy: I got 75! (Randy seems pleased to share this information again.)
Lily: Yeah. 75.

I knew that Lily's partners were eager, confident participants, but I was still unsure about Lily's understanding, so I asked her to show me a way to count the eyes. She picked up the pile of aliens and counted "5, 10, 15, . . . 75," as she placed each picture down. I debated about whether to be satisfied with this. Lily is a child who rarely appears very involved. Most often, she is distracted by something physical about herself or something going on nearby. Her eyes never seem completely focused on her co-workers as they speak. She rarely becomes involved in a discussion with her partners. So, as I observed her counting, I decided, "That's pretty good."

However, I hadn't been pleased with the questions I'd asked Lily. Later in the day, as I thought back on them, I realized that my questions had required Lily to do little more than parrot back what her partners had already said. I continue to struggle with ways to involve all learners, especially the less self-motivated students. How can I increase Lily's feeling of accountability without making her feel anxious?

I continued around the room. Alison and Nate were kneeling on the carpet, leaning close to their work, counting dubloids. I overheard Nate saying, "We got 26 eyes." I wanted to be sure that Alison wasn't left behind, so I asked her to explain to me what she and Nate were doing.

Alison: Well, we divided the pile into two groups. I counted one and Nate counted the other. Then we added the two groups together, $14 + 12 = 26$. We counted the aliens' eyes by 1s. See, 1, 2, 3, 4, . . . 26. (Alison holds up one alien at a time and tilts her head as she counts each eye.)
Nate: Now let's count by 2s! (It makes sense to count these aliens by 2s because they are the dubloids—the 2-eyed aliens.)
Alison: This time we're going to count by 2s? So, we'll start with 2

and go to 4? (Her voice rises at the end of her sentences, making the statements sound like questions.)

Nate nodded at Alison, and they both began to count their piles. Nate counted silently and quickly while Alison counted aloud and slowly. When she finished, she looked up at Nate and said, "I got 14 again! Did you get the same as last time?" When Nate said he did, Alison looked surprised and a little confused. She looked at me, with her eyes wide and her mouth smiling, and exclaimed, "Mrs. Redman, we counted by 2s and I got 14 and Nate got 12 just like last time!"

Teacher: Does that surprise you, Alison?
Alison: Yeah, I thought we'd get different numbers.
Nate: I knew we'd get the same because we still have the same number of aliens in our pile.

I assumed Alison would have some interesting thoughts about why she'd expected different numbers, but as I began to ask her about it, she turned away. She couldn't wait to start writing in her notebook about what she'd found. I left our conversation here, but I do wish I could have gone back to it.

Although Alison and Nate were in different places with understanding skip counting and counting in general, I could tell that they'd both grown from where they'd been earlier in the year. Alison had demonstrated her understanding of one-to-one correspondence as she nodded her head while she counted. Instead of pointing, she'd been using the movement of her head to connect with each eye as she recited each number. And she had shown an understanding of how to count by 2s, seeing two eyes as one pair to be counted together as a single unit. She wasn't familiar enough with the idea to predict that the outcome would be the same, but she will get there.

Nate, on the other hand, had been quite a mature counter when he'd entered second grade. He had already displayed an understanding of one-to-one correspondence and skip counting, and expected consistent answers. However, Nate had come into my classroom preferring to use algorithms. He wanted immediate, clear-cut feedback; he needed to know if he was right or wrong. When I asked him to work on more complex problems, he said things like, "Do we have to do that problem?" and "Why can't you just give us a worksheet?" Although, once in a while, Nate still commented negatively, he had become very involved in some of our counting work. The example of Nate and Alison working together shows that he had become willing to search for more than one way to solve a problem. Nate had also begun to progress in other ways. He'd been patient working with Alison, taking time to be sure that she understood. Nate's record of his work, in his notebook, was becoming more detailed. Instead of a terse, ''I counted,'' as he'd written earlier in the year, he described his and Alison's work in numbers and words. Then he wrote, ''Next we counted again by 2s. We got the same answer. I knew we would.''

REFLECTIONS ON COUNTING AND MORE

As I look back on the last couple of months and the counting work my class and I have done, I have mixed emotions. I am sure that the experiences have been worthwhile for me. I have learned much about second graders and their thoughts about numbers, counting, and mathematics. I have also learned a lot about myself and what I believe good teaching entails.

My personal growth as a teacher feels noteworthy. I have seen the value of watching what children do and listening to them discuss their ideas. My experiences support my beliefs that listening to children is the best way to formulate successful teaching plans. This year I have attempted a compromise between a set curriculum and a flexible one based on the class' needs and interests. While keeping the expectations of the school district in mind, I have tried to organize my class' mathematics curriculum primarily on the children's actions and discussions.

I began the counting exploration mostly to better understand how the children were looking at numbers, but I continued the exploration because of the thought-provoking situations and dilemmas encountered. It seemed that with each activity a new, potentially engaging mathematical concept emerged. From the counting stations came the important question about one right answer. ''Is there a right answer, anyway?'' Counting aliens' eyes led the class to a discussion (and possible future exploration) of odd and even numbers. The aliens' eyes problem and counting noses, feet, and fingers led some children to discover repeated addition and the beginning of multiplication. If I hadn't been observing the children so closely, I might have missed these connections.

Although I can see clearly what I am taking away from these experiences, it is more difficult to assess what the children have gained. They have become more confident in their mathematics work, particularly the ''weaker'' students. Each day, almost every child volunteers to share his or her solution to the day's problem. No one seems afraid to try or fearful of having the wrong answer. The children also seem to place greater value on finding different methods for solving the same problem than they did early in the year. They have become better problem solvers because they are able to analyze a problem and work out a reasonable answer. However, they are still struggling with their math facts. So while they discover new ideas about math concepts, they still need to use blocks to add two numbers. I wonder how to achieve a balance between concepts and skills.

I will continue observing, listening to, and talking with the children to learn more about their mathematical thinking. I haven't found all the answers, but I have learned a lot about how second graders count.

+   —   ×   ÷

TEACHERS BECOMING INVESTIGATORS OF THEIR STUDENTS' MATHEMATICAL CONCEPTIONS

Stephen Lerman

Teachers continually assess and evaluate their students' mathematical knowledge. Determining what students have learned in order to be able to decide what to offer them next is an ongoing and essential aspect of the teacher's role.

However, interpreting what students know from what they say is far from straightforward. Consider, for example, the following reported situation: A child is shown a picture of nine dots and asked to count them. "Seven," she replies. When asked to take her teacher through the counting, the child correctly numbers 1, 2, 3, . . . up to 6, and then, pointing to the remaining three, says, "And those make 7."

The child's first response, "Seven," might have suggested that she couldn't count. However, once asked to show the teacher how she came to that answer, we see that such a conclusion would have been quite wrong—after all, she counted correctly up to 6. Since her teacher did not investigate further, we do not know more about what the child was thinking, what other idea in her head dominated her response.

In the three narratives in this chapter, one reads the outcomes of investigating such incidents further. All kinds of insights and understandings emerge from such investigations—about the nature of learning, about how mathematics manifests and functions in students' lives, and, of course, about the teaching of mathematics.

Implicit in these teachers' investigations are beliefs about learning and about mathematics that contrast sharply with those that govern typical classrooms. To these teachers, mathematics is not a fixed body of knowledge and skills to be taught through presentation and learned through drill, as has been done for decades. Rather, learning even the most basic mathematical concepts—number, counting, shape—involves complex processes as young children actively engage in mathematical tasks. The role of the teacher is to investigate students' understandings in order to help them appropriate and internalize mathematical thinking and doing and mathematical conceptions.

At the beginning of the year, these teachers' questions are quite general. Redman says, "I wanted to know more about what second graders thought about numbers, about counting, and about mathematics in general.'' And Szymaszek asks, ''How do children work through such confusion as they untangle the multiple meanings numbers have?'' As they pursue their investigations, their questions and observations become more specific. But the evidence they acquire, in turn, supports more general principles.

TEACHING AS INQUIRY

Inquiry into students' mathematical conceptions has significant implications for practice. Here I will discuss just three points, as illustrated by Szymaszek, Anderson, and Redman.

What lies below the surface?

When a teacher views her task as training students to provide correct answers to particular problem types, she is satisfied once a correct answer is given. She is unlikely to ask further questions that might ''confuse the child'' or ''throw the child off track.'' That would simply make everybody's life more difficult. And if a child responds with incorrect answers, then the teacher concentrates her efforts on taking the child through the steps that lead to correct ones.

The practice of Szymaszek, Anderson, and Redman contrasts sharply with such a goal. Upon hearing correct answers, they look further; in fact, they are often suspicious of what might *sound* right. For example, Redman writes:

> I asked Lynn how many cubes the snake had had. ''Eleven hundred,''
> she answered. Immediately I thought, ''What an adult way to use numbers,'' but then, since I knew something that sounds like a ''right'' answer may actually be a misunderstanding, I questioned her further.

Once these teachers begin looking below the surface, they discover that responses that might seem perfectly reasonable can mask considerable confusion. With the goal of teaching for understanding, they work to develop more complete pictures of the mathematical ideas and connections their students hold.

When Redman sets up counting stations in the room, she discovers that the children do not seem concerned that different groups came up with different counts at the same station. That is, given a single set of crayons, one group counted 44, another 41, and another 50. In most traditional second-grade classrooms, a teacher would set as her goal to make sure that the children were able to name the counting words in one-to-one correspondence and would have the children practice until they came up with the correct count. However, Redman looks further: ''If they could believe that the same pile of crayons is 44 for one counter and 50 for another, what does that say about their sense of number—how much a number really is?''

Redman's goals go beyond helping her students "realize that a careful, correct count should yield only one answer"; she aspires to have them develop a stronger sense of number. In order to do this, however, she must first learn more about what her students currently believe. Thus, she sets herself the program of unpacking their understandings and then taking them further into mathematical ideas.

At each stage, she does this by offering the children a task that draws on their conceptions and by asking questions to extend those conceptions. She notes carefully the children's responses and uses that feedback to determine the next set of questions and tasks. Her practice is based on the belief that children develop new ideas on the base of their existing understanding, and that to ignore their conceptual states is to risk losing contact with them.

While these teachers believe that developing pictures of their students' conceptual states is central to their work, they also understand that those pictures are necessarily only partial, to be considered hypotheses. Thus the teacher must be willing to alter her hypothesis when the child offers new evidence. For example, in the following passage Anderson revises her hypothesis about Nikima's understanding of the difference between a square and a triangle several times:

> *Nikima:* But they're twins.
>
> Egad! Nikima had been quiet up to this point, but I thought from the expression on her face and the occasional nod of her head that she was following right along with the differences that had been noticed.
>
> *Teacher:* How are they like twins, Nikima?
>
> *Nikima:* They're both yellow.
>
> I had purposely used two yellow shapes in order to provide a common characteristic. Then, when Nikima noticed the colors were similar, I thought she was totally confused. I hope that my feelings weren't obvious to the children, since Nikima continued, "This is a yellow square and this is a yellow triangle."
>
> . . . I realized [then] that Nikima's previous body language had not been misinterpreted by me.

Szymaszek is explicit about the limits of a teacher's knowledge when she discusses Jenny's representation of a "pretend family that has 12 legs."

> I wondered what this indicated about her interpretation of the problem and about her sense of numbers. Did she want to include both people and animals? . . . Or was she going along by trial and error, without a bigger plan? Because I didn't ask her during her work, I could not know for sure.

Appreciating multiple meanings

I remember my daughter, when about five years old, asking me, "What is 1 and 2?" If I answered "3" she would say, "No, 12," and if I answered "12" she would say, "No, 3." I couldn't win! My daughter was intrigued by these two ways of thinking about "1 and 2," and used this idea to play with me.

The common view that mathematical concepts have fixed meanings and that the teacher's role is to convey them to children ignores the nature of children's experiences of number (to say nothing of the nature of mathematics itself). The investigations pursued in the narratives in this chapter explicitly address the multiple meanings students confront and construct.

Szymaszek tells the following story:

> The teacher invited [her preschool class] to join her as she began to count: "One, two, three, four," but she was interrupted. "No, no. I'm not four. I'm three."

Szymaszek is struck by the multiple meanings of number—number used to count objects, to represent age, as code (as in a telephone number)—with which her young students are confronted. She sees that children need to learn how to "call up" the appropriate meaning for any given task.

Furthermore, they need not repress other, less formal meanings. It's not wrong to say, "My half is bigger than your half," so long as one recognizes that there is an everyday context in which that is perfectly sensible and a mathematical context in which it is not. Children need to play with meanings as they struggle to make connections within particular categories. Language, communication, and knowledge are about meanings (Lerman, 1994), and one learns them through experimenting, trying things out, playing. This is no less appropriate for mathematics than for any other realm.

Anderson finds herself confronted with various interpretations for the word "side" when she asks about the sides of geometric shapes. Her students tell her that a rectangle has four sides—unless that rectangle is composed of two squares, in which case the rectangle has six or eight sides (they are not sure which). To these children, the word "side," when applied to a rectangle composed of two squares, means the side of a square—a different interpretation from that of most adults and older children. Once Anderson investigates just what the children's arguments are, she decides it is not appropriate to "challenge them [on this]. The notion that something can be a side and not a side at the same time is a sophisticated one." This is an idea they will come across again.

Autonomy in learning

The teaching in these three classrooms is, in Szymaszek's words, "learner-driven, with the teacher 'leading from behind.'" Teachers pose questions, offer tasks, and then watch and wait as students respond. Rather than being led through the task or being told what they should remember, the children are given autonomy as learners—they are the ones who seek out solutions and give voice to ideas.

For example, Anderson has laid out three triangles—one red, one blue, and one yellow—placed in different orientations. The children recognize the red one, with one horizontal side and a vertex pointing up, to be a triangle. But to them the blue one, with a horizontal side and a vertex pointing down, is an "ice cream cone," and the yellow one, with a vertical side and a vertex pointing to the right, is a "flag." These kindergartners develop their own vocabulary to express their thoughts—"twins" is their word for sharing an attribute. Only after one of the children turns the "ice cream cone" upside-down do the others realize that it is "twins" with the red one; that it, too, is a triangle. But when the children still do not recognize the "flag" as a triangle, Anderson (calling upon restraint) decides not to push it. At the last moment, however, as Megan is putting the shapes away, she discovers that all three are congruent. "Wait! Look!" she says to the others. "They are all the same." One senses that the learning that took place at that moment for all the children was of a different order from what might have happened had the teacher pointed it out for them. As Anderson says later, "The approach that I used with the children this year, when discussing the properties of the four basic shapes, seemed to give them more ownership of the mathematics involved."

FROM OBSERVATION TO INQUIRY TO RESEARCH

> *Redman:* I tucked that information into my brain for further reflection. . . . The evening after that lesson, I sat down and thought it over.
>
> *Szymaszek:* Every time I have one of those bewildering moments, I am forced to reflect on and to analyze how the problem looks from the perspective of a five- or six-year-old.
>
> *Anderson:* I puzzled for several days, reflecting on their idea that a rectangle could have six or eight sides. About a week after this discussion, I decided to use a different approach.

Practice as inquiry centers upon consciously focusing one's attention on what is happening in the classroom and recording, in writing or mentally, special incidents for later evaluation, self-criticism, and decision making. The process is sharpened by articulating to others reflections, plans, conjectures, and, most of all, one's own learnings. All teachers observe significant events in the classroom, but the main activity that shifts one from an observer to an active inquirer is the articulation of those events and subsequent reflections. Oral discussion with like-minded colleagues (as emphasized by Schweitzer in Chapter 2) is critical, but the process of writing for an audience often forces even deeper reflection.

As one writes (indeed as I write this piece), one attempts to capture for oneself what is taking place. At the same time, one is acutely conscious of audience, which is in one's head; the audience may be composed of colleagues, other students in an in-service course, tutors assessing the writing, the anonymous readers of books and journals, or, indeed, a significant other to whom in a sense one "speaks" in writing. The narratives in this chapter confirm the richness that writing can bring to the process of inquiry.

The writers are searching after their students' conceptual development in mathematics, looking at the ways the children construct and elaborate meaning. They treat the learning of mathematics as problematic—one has theories and beliefs about children's learning, which need to be questioned and challenged. Teachers learn through continuing to inquire into the processes involved in mathematical activity, mathematical thinking and doing, and the learning of skills and concepts. Reading articles and books contributes to the grounding of theories and beliefs against which they can reflect on the outcomes of their inquiries.

There is no distinct line between what constitutes research and what does not, and criteria used to make such judgments are those of the academic community. In recent years in education, there has been a shift away from the view that research is what is carried out by people in universities with access to funds and with knowledge about research that can be acquired only by joining that group. Research is about knowledge production: in the case of the narratives in this chapter, about children's mathematical thinking and learning as they take place in the classroom. Teachers, rather than university-based researchers, are best placed to incorporate into such research the richness of the complex sociocultural setting of the school classroom.

Sharing those findings—putting them into the public arena through writing and disseminating that writing—is an essential aspect of knowledge production. The whole mathematics education community benefits by sharing teachers' learning through such inquiries and research in the classroom. Other teachers not yet engaged in this process will gain a sense of its potential and may be inspired to join in. Those who are engaged in the process gain a sense of community. Specific activities and focuses of study are offered to others. Readers may well find that the hypotheses and conjectures about the process of children's learning of mathematics resonate with their ideas and experiences, and this may be the major criterion of what constitutes knowledge production and research.

REFERENCE

Lerman, S. (Ed.). (1994). *Cultural perspectives of the mathematics classroom.* Dordrecht, The Netherlands: Kluwer.

CHAPTER 4

The New Mathematics Pedagogy:
An Open-Ended Practice

The narratives of changing professional identities presented in earlier chapters address crucial initial challenges facing teachers determined to construct new mathematics instructional practices. By contrast, the stories that follow—by Valerie Penniman and Deborah Carey O'Brien—invite us to consider what kind of practitioner emerges as these initial challenges are worked through. In an essay touching on a number of important issues, Susan Jo Russell suggests that these "reflective practitioners" work by "construct[ing] hypotheses about what is going on in the classroom and what to introduce into the learning/ teaching situation to change it": Penniman, in response to her students' failure to grasp the logic of graphic representation; O'Brien, in acting on her conviction that writing about their ideas will enhance her students' understanding of the mathematics they are studying.

Contextualizing Russell's insight, one might add that precisely because Penniman and O'Brien have become comfortable with new routines of classroom management and are skilled at monitoring their students' learning, they are now free to concentrate on the mathematical ideas their students are constructing and on the means that will best serve to deepen and extend those ideas. Within the horizon of the new mathematics pedagogy, this means being open to novelty, committed to self-scrutiny, and prepared to continually rethink one's practices.

Both Valerie Penniman and Deborah Carey O'Brien teach third grade in western Massachusetts college towns.

$+ \quad - \quad \times \quad \div$

MAKING GRAPHS IS A FUN THING TO DO

Valerie Penniman

"I don't get it," Jeremy complained as he pointed to a bar graph and a few accompanying questions.

"What don't you get? Here is the graph and here are the questions that go with the graph," I replied, using my best teacher voice.

"I don't get how to answer this question," he said as he looked up at me, worried.

"I can't give you clues or tell you how to solve this, Jeremy, because this is a test. I suggest you study the graph a little longer and think about some of the graphs we made last year in class. Keep trying," I suggested. I couldn't say any more since this exercise was part of the standardized tests third graders were taking.

Just as I finished answering his questions, two more hands shot up. I went over to Virginia, who looked quite unhappy. "I don't get this," she said in a rather unsteady voice as she pointed to the bar graph. After giving her my "I can't tell you the answer" speech I moved on to Karen.

"I don't know how to answer this," she groaned. When she also pointed to the bar graph section of the test, I started to wonder what was happening.

After responding to what felt like a million more "I don't get it" questions about the graphs and corresponding questions, I realized *I* didn't get it!

When my students finished taking the tests I checked the bar graphs and the questions. The graph looked fine. It was a typical bar graph, clearly labeled and clearly unexciting. The questions were also clearly asked: "The classes in Woodlawn School were collecting soda cans for a school project. Use the graph to tell how many more cans Miss Stanley's class collected than Mr. Smith's class." It was all very *clear*—except to my students.

What was the problem? As a second-grade teacher, I had taught most of these students last year. When I moved to the third grade this year, the majority moved with me. We had studied graphing, we had created graphs, we knew graphs! Could it be my students really didn't understand them? And of all places for me to discover this, in a standardized testing situation! As I reviewed this test and reflected on my pupils' inabilities to answer the questions, I thought back to . . .

. . . last year. My second-grade students made graphs and answered comparison questions about them. They created a class graph on a large bulletin board using emptied, personally decorated, half-pint milk cartons to represent their responses to questions like, "What is your favorite color?" Later, as they colored in the boxes in predesigned graphs, I noticed how well one-to-one correspondence was developing in this group. They also used unifix cubes to answer "more than, less than" questions about the graphs. They had solved problems with confidence, showing how they arrived at answers and, if challenged to explain their thinking, proving their conclusions. I thought I had made available the experiences and opportunities that would allow students to make sense of bar graphs. I never told them what to think or how to proceed. I thought they understood graphs.

After reviewing and analyzing last year's activities on graphs, I concluded that they had never experimented with, invented, or interpreted graphs. I, as the teacher, had structured these concrete and pictorial experiences, including discussions about the graphs and the story problems they had solved with their partners. My students didn't need an easier lesson or a review of graphing to help them understand graphs; they required something more difficult, a challenge, to make them think about and make sense of graphs. They needed an experience to encourage them to invent, compare, contrast, question, analyze, and interpret. My task was to create such an experience so my students could construct new meaning by building on and extending their earlier knowledge.

THE CHALLENGE

After perusing a variety of materials, I decided to use AIMS's *Primarily Bears* (Wiebe, Youngs, Hillen, & Sutton, 1987) activities on sorting and graphing gummy bear candies by color. I liked the sorting, tally, and graphing sheets (see Figure 4.1) because they were clear and attractive, but decided that the Teacher Instructions were too directed and limiting for my purpose because they reduced graphing to an activity requiring only one-to-one correspondence between the gummy bears and squares on the graph paper. My plan was to give my students more gummy bears to sort and graph than would easily fit on the graph paper provided. Consequently, they would have to devise their own methods to make the graph meaningful and would, I hoped, come to a deeper understanding of the structure of bar graphs.

My lesson plans were quite different from traditional plans. They were flexible, fluid, and dependent on the children's progress. The objectives were to invite students to invent a way to include more objects on a graph than could easily be accommodated, to make a graph that included a title, key, labeled axes, and accurate information, and to clearly communicate that information to others. I planned to start concretely, with the children sorting and tallying gummy bears. Then they would graph the results on the gummy bear graph paper, inventing ways to fit them all on the graph. My pupils would discover through discussions the important aspects of creating graphs and later would make improved, final versions on traditional graph paper. During our

FIGURE 4.1. Sorting, Tally, and Graphing Sheets

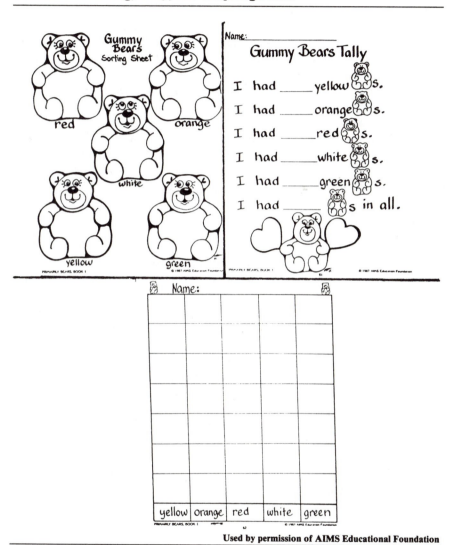

Used by permission of AIMS Educational Foundation

discussions, we would compose a graphing guideline list. Finally, when the students were ready, I planned to find alternative examples of graphs in books and newspapers so they could experience a variety of graphs.

I prepared for the activity with excitement and trepidation. I arranged the students in groups of three or four and carefully mixed and sorted the gummy bears into plastic bags, one for each group. The graphing sheet allowed only seven candies of each color to be recorded, so I had to make sure that in each bag a few colors were represented by more than seven. Although I didn't want the groups to have equal numbers of each color, I did want the groups to have equal total amounts of candy because later they would eat it. I planned on listening very carefully to the children to assess their progress and make decisions based on that information. Would this activity provide the necessary stimulus for probing and thinking about graphs? In time, I would know.

THE PROCESS

Day 1

My students loved sorting gummy bears by color on the sorting sheets. They counted them easily and recorded the number of each color on the tally sheet.

Everyone agreed to use purple on the graph to represent the white gummy bears because white crayon would be impossible to see against the white paper. Each group used a different method to record the results on a graph. Jeremy's group took a second sheet of graph paper and taped it to the first. "We ran out of squares but this way one square equals one gummy bear," he explained. While all the members of this group agreed to use this system, one of them looked unhappy.

Josh was easy to spot because he was frowning, and his hair was arranged in an unusual, messy way, as if he'd been running his hands through it. I asked him if there was a problem. "No," he responded, "but I have another way and no one gets it. You see, you make each square count for three gummy bears. I tried it on the reds and it's perfect."

"But that's too hard," argued Jeremy. "You only know it'll work on reds. What about the other colors? This way is better because you know it's gonna work and it's easy."

Josh looked up at me with his big eyes and quietly said, "See what I mean?" I did. He had lost his argument and agreed to comply with the group decision. I moved on, realizing he didn't want me to interfere. However, I registered his idea of using ratio and knew I would be looking for an opportunity to bring it up again or let him explore it at a later time.

By drawing squares on the sides and top of the graph so each square could also equal one bear, Jon's group showed it, too, clearly understood the one-to-one correspondence between bears and squares.

Karen's group used a variety of horizontal, vertical, and diagonal lines to divide squares, each half square representing one bear. Karen was very proud of her group's creativity. "We used lines going in lots of directions to split boxes because there weren't enough boxes for the candy," she told me.

Elizabeth's group colored in as many squares as there were and didn't worry if they ran out. Even though they had 12 green gummy bears, they only colored in the seven squares provided on the graph paper. They told me this was the easiest work they'd done all year in math!

Day 2

When the students were ready, they shared their graphs with the class. I asked that the groups be given a chance to show and explain their graphs before others offered comments and asked questions. At the end of each group's presentation, I asked what the class liked about the graph, and I made a list of the comments. By structuring the sharing session in this manner, I hoped my students would notice the properties of graphs and discover those aspects that made them meaningful to the group. I had seen enough well-done graphs to be fairly confident the positive comments would highlight those aspects and at the same time provide us with several different models.

Jeremy's group shared first. With pointer in hand, Chris showed how they taped the graph sheets together and how the tally sheet agreed with the graph sheets. Virginia offered, "The squares are the same as the amount of gummy bears." Josh looked at me with a little smile on his face as I recorded this comment on our list.

After Jerome's group explained their method of adding squares to the sheet, Alex said, "It's easy to tell how many gummy bears there were even if they don't fit exactly on the graph."

The only comment anyone could offer to Elizabeth's group, since they had incorrect information recorded on their graph, was that they colored their squares the same color as the rows were labeled.

The problem with this experience was that some graphs were clearly readable and understandable, while others were not. Because I accepted only positive comments, the groups with inaccurate or confusing graphs were not necessarily made cognizant of their shortcomings. After all, the people who made the graph understood it! The group that really bothered me was the one that just didn't worry whether there were enough squares. When I checked in with them at the end of class, they told me, "We just ran out of squares, so we stopped coloring."

When I asked what they were going to do about it, they just gave me blank stares. I said, "If we put your graph on the bulletin board, how many red bears would classmates think you had?" They admitted that others couldn't get that information from their graph. But they really didn't care! I was surprised and, from a teacher's point of view, disappointed.

That evening, I did some hard thinking about setting up an environment that was positive and safe yet fostered critical thinking. All we really had done in that day's session was observe, not analyze. It had been positive and comfortable, but it did not encourage students to look at aspects of their graphs that did not work.

Day 3

The more I thought about the discussion, the more I realized that we had, in fact, created a very positive, supportive atmosphere in our classroom. The ground rules of respecting and valuing all individuals, their ideas and their work, were understood, accepted, and practiced consistently. Here was an environment where students could take risks, critically analyze their work, challenge one another's thinking, and take those necessary next steps to learn something new. We obviously had a *safe* place. But by accepting only positive comments I had created a *protective* environment. Yet students don't need to be protected when they are safe. I used this insight to take the next step. I devised a questionnaire that asked pupils to respond to each other's graphs.

The students received the questionnaire with delight. Each group understood they would read all the other groups' graphs and answer the questionnaire concerning the color and number of gummy bears. As students dashed around the room to answer the questions, they discovered some graphs could be read with ease and some were confusing. After we surveyed them, we found that many were accurate, but a few weren't. I asked the class, "What made some graphs easier to read?" As they answered, I again recorded their responses and added them to the previous day's list.

Ann commented, "Adding a square on the side means there is one more bear. I understand that, but it usually got squished, so it was hard to see. New squares need enough room."

Susan added, "Dividing a square by lines means there are two gummy bears for that square."

Laura jumped in with, "Dividing squares the same way would make it easier to read." Lots of heads nodded in agreement.

In a quiet voice, Elizabeth told us, "The number of gummy bears on the tally sheet should be the same as on the graphs." This is what I had been looking for earlier. Elizabeth realized her graph was inaccurate and she knew how to correct her information.

At the end Chris offered, "Crossing off squares confuses people. Do the graph over instead of crossing off."

These comments illustrated the big leap my students had made in understanding. When no one could read their graph correctly, even the group that hadn't cared about accurate information understood the problem. I tried to keep the atmosphere as positive as possible, yet I know a few groups felt some discomfort during the discussion and were unhappy with their work. They would have a chance to revise their graph, however, and they had learned some valuable information about graphing. I had to create some tension in the environment before learning could take place. When it was too comfortable, my students didn't make the effort to learn. I, too, learned from this experience. The classroom environment was definitely safe enough for the children to take risks, feel a little uncomfortable, and take the necessary next steps.

Day 4

In the main corridor of the school I had noticed some graphs created by sixth graders about their classmates' favorite candy bars, TV shows, cars, books, and so on. Although I had passed by them several times, it wasn't until now that I thought of using them to help my class learn more about graphing. Rather than using graphs from newspapers and books, I could use graphs created by people my students knew and respected. The sixth graders' graphs had titles, labeled axes, and keys. They were quite polished and creative. These graphs would introduce more valuable information to the class. I decided to bring the children to the hall and see what else we could discover about the world of graphs. Students noticed many different elements of the graphs, and, after we studied and discussed them for a while, we returned to the classroom and added more comments to our list.

Jeremy liked the titles that were written neatly and in color. Laura noticed, "There is a key, so the reader understands the graph. It said two squares equaled one person."

Virginia, Elizabeth, Susan, and Josh commented on the numbers on the side of the graph and the words on the bottom of the rows. They thought it made the graphs easier to read. Sarah, a very artistic student, added, "Pictures make the graph look interesting, especially when they're in the bar part."

We were near the end of this session and no one had made a comment about the uniformity of the sixth-grade graphs. All the squares represented the same amounts. In the graphs my third graders made, they had divided the squares only when they had run out of room, so the bars were all different. I raised this point to the group but, because no one considered it very important, let it drop. At least I could take comfort in the fact that they didn't think everything I said had to be followed just because I was the teacher. They were independent learners, taking control of this situation, accepting what they thought was important and rejecting what they thought was not.

Day 5

During the past four days, I had recorded the comments students made about graphing. This list was to act as their guide as they revised their first graphs and created their final ones. I wanted them to reread the list and prioritize it. I was asking them to analyze the most important aspects of graphing.

Each group met to choose the three most important ideas from our list.

Then we pooled the results and discussed them, keeping in mind they would be making their own individual gummy bear graphs the next day.

As I observed the children discussing the most important elements of graphing, I realized how much information they really had discovered in the process of making their gummy bear graphs and analyzing the work of the sixth graders. If I had created the graphing guidelines, I probably wouldn't have done as thorough a job and the students would have accepted them passively. Instead, they had power and purpose as they actively created this list from their experiences, observations, analyses, and errors. Since it represented what they had learned about graphing so far, they valued and owned this list in which they had invested so much time and energy (see Figure 4.2).

However, I wished I could have added to their list, "If some squares are divided, all the squares must be divided." This point still bothered me. Why couldn't the students see this? I thought about imposing my idea on the class, but then I realized that probably it was important only to me, so I let it drop. Perhaps there would be another time when I could mention it.

Days 6 and 7

I originally had planned to use traditional, one-half-inch graph paper for the final project, but changed my mind and instead prepared the same gummy

FIGURE 4.2. Students' Graphing Guidelines

Graphing Guidelines

1. The number of bears on the tally sheet is the same as on the graph.

2. The squares are colored in neatly.

3. The colors of the squares match the labels on the graph.

4. A key tells you if colors or squares are different.

5. Crossing off squares confuses people; do this graph over instead of crossing off.

6. The title is written neatly and in color.

7. The numbers on the side make it easier to read.

8. Dividing squares the same way makes it easier to read.

9. Pictures look nice in and on the graph.

bear graph paper the children first used. If my students had made their final graphs on traditional graph paper, they would have missed the chance to process their inventions and discoveries, because all the data would have easily fit on it. Using the original gummy bear graph paper forced them to make choices about their methods and apply what they had learned. They had some interesting decisions to make about how to deal with the lack of space, and I was curious to see what would happen.

As I walked around the room observing the students working on their individual graphs, I noticed that Elizabeth was using the same method Jeremy's group used originally—adding a second sheet of paper to the first. She was careful to color in the exact number of squares. She even asked a peer to check it. Virginia calmly commented, "We didn't have enough squares but now we do, so we can color in the right number. No big deal."

I was curious about Josh. Would he develop his idea about making one square equal to three bears? When I questioned him about his graph he explained that the group's way was easier even though his was "pretty good, too." He surprised me by using a diagonal line to divide his squares. "This is almost like my first idea except the line makes it easier to read. Each square is really for two gummy bears, but the line shows you without thinking about it." He was right! He was applying the same mathematical idea of ratio to his graph and at the same time using a method that his classmates would understand. Communication was a primary function of his graph.

I noticed he had divided *all* the squares and I was quite surprised. Nobody had done that in the first draft or reinforced my idea when I brought it up after we had analyzed the sixth graders' graphs. When I asked Josh about this, he explained, "I wasn't going to divide all the squares but when I made a key like this, I knew I was in big trouble. So I made them all the the same and it was okay." (See Figure 4.3.) I was surprised.

When I stopped by Karen she told me, "I wanted to use all different lines to divide the squares, like on the first graph, but our list said it was too confusing so I'm just using corner lines [diagonals]."

Karen also had divided all her squares. "Why did you divide all the squares instead of just the ones you ran out of?" I inquired.

Karen smiled at me and admitted, "I was going to divide just the yellows,

---

FIGURE 4.3. Josh's Indication That One Square Represents Two Bears

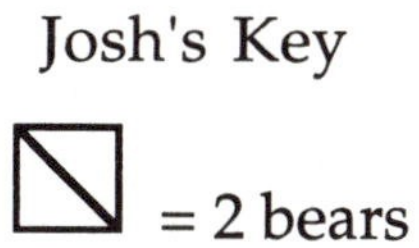

Josh's Key

= 2 bears

---

greens, and whites because they're the only ones that don't fit on the graph paper. But when I made the key I knew something was wrong. Maybe I could have made two keys, but this made sense and it was easier.''

"Amazing," I responded. When will I begin to trust my students to make the decisions necessary for their learning? They discovered the reason for uniformity because they had a need for it. They figured out the problem and the solution. To think I almost took that away from them.

Day 8

The graphs were finished and they looked wonderful. Many were quite similar to one another, yet many were not. To record the numbers of gummy bears, the method of choice was to divide each square by a diagonal line to make a total of 14 spaces. Sarah drew a bear face in each square in the corresponding color. She was proud of her work and knew it looked great. Susan colored too dark and her graph looked messy. "We should have put 'to color lightly' on our list," she grumbled.

Roberto counted incorrectly and couldn't understand how he could have made a mistake. He was very upset and asked to do it over again for homework. Ann decorated hers with bears around the outside of the graph. Most graphs were accurate and looked very attractive. I was quite impressed with the results because they showed how much the students had learned about graphs. I knew the graphs would be hung with pride on our classroom bulletin board.

Now my pupils wanted to graph class favorites (TV shows, food, etc.). If they were ready, so was I!

The students went on to create their own individual graphs of class favorites. They chose topics, took surveys, and, based on our original list of the qualities of graphs, set up their own on traditional graph paper. Their topics ranged from favorite birds, to favorite flags, to favorite Star Wars movies. The most difficult part of this activity was learning to limit the number of choices they gave as they surveyed their classmates. Many students performed an initial survey, discovered they had 15 or more answers, then limited the choices and asked their questions again. Students made rough drafts first. Together, the class and I created a peer editing checklist (see Figure 4.4) out of the class' comments about graphs. It worked quite well in focusing the comments and questions of peers in regard to the rough drafts. Then students made their final drafts and, again, they were very careful and creative in their work. There was more room for innovative ideas in this project, and I was pleased to see the children so involved. When the graphs were completed, the students displayed them in the hall for the school to see. The ownership and pride they showed were exciting. Jeremy summed up his experience by saying, "If we can do these graphs this well now, just think how great we'll do in sixth grade!''

FIGURE 4.4. Peer Editing Checklist

Peer Editing Checklist Graphing	Name_____ Peer_____	
Questions & Considerations	Editor	Peer
Do you have a title?		
Does it explain what you are graphing?		
Is your information accurate?		
Is your graph clearly labeled?		
Is your key neat, complete, and easy to read?		
How are you planning to color your graph?		
Does your graph look the way you want it to?		
Underline misspelled words. Look up five words in the dictionary.		
Additional comments, questions, and concerns:		

THE STUDENTS' COMMENTS

After both graphs were completed, students wrote in their journals. The following excerpts are in response to this prompt: "Please write everything you know about making bar graphs." (The spelling has been corrected for ease of reading, but the wording and punctuation are the original.)
Virginia wrote:

Graphing is another way of showing how many things or living things you may or may not have. Graphs are some ways of showing about things such as how many black cats you have and how many brown cats, gray cats, orange and white cats. And how you make a graph is not to write down that information but to show it on squared paper. It should probably have a key box that shows what equals what such as red = Robin. And on the top write down what the graph is about and on the side of the graph different levels. Then write your name.

Josh included these comments:

People make graphs because it tells them things easier. Graphs tell you about things like what your favorite thing is and how the stock is doing. They usually have keys to tell you what the letters or colors mean. They have numbers on the side and have boxes to tell you how many people vote/want that thing. Some have letters to tell you what it is. You have to make a rough draft first. Sometimes a square can mean two or three things.

Karen wrote:

The first thing you have to know is how to group. Then you have to know how many you have and then you color in how many of each thing you have. Then you label them. Then you should tell what you are graphing. Then you number the side so other people know how many boxes are colored in. Have a key that tells what and how many boxes equal such and such. Then you should use punctuation after you ask a question. Example: What is your favorite flag? It is easy to read graphs because you don't have to count up you just look at the side and then you figured it out. People make graphs because it is easier for people to read.

Jeremy explained:

If you want to read a graph and you don't know how you should look at the key and it should show you how and give you a little information. Making graphs is a fun thing to do. It can also help people to understand what people like.

Reading the children's journals was such fun! All of them understood that graphing was another means of communicating information. They felt graphs were easier to read, but they didn't say with what they were comparing them. I would guess they were thinking of text, because of Virginia's comment, "And how you make a graph is not to write down that information but to show it on squared paper." Since the entries were written after all the graphs were completed, my students wrote about their most recent graphing experience, class favorites. Keys, titles, and labeled axes were included in the majority of journals. Making rough and final drafts and editing with a peer were also mentioned fairly often.

The journals, written individually during about 20 minutes of class time, provided evidence of the graphing knowledge my students now possessed. Taken together with their graphs and my observations of their class performance, the journals made it easy for me to assess each student's progress during this project. We were all pleased with the results.

IMPLICATIONS

The AIMS *Primarily Bears* materials worked quite well as a starting point for graphing. By listening to my students, using the resources around us (such as the sixth graders' graphs), and observing their conversations and actions, I made conscious decisions about next steps. I learned, rather painfully, to trust my students to make choices important to their learning. They discovered what they needed to know in order to make successful graphs. By analyzing their first graphs, making observations that were important to them, and sequencing them in a meaningful way, students created their own guidelines and rules for graphing.

Some pupils progressed further than others in their mathematical understanding. Elizabeth's group was slow to understand that a graph must represent an exact number. Finally, when members of that group did accept this basic concept, they attached another sheet of graph paper onto the first paper to ensure there were enough squares for their final gummy bear graph. Most other students took a bigger leap in understanding when they divided squares so that each would represent two candies. Josh developed his idea of ratio so it could be understood by his classmates. All the students improved and further developed their graphing skills at their own speeds and levels of development.

The decisions I made were important in this project. First, I decided to give my students a complex graphing problem rather than a simple one. Second, I distinguished between a protective environment and a safe environment, and this understanding enabled me to create the opportunity that allowed the students to analyze their work. Consequently, they discovered important aspects of graphing. Third, since traditional paper had more squares than they needed for the candy, I asked the students to graph their final gummy bear graphs onto the gummy bear paper. Using it gave them the opportunity to make improvements and corrections, applying what they had just learned. Fourth, I made a decision about Josh's ratio scheme, which was probably fine, but I still wondered if I should have encouraged him more. He learned from this experience and seemed very happy with the outcome; those were my first priorities for him. Last, because I respected the children's desire to create meaningful graphs, the issue of dividing either all or none of the squares resolved itself nicely. When they needed a uniform scale in order to communicate information to others, they created one themselves.

Will I do this project the same way next year? I doubt it. I may begin the same way, but its development will depend on the students and their needs. I now have some experiences to draw from and some ideas for further planning, but I'll make decisions based on what is most appropriate for the students. I've learned I can trust them to make decisions important to their learning. If they are to discuss, interpret, and evaluate mathematical ideas, they have to make their own decisions. They are the active ingredient in any learning situation.

Later in the year, during another standardized test, my students answered questions about graphing. As I anxiously watched them choose answers, I felt like a mother hen. There had been another time when I thought they understood graphs and I had been wrong. All the indications I'd had assured me they knew graphs. "After all," I reasoned, "standardized tests don't really show what my pupils do or don't understand." But still, I was worried.

When Rebecca raised her hand during the test, I quickly joined her, wondering if she was having difficulty. She whispered, "These graphs are boring. Ours were much prettier and more interesting." Then she flashed me a big smile. With a sigh of relief and a feeling of pride, I saw the children answer most questions correctly. Now I could relax, too.

REFERENCE

Wiebe, A., Youngs, D., Hillen, J., & Sutton, K. (Eds.). (1987). *Primarily bears.* Fresno, CA: AIMS Education Foundation.

MATH JOURNALS: FIRST ATTEMPTS IN THIRD GRADE

Deborah Carey O'Brien

In March, I made the decision that the following September my new class of third graders was going to use math journals. Since I began teaching eight years ago, I have been on a quest to find ways to help children really understand mathematics. Perhaps math journals would be the key to the understanding I was looking for. This was a totally new teaching idea for me.

This approach came to me as a result of using a math journal myself in a geometry course I was taking, in which I was asked to solve problems not by memorizing formulas and steps, but by making sense of them instead. In the process of writing about new, vague, and confusing concepts, concepts I sort of understood, and even concepts that were clear to me, I discovered that writing was a powerful means for sorting through ideas. I felt that I really understood what I was doing. Through my journal, I was able to clarify my thinking. I didn't always find the answers but I always got a clearer sense of my questions and my confusions.

I thought my students might reap the same benefits. They, too, should be able to move to a deeper level of understanding by writing about their math thinking in their math journals.

SETTING

I teach in a public school in a town that has a mixture of college and working-class families. I have a class of 27 children (18 boys and 9 girls) heterogeneously grouped, based on academic and behavioral abilities.

Last March, when the math journal notion came to me, all school budgets were frozen. This posed a problem about materials for journals. That situation, and the fact that I thought this new teaching strategy would need careful consideration, led me to decide not to jump into math journals with that year's class. I would allow myself to take five or six months to carefully plan this change.

PLANNING

One of my initial goals for my class this year was to have the students think about thinking. I envisioned math journals as a part of this process. In deciding how to start, I found myself coming up with many more questions than answers. What do I want students to get from keeping a math journal? What do I want to get from their journal writing? Will journals help children in their thinking? Where should we start? Can third graders write valuable journals? How could or should they be used to demonstrate student learning to parents? What difficulties will be encountered? Will journals increase children's ability to communicate about mathematics? How do I teach them how to write math journals? Are certain levels of skills needed? Should I be thinking about beginning to use journals in ways that are painless and fun, that have a high success rate built in, and only then move to more abstract and challenging assignments? Should I expect the journal entries to move gradually from concrete to more abstract? Will journals help me to know what to plan next? How do I set my expectations for children with a wide range of skill levels?

These were just some of the questions that were going through my mind. I expected to have even more questions to resolve as I gained experience using journals. Out of all of my questions (and doubts), two matters stood out from the rest: What did I want kids to learn by writing journals? and, What could I learn about their mathematics thinking by reading the journals?

An important goal for students of doing math journal writing was that members of the class come to view their thoughts, ideas, and work as important matters worth sharing and discussing. I had seen evidence that third graders could think about thinking. I now wanted them to develop ways of thinking that were more flexible, more logical, and more reflective. I wanted math journals to become a vehicle for this. If these things did happen, the children would benefit greatly. Journals could be my *teaching* tools and their *learning* tools.

I also wanted some kind of physical evidence of what was going on. With journals, I'd have a record of their ideas over time. With the traditional math book or worksheet routine, a teacher gets a score, a number of questions with right and wrong answers, and clues about where the errors are occurring. When I teach math in problem-solving groups or through partner work, I can't possibly be at every group or hear every idea spoken. Groups can spend blocks of time doing work that would be considered "wrong" and I might not know about it. I hoped math journals, along with monitoring the groups and listening during class discussions, would provide a periodic and systematic way of checking in with individuals. My fear that whole class discussions might not click for everyone would be alleviated. Journals would permit me to keep discussions going for the whole class and still allow students individual private times to work on the same problems.

I had the feeling this change, like many others, was not going to be easy. I was going to need to stay on my toes. As is often the case when trying something new and different, I had thousands of doubts creeping in about this new plan. Any change in the status quo is kind of scary. I thought, "What if they don't like writing? Will limited vocabulary restrict them? What if this? What if that? But . . . But. . . . " As September approached, I decided to put the doubts aside and treat this as a learning experience for my students and me, too. So without total confidence, I set to work. (No doubt I will continue to search for the best way to introduce math journals next year, and the year after that, and for many years to come.)

GETTING STARTED

I found out the week before school started that there would be no extra money in the budget for journals or notebooks. (Problems before I even started!) Undaunted, I decided to make my own journals using our school's book binder. I put the journals together in such a way that however they were opened there was a blank sheet on one side and a lined sheet on the other. I hoped the students would use drawings, calculations, and, gradually, more writing to explore and explain their thinking.

Once school started, introducing journals to the class was the next step. I felt I had to be very precise when I explained journal use the first time. I didn't want to be too intense or make math journals seem too imposing. I wanted the students to get a sense of the importance and value of recording their thoughts. I wanted the class to feel that they could do what was asked and still feel the importance of doing something new and more grown-up than second graders were usually asked to handle.

During the first week of school I asked the students to do their *"impor-tant* figuring out and math thinking" in their math journals instead of on sepa-rate sheets of paper. I said it would make it easier for us to look back at our ways of thinking later in the year. A journal would allow us to keep all of our ideas in one place.

The children began by working on the following problem:

A farmer owns 3 cats, 4 chickens, and 6 cows. The farmer is trying to figure out exactly how many animals there are on the farm and how many animal legs are walking around the farm. Can you help answer these two questions? Be sure to show your ideas clearly.

When I looked at the entries, I found some addition (showing sound and not-so-sound reasoning), pictures of animals, dots (arranged like footprints), some "numbery" work erased or crossed out, and some numbers (which I as-sumed were meant as totals). There were several different ideas and answers to talk about, but nothing specifically about their thinking. I was somewhat disappointed, but not all that surprised that the children wrote only answers. I knew it would take some training and practice to acquire the skills to write about thinking. A new approach was necessary. A change was called for. I decided I needed to be much more specific with the children about what I ex-pected.

In the next few days, we spent a good deal of time talking about thinking, using various content areas as examples. In reading we made predictions about what characters would say or do next in novels we were using. In science we predicted changes we expected to see taking place with our caterpillars. For any idea or answer, I asked the children if they could think of their brain with a "pause" or "reverse" button. We tried to slow down discussions to find out where ideas came from. I hoped all of this would give us the experience, language, ideas, and format to talk about thinking with each other. This was a change in how I talked to my classes. It seemed like a new concept to them, too.

Several days later, I assigned another problem, one similar to the farmer's animals question. Again I asked them to work on it in their journals. This time I was very specific about asking them to also write down their thinking as they solved it. I pointed out to them there was plenty of room for numbers or pictures as well as space for writing in words. I distinctly remember my phrase, "See if you can *write* what you are thinking."

Looking back, I see they took this to mean, "Tell what your *opinion* is of this problem." As I looked at the journals, I found: "It is fun." "It is easy doing this." "It is hard." "No sweat man." "I *love* problems like these." "The beginning was easy but when I got to the feet it was really hard."

This was not turning out at all as I had hoped. The thought crossed my mind, "This didn't work. Do I have time for this? If my efforts so far haven't produced some magic, should I forget it?" At the first sign of trouble, it is very easy for teachers to give up on the latest new thing they try! With a class of 27 it would have been easy to let what seemed like dozens of other pressing matters, with easier solutions, be the ones I stuck with and thought through.

But I quickly regrouped. Giving an opinion was a natural thing for them to do, since I had asked them a series of opinion-type questions in the first few days of school. I decided these journal results were a small setback, maybe even one I should have seen coming. I would try to retain this journal writing as a high priority. I knew I should be looking for only small or gradual improvements.

TALKING ABOUT THINKING

I had work to do. I had to teach what it meant to show thinking and what it meant to talk about thinking. As a whole, the class seemed to be unaware of the importance of their math thoughts. Through several conversations I got the message from my kids that math was something to do with just numbers. You get a number, the answer, the end.

This really didn't surprise me. *Fast* and *finished* were frequently key objectives in math. What could I do to change my students' notions of what math was all about? I wanted to shift the focus away from fast and finished. I needed to let the class know I was extremely interested in taking time to explore the different ways a problem could be approached. I decided all of my questions and comments should reflect that interest. So, during math time, when they were working with partners or in groups, and in every discussion and whole class sharing, I tried to restrict my questions and comments to the topic of thinking. For example, I would say, "What were you thinking as you did that?" or "What do you think about what was just said?" or "Who can say back to us the thinking we just heard?" I was able to model good questioning to show the class how to politely and productively check to see if they understood the other person's ideas. I also was able to model appreciation of ideas that might be new or different from my own.

After several days of modeling attention to thinking, I asked the kids to use their journals to think about our seashell problem:

> *Some kids spent three days at the shore. They collected seashells each day. On the first day they found 17. The next day they found only 14. Before leaving they gathered 9 more. How many did they have to take home?*

After working on the problem in small groups, we had a whole group discussion. Some children explained work that surprised most of the rest of the class.

Jed volunteered to copy some of his journal work onto the board for all of us to discuss. He had done his calculation of the ones place out to the right-hand side of his addition problem (see Figure 4.5). Many kids were surprised by this physical arrangement.

Jay had drawn a series of slash marks to stand for 17, 14, and 9. Because his work tends to be rather fast and messy, his answers are often approximate. Using his own diagrams, he didn't get the same answer twice.

Bob had drawn a series of 17 boxes in a row, 14 boxes alongside the 17, and 9 beside the others. Then he numbered each box consecutively until all boxes were accounted for.

Tanya had taken unifix cubes apart and placed 17, 14, and then 9 into a big pile. Next she snapped them back together in groups of 5 and counted by 5s to 40.

I asked everyone to do some thinking and to write about ideas they had heard from others during our discussion. I was thrilled later to read that kids

FIGURE 4.5. Jed's Solution to the Seashell Problem

$$
\begin{array}{cc}
2 & \\
17 & 11 \\
14 & +\ 9 \\
+\ \ 9 & ---- \\
---- & 20 \\
40 &
\end{array}
$$

expressed some confusion over so-and-so's idea, or really understood a new idea talked about by so-and-so, or liked the way so-and-so showed an idea that was different from their own. These samples from journals illustrate the progress I was beginning to find: "I did not get when Jed did this because I never saw anything like it." "Most people added the shells and I agree. Jed's way was different but it works. I really didn't get what Jay did. First he counted lines to 39 and the next two times to other stuff. I thought that was weird." "I have two different ways. I didn't get Jay's idea. Jed's was new but it works because he was counting the ones." "Using cubes or numbers came out the same and I didn't think for sure they would." "Bob's way was really different from what my partner and I thought up." "I had two ways to get the answer 40. Jay got 40 doing his way and Jed got 40 doing his idea but they both still feel unusual." "I found out $17 + 14 + 9 = 40$, $14 + 17 + 9 = 40$, $9 + 14 + 17 = 40$ and I could even do more. There are lots of good different ways to do these. Jay's idea would work if he was careful." "Tanya had a different way when she put 17, 14, and 9 cubes all together and counted by 5s. We both got 40."

This was progress! Changes were beginning to happen!

CHANGES IN STUDENTS' CONVERSATIONS

About a week later, on an early October day, and amidst at least a dozen other things that were going on during math class, one sound separated itself from all the other noises, voices, and sounds. I heard one of my students say in class discussion, "I never thought of doing it that way. I like that new idea. I tried it myself. It works." The class discussion went on, but I was mesmerized. Had the voice come from my class? How had that change come about? No one was talking like that earlier this year. One comment by a student to another student about a math solution demonstrated listening, considering, experimenting, evaluating, and agreeing. Something *big* had been happening!

That voice, which separated itself from all the other noises, sounded to me like a big change. But I didn't let myself get too overwhelmed with joy. This could have been a fluke. I calmed my excitement by recalling the example of the sing-along. When the music plays and people start to sing, almost everyone joins in for at least a few words. Because they had heard me singing that song so often, maybe someone was just saying, "I never thought of doing it that way," to be singing along.

Yet even that would be a change. It was a start.

Were math journals helping students develop their thinking? The plain truth was I didn't know, yet; it looked like it was happening and I hoped so. I was going to keep working on it.

MORE RECENT RESULTS

Early in December, after three months together, I was beginning to find journal entries different from earlier ones. The writing was starting to be more thoughtful and reflective. It showed movement toward greater abstraction. Quite a few kids were able to talk about their math thinking. They were beginning to be able to talk about math concepts, not just specific math calculations.

For example, the class had been working on the following math problem:

> *You decide you really want three books from a new book order. The prices of the books are $2.95, $2.75, and 95 cents. Your mom says okay to the idea, but she is going to give you only $5. You are allowed to buy the rest but you will need to use your money if they cost more than $5.00. Do you need to spend more? If so, how much of your own money?*

After working in small groups, the class came together to share their work. This time there was no consensus. The class had come up with several different answers, and though the problem was unresolved, I set it aside. A few days later, I went back to it and asked the kids to think about the book-order question. I asked how it could have happened that, when we had gathered previously for discussion and sharing time, people had different answers. I told them to think about whether there could be more than one correct amount of money for the books or for them to chip in. After giving them a short time to think about those questions, I asked them not to tell me their answers, but to *write* about doing that book-order problem.

Excerpts from their journals demonstrate development in their thinking. I found evidence of students making comparisons between current work and previous work: "First I had to find out the total cost of the books and I did that by adding. You have to think money. . . . To me this was like the piggy bank one."

Some children were considering other people's solution strategies. For example, Jay and Eric had each shown a way that involved setting up an addition problem and then using some mental math to extract $5.00. This was too different for some of the class: "I think $1.65 is the one right answer. It was all easy to understand until Jay's way and Eric's way. I couldn't really understand those two. And Jay's $5.00 is too much."

Other students were expressing an appreciation for differences in others' ideas: "I think people figured it out in lots of ways and got the same amount. You will really need $1.65 but some people could have made adding or subtracting mistakes."

There were signs of children contemplating the places where someone might have made mistakes: "I think the different answers are because some people could have mixed up adding 5 + 5 + 5 or 9 + 7 + 9 + 1 or about where to put the 15 and 26 from the columns when they added up the total cost of the books."

I found many journals talking about the value of having help and of hearing other ideas. Some journals indicated that working with someone else had helped in finding the ideas: "It was easy for me to think about the problem because I had help from my partner. There can be different ways, but only one right answer to the money it will cost you. There were many different ideas being considered. I think me and Lorna had more than three ways to do it. But all of the ways show you still have to pay $1.65."

I read about feelings of confusion that showed efforts to try some notions that weren't solid yet, but there was some thinking about them: "The other day's math problem was very confusing! As we worked more we came up with lots of different answers. I had to think of the cost of books and then the money of your own to get them. I still have questions."

I found evidence that ideas were valued, whether they were one's own or one's partner's: "This math was hard and easy. We ended up with lots of ideas by working together."

I saw how the children's ability to reflect continued to develop when, in mid-December, the class worked on a shopping problem:

> *You have $19.50 to spend on gifts. Mom's gift is $4.95. Granny's costs $3.70. Your best friend's is $7.38. The gift you pick for dad is $3.00. Do you have enough for all of these? Will you have any money to do more shopping?*

As the children shared ideas, the question arose whether the way to get the answer was by adding or subtracting. We used several math periods to explore that question, which had been initiated when Tanya went to the board and wrote $19.50 - 4.95 = $14.55. This sparked lively conversations all over the room. After several minutes, we wrapped up math for the day by acknowledging Tanya's idea had given us some important things to think about until the next day.

The following day I asked the children to each write in their math journals about their thoughts on the matter. Was the shopping problem an addition or subtraction question?

Dora's journal showed two ways to find the solution. First, she added up all the gift prices and compared the sum to $19.50. Then she did a series of subtraction problems starting with $19.50 and taking away the price of each gift. She wrote, "There is nothing weird about this being add OR take away."

Karrie wrote, "Lorna and I did the math problem by just adding and we can spend 47 cents. I think Tanya's idea is confusing because she started doing lots of steps and lots of crossing out."

Jean's journal showed she had tried to find the total of the gift prices at least three times, each time coming up with a different total. She said, "I agreed with the kids who thought it would work to add but I'm having trouble." (When I find things like this in journals, I can either work with a particular child or bring that kind of skill question to the class for some work.)

After writing their thoughts in the journals, members of the class demonstrated their ideas to one another. About a third of the class thought the solution could be found by adding, another third thought they had to subtract, and the rest saw that either way could work. They ended consideration of this problem by proving it could be done with either operation.

REFLECTIONS ON CHANGES

These later writings show more thought and skill than the earlier journal entries. Math calculations were shown primarily as a means of illustrating some bigger ideas that were being considered.

Several years of teaching experience, and many years of working with children, have brought me to the firm belief that there are levels of knowing. Children may be able to do something, may be able to show someone else and explain it, may be able to just tell someone else, or, finally, may be able to explain clearly in writing. To me these are distinctly different skills or levels of understanding. I hoped the journals would be a way to help the students toward the highest level of knowing.

It would be hard for me to pinpoint proof, but many experiences have left me with the opinion that writing does affect thinking. I believe that as one mulls over ideas that are being put on paper, the ideas need to be explored, explained, and organized. Language needs to be precise and ideas need to be clarified. All of those steps involve lots of mental processing. Try to write a "how-to" paper without pictures, diagrams, objects, or props, to see what I mean.

ALONG THE WAY

After several months, my original barrage of questions and doubts about journals was transformed into two critical questions: What did I want kids to learn by writing journals? and, What could I learn about their mathematics thinking by reading the journals? Those two key questions became intertwined as I worked on making continual assessments of what the children understood about the mathematics they encountered. Their journals were allowing me insight into what they knew and what they didn't know. Their writing was showing me their procedures and, more important, their understandings and misunderstandings.

I began planning the next lessons based on what happened in groupwork, discussion periods, and what I read in individual journals. By listening closely, I found myself continually assessing understanding.

I was able to use my ongoing assessments and the physical records of math thinking, the journals, to learn more about my students. The journals were also valuable as springboards to conversation at the first parent-conference week in early November. The journals provided a tangible way to show parents what big ideas their children had been exploring and the directions students' thinking had taken. At the parent conferences, I was able to use the journals to show growth in thinking and to learn for myself more about the kinds of thinking parents saw in their kids. I felt parents learned more about their children and the kids' ways of thinking, and I learned more about the students from parents by opening this avenue of conversation. Parents were able to share incidents that revealed strengths or weaknesses in the kind of thinking they had noticed at home.

As a bonus, I was able to use the journals as a way to clear up any misconceptions parents might have had about "playing with blocks" instead of doing real math. I was able to show parents how I'm working on having kids learn from each other and having them learn to think of math as the process of "getting there" and not just "right answers."

CONCLUSIONS

I have set a process in motion. I'm sure I will continue to change the way I use journals. Now I use them to check on initial starting points in problem solving and to check on performance levels. I ask the students to use them to consider new ideas they hear from partners or in whole class discussions. I use journals to check on the children's ownership of new ideas days after they have been exposed to those ideas. I'm still discovering uses for journals.

I know for certain I want my class to understand—really understand—the concepts in the third-grade curriculum. I want them to enjoy math. I want them to see that there is more to math than just right answers. I want them to enjoy exploring numbers and how they can be used. I want them to pose questions for themselves and each other because they are curious. I want them to think about their own ideas and the ideas of others. I want them to feel comfortable talking about ideas. I want my class to see the value of looking at "wrong" answers. This list could go on and on. All of these relate to children having positive feelings about math and expecting math to make sense.

Over the course of time, I want my class to use their journals to see how their math strategies might change. They will have a record in one place of what and how they used to think and solve problems. I can also use these records in planning and assessing.

Finally, I want the class to develop writing skills. I want to start in an area that I expect to be weak and help the kids improve their writing about what they are thinking. I want the students' thinking to be clarified by the writing. I see this activity as having the potential of setting a cycle in motion: better writing leading to clearer thinking, leading to still clearer writing, and so on.

Perhaps these goals are too high for third graders. On the other hand, perhaps they are not.

$$+ \quad - \quad \times \quad \div$$

REFLECTION ON PRACTICE: TWO STEPS FORWARD, ONE STEP BACK

Susan Jo Russell

"Reflection on practice" is one of the terms currently in vogue in the mathematics education world. And, like many others who work with teachers, I am involved in efforts to support teachers in reflecting on their own learning as well as their students' learning. What does it take to be a reflective practitioner in the world of schools? An elementary school teacher spends six hours a day within the confines of a single room with perhaps 25, perhaps 35, other people. A secondary teacher sees perhaps 100 to 200 people each day. Each is responsible for orchestrating educational activities that will meet the needs of all of those other people, as well as for maintaining a relatively calm and safe environment.

In order to keep the classroom functioning and to teach, a teacher must interact many times a day with each of the other people in the room over issues ranging from lost lunch money to bruised feelings to the nurturing of creative writing or the development of mathematical understanding—hundreds of interactions each day. Although I have been out of the classroom now for many years, I can still bring back the feelings of being overwhelmed by the human activity of a single day and the sheer difficulty of remembering what had happened at 10:00 in the morning by the time it was 3:00 in the afternoon.

The commitment to becoming a reflective practitioner is a serious one, and both of the narratives in this chapter illustrate the long-term nature of this commitment. Valerie Penniman and Deborah Carey O'Brien are at points in their thinking about the teaching of mathematics where they view their practice as problem solving, a piece of research into their students' mathematical development. Despite the pressures on teachers to "cover" topic after topic in mathematics, these teachers are willing to observe and experiment, withhold judgment, and let time pass without immediate results.

Their teaching is truly reflective—that is, it assumes that by thinking hard about a problem, it is possible to understand it better: to construct hypotheses about what is going on in the classroom and what to introduce into the learning/teaching situation to change it. While this may sound simple, it often is not the way teaching is done. In mathematics in particular, students' lack of understanding is frequently attributed to simple causes. If students do not seem to know what has been taught, the reasons are that they "forgot," they "just can't get it," "they're not developmentally ready," they "can't think abstractly." None of these explanations illuminates anything about what the students *do* understand or what the next teaching step might be. Taking responsibility for the teaching of mathematics means examining the complexity of students' knowledge, beliefs, and experience to try to make good guesses about their views of mathematical ideas, rather than blaming them for being unable or unwilling to learn.

Like any other researcher, these teachers then develop interventions based on their good guesses, but are prepared to revise or refine those hypotheses if their attempts do not bear fruit (Cobb & Steffe, 1983). When Penniman notices with mounting horror the number of students who are unable to interpret graphs on a standardized test, despite what she has felt was reasonable time and attention paid to this area of mathematics, she begins to analyze the problem. When O'Brien's students' first attempts at journal writing do not yield the results she hoped for, she considers how her students are understanding the assignment and what kind of work she can do with them to help them shift their views about what is important in mathematics.

In order to do this, both teachers must rise above what I might call the "cult of the individual child" in the school culture. Many teachers are attracted to teaching because of their abilities and interests in building individual relationships with children. In fact, in a profession with few rewards—certainly, respect and appreciation from the culture are not among them—response from individual children is key in providing job satisfaction for teachers. In elementary education, in particular, there is a great deal of focus on the individual needs of each child and the creation of educational environments that support individual needs. However, this cult of the individual may undermine a critical part of teaching—stepping back from the quirks and intricacies of each learner to view the learning of the class as a whole.

In the case of mathematics, the teacher needs to ask not only questions like, "What does Kim understand about this mathematical idea?" but also, "Why is this piece of mathematics difficult for many of the students in my class?" What is even more difficult than asking such a question is the close observation and analysis needed to develop conjectures that lead to specific teaching actions rather than to vague or overly simplistic generalizations.

Reflection on the practice of mathematics teaching requires not only reflection on students' thinking, but also reflection on mathematics content and pedagogy. What mathematical ideas are important for students to encounter, and what kinds of problem situations will engage students with these ideas?

Again, this means, for the truly reflective teacher, going beyond a superficial interpretation of the recommendations of the mathematics reform: Turning to the use of "real-life problems" or "concrete materials" in the classroom does not magically transform mathematics learning (Ball, 1992).

One of the red herrings of the reform movement in mathematics education is the focus on making problems "real" for students in the elementary grades (Mokros, Russell, & Economopoulos, 1995). "Real" in this sense is taken to mean relevant, familiar, about the world that students know, built on and applicable to their everyday experience. Teachers feel the need to demonstrate through realistic problems that mathematics is useful in the "real world" of students' lives. Therefore, if students bring in empty food cartons and play store in a corner of the classroom, they are doing "real" mathematics. If they are doing made-up problems on a textbook page, they are not.

It is probably—although not necessarily—true that the students involved in the play store are doing more real mathematics than the students solving problem after problem on a textbook page. However, if it is true, it is not because the play store is a true-to-life re-enactment while the textbook problems are not, but because significant mathematical issues are being faced in the one situation and not in the other. It is possible for the students to be playing store without engaging in interesting mathematics while the students solving the textbook problems are working on critical mathematical ideas. It is not the context of the problem itself, but the context of mathematical inquiry that determines whether or not students are engaged with mathematics.

Both O'Brien and Penniman are grappling in a deeper way with the question, What is the nature of real mathematical work? In both narratives the problems themselves are unremarkable—and even unrealistic. Consider the seashell problem O'Brien uses in her classroom:

Some kids spent three days at the shore. They collected seashells each day. On the first day they found 17. The next day they found only 14. Before leaving they gathered 9 more. How many did they have to take home?

This problem is a typical textbook-like "word problem." Without any mathematical context, it can be viewed as merely an excuse to practice addition in a way that looks "real." In fact, it is not even a very realistic problem: adding 17, 14, and 9 is unlikely to be the way that the children at the shore would have solved this problem; the shells would have ended up all together in a container, and if the children had been interested in how many there were, they would simply have counted the shells one by one. As an avid shell collector in my childhood years, I was much less interested in counting my shells— despite a mathematical bent—than in sorting them by color or shape, and exploring their textures and the sounds of the ocean I could hear inside them.

The "real-life context" is a stretch. The shell problem is not, by its nature, a fascinating one. Yet significant mathematical work happens in O'Brien's classroom around this problem. Why? Because she sets a *mathematical* context that makes the students' explorations interesting. The mathematical question quickly moves away from "how many shells?" to questions about how this type of problem can be solved: Which methods worked? Which didn't? Why or why not? Students writing about the problem rarely mention the initial contextualization of the problem (the shells). Their focus is on the relationships of the numbers and the processes used to solve the problem; their writing shows that they are considering mathematical issues.

> Using cubes or numbers came out the same and I didn't think for sure they would.

> I found out $17 + 14 + 9 = 40$, $14 + 17 + 9 = 40$, $9 + 14 + 17 = 40$, and I could even do more.

O'Brien continues to shift the questions from the everyday context to the mathematical context in her problems about spending money as she asks students to consider whether a particular problem can be solved by addition or subtraction.

In Penniman's narrative, we see the same struggle to connect her students with significant mathematics. When I first read the piece, I felt uncomfortable at her choice of problem—graphing the number of each color of gummy bears in a bag. In work on developing data analysis materials for elementary grades, my colleagues and I too often have seen students making uninteresting graphs of uninteresting data on which no conclusions or inferences can be based (Russell & Friel, 1989). In this problem the proportion of colors in each bag of gummy bears was manipulated in advance by the teacher, so that there were certainly no conclusions to be drawn about the distribution of colors in the population of gummy bears. However, Penniman makes it clear from the beginning that the investigation is not focused on the question "how many gummy bears of each color are there?" Rather, the focus is on a general issue of representation: how to graph categorical data clearly and, more specifically, how to represent data when there are not enough squares on the page for one square to represent each item.

The problem context (gummy bears) does its job of providing a fun and pleasant (and edible) source of data, but again in this narrative the clear, intended focus is on the mathematical context. Without the challenge of the mathematical issues deliberately emphasized by Penniman, it is unlikely that the students' work would have risen out of the "real-life" context into the mathematical realm. We would expect to hear the flat, repetitive responses of students as they consider graphs of categorical data: "red has 6, yellow has

4, green has the most, white has the least.'' Instead, what we hear from the students is reflection on substantive issues of data representation—what makes a graph clear to the audience; why if *some* squares represent 2 pieces of data, *all* the squares should represent 2 pieces of data. (For more about the development of ideas about categorical data in the elementary grades, see Berle-Carman et al., 1995; Russell & Corwin, 1990.)

The two narratives in this section illustrate the work of teachers who have made a critical decision about the way they teach mathematics. They have committed themselves to focus on mathematical *thinking* rather than mathematical *activity*, and they have decided to take the long view of their mathematics teaching. Does this mean that these two teachers are ''stars,'' that they always know how their students are thinking and how to shape their teaching in response? Of course not. This stance is, by its very nature, accompanied by uncertainty: Is this a good decision? What if my students don't learn what I'm hoping to teach? How much longer should I try this? In these narratives, the teacher-authors expose their own practice to the reader in the same way they are willing to expose it to themselves by reflecting on their students' understanding, facing up to what is not working, developing hypotheses about their own teaching and their students' learning, and taking action based on these hypotheses—which they then continue to evaluate and re-evaluate. It is a matter of taking ''two steps forward, one step back,'' in a continual cycle of experimentation, observation, reflection, and revision.

REFERENCES

Ball, D. L. (1992, Summer). Magical hopes: Manipulatives and the reform of math education. *American Educator*, pp. 15–18, 46–47.

Berle-Carman, M., Economopoulos, K., Rubin, A., Russell, S. J., & Corwin, R. B. (1995). Three out of four like spaghetti: Data and fractions. A unit of the series, *Investigations in number, data, and space*. Palo Alto, CA: Dale Seymour.

Cobb, P., & Steffe, L. P. (1983). The constructivist researcher as a teacher and model builder. *Journal for Research in Mathematics Education, 14*(2), 83–94.

Mokros, J., Russell, S. J., & Economopoulos, K. (1995). *Beyond arithmetic: Changing elementary mathematics*. Palo Alto: Dale Seymour.

Russell, S. J., & Corwin, R. B. (1990). Sorting: Groups and graphs. A unit of the series, *Used numbers: Collecting and analyzing real data*. Palo Alto, CA: Dale Seymour.

Russell, S. J., & Friel, S. N. (1989). Collecting and analyzing real data in the elementary school classroom. In P. R. Trafton & A. P. Shulte (Eds.), *New directions for elementary school mathematics: NCTM 1989 yearbook* (pp. 134–148). Reston, VA: National Council of Teachers of Mathematics.

Conclusion:
Throwing Open the Doors

Deborah Schifter

Mathematics education in the United States is currently in a state of ferment: New standards and policies have been promulgated, new kinds of teaching materials are beginning to appear, and new assessment measures are being debated. But if all this activity is to result in a transformed mathematics pedagogy, it must be acknowledged—concretely, in programmatic terms—that, in the end, it is the classroom teacher who will interpret these standards and policies, who will decide how the new curricular materials are to be used.

This book and its companion volume, *What's Happening in Math Class?, Volume 1: Envisioning New Practices Through Teacher Narratives*, grew out of a project designed to allow a group of teachers from western Massachusetts to share with others what they are learning as they work to transform their mathematics instruction. By describing scenes from their own classrooms, and reflecting on what they describe, they have created narratives intended to provide grounding for much-needed discussion of the meaning of the rhetoric of mathematics education reform.

One lesson emphatically driven home in story after story is that the new mathematics pedagogy is not simply a matter of implementing the latest set of fashionable techniques or adopting a fun textbook. Instead, constructing new practices along the lines of the reforms poses profound challenges to extant professional identities—as mathematical thinkers, as managers of classroom process, as monitors of student learning—and continuing challenges to reconstructed ones, if for no other reason than that students will continually surprise us with their own discoveries. In place of the comforts of arrival and repetition, there is the prospect of further change and the promise of deepening insight.

However, the notion that even experienced teachers can and should be expected to continue learning in their own classrooms contrasts sharply with the traditional assumption that becoming a teacher marks a sufficiency of learning. It is no great exaggeration to say that, according to the conventions of school culture, teachers, by definition, already know—know the content domain they are to teach, the sequence of lessons they must go through to teach it, and the techniques necessary for imposing order on a roomful of students.

Burdened by these assumptions, teachers generally keep their doubts, questions, confusions, and failures hidden behind the closed doors of the classroom. To peers, supervisors, and parents, they offer a face of competence and confidence. Although surrounded by people daily, in the absence of discussion about the heart of their work, they are practitioners in and of isolation.

If we now reconceive teaching as a form of open-ended inquiry rather than as an enactment of repetition aiming at closure, then teachers will need communities of peers within which to explore issues arising from their instruction. For just as their own classrooms are to become communities of mathematical inquiry, so must teachers come together to pose questions about their teaching, formulating conjectures about their students' learning, and considering alternative instructional strategies. But in sharing with their peers what is happening in their classrooms, they are constructing new practices of collegiality—new identities as colleagues.

As Ruth Heaton points out in Chapter 2, it takes courage for a teacher to dare expose problems from her own classroom. Heaton suggests that, to the teacher who voices her concerns, one of two things is likely to happen: Either others hurry forward with simple answers to complex problems; or she is judged incompetent. As a result, the problem never becomes an occasion for collective reflection; instead, in the rush back to familiar routine, it is quickly dismissed.

In the culture of inquiry envisioned by the reforms, one supportive of the reflective practitioner, such tendencies will be curbed. Teachers, supervisors, administrators, and parents will have learned to cope with the anxiety that comes when issues are opened up and exposed to sustained discussion.

The teachers whose stories are included in this volume have stepped forward to challenge the culture of isolation. Even as they make public the self-doubt, confusion, and failure they experience in addressing the demands of mathematics education reform, they exemplify the new culture of inquiry.

Stories like those collected here must become public; their telling, commonplace. For the kind of transformation teachers are being asked to undertake is so profound, the challenges to their professional ways of being so threatening, that without some larger perspective that contextualizes their difficulties, and without the reassuring knowledge that others have worked through similar confusions, most will despair of success when the going gets rough, and many once again will retreat behind the closed doors of the classroom.

With the propagation of the rhetoric of mathematics education reform outward from the centers of policy making to the school systems of the nation, teachers have begun to enact—to construct possible meanings for—the rhetoric's still largely abstract principles. As I have argued, in attempting to translate such phrases as ''teaching for understanding,'' ''facilitating the construction of mathematical concepts,'' or ''problem-generated instruction'' into the day-to-day life of their classrooms, these teachers are also and necessarily reconstructing their professional identities. While the narratives included in this volume speak out of and to these new ways of being a teacher, only one author, Karen Schweitzer, remarks on the importance of her changing relationship to her colleagues. Yet, without the weekly meetings of the Mathematics Process Writing Project, at which participants shared with one another their classroom narratives, their reflections on the content and style of their colleagues' writings, and their thoughts on where next to take their instruction, these papers would not have been written. And without the willingness of their authors to share their struggles, throwing open the doors of their classrooms to an anonymous public, the papers would not have appeared in print. By taking such risks, the authors of these narratives enter the national conversation about the process and goals of the reforms as researchers into learning and teaching school mathematics. No longer just consumers, or objects, of the research of others, they have refashioned their relationship to the wider educational community. This opening out from straitened identities of collegial isolation and cognitive closure to expansive ones of collegial exchange, continuing inquiry, and knowledge dissemination can be seen as both a subtext of these papers and the context that enabled their production.

A Writing Course for Teachers

Deborah Schifter

In 1990, the Mathematics Process Writing Project (MPWP), whose participants produced the narratives collected in these two volumes of *What's Happening in Math Class?*, brought together the first of three groups of teachers
who were already engaged in transforming their mathematics instruction.

MPWP was an experimental course conducted by SummerMath for
Teachers, an in-service program for K–12 teachers located at Mount Holyoke
College. Founded in 1983, the program has offered summer institutes and aca-
demic-year courses based on constructivist perspectives on learning (Schifter,
1993; Schifter & Fosnot, 1993; Simon & Schifter, 1991).

PROJECT GOALS

The purpose of MPWP was to produce detailed, reflective, first-person
narratives exploring classroom process and instructional goals and decision
making for use in teacher education courses. The idea for the project came
from the recognition that although a significant number of SummerMath for
Teachers participants—having engaged in summer institutes, semester-long
mathematics courses, and/or a year-round classroom supervision program—
had made considerable progress in transforming their teaching, many others
were unable to move forward. The reasons were varied, but the need for curricular materials was frequently cited.

In trying to address these teachers' needs, the quandary of the staff was
that there were so few innovative published materials available and that traditional formats were of little use. For example, a powerful lesson often is
launched by a single question. Yet that same question, baldly stated and lacking context—as is usually the case with traditional materials—may yield no
more than a mechanical exercise in computation. The ability to position such
questions in the flow of classroom process clearly would be of far greater
value.

MPWP was designed to address this issue, taking advantage of the knowledge and experience of teachers who had been working to enact the new mathematics pedagogy. Each year for three years, 14 to 19 teachers (a total of 44

women and 4 men) who had previously attended at least one SummerMath for
Teachers offering were invited to become teacher-writers in a one-semester
course that met weekly for three hours and additionally for two full-day workshops.

COURSE STRUCTURE

The course comprised two major activities: reading assigned materials
and writing. The reading materials were written by teachers about their own
teaching—for example, articles by Ball (1993a, 1993b), Heaton (1991), and
Lampert (1988, 1989), as well as articles coming out of the current movement
to reform the teaching of reading and writing (Atwell, 1985; Hillocks, 1990).
In addition to such works, the second and third groups of teacher-writers read
papers written by their predecessors. All readings were critically examined for
both content and writing style.

The writing component of the course was fashioned after the process
writing model that many of the elementary teachers already used in their own
classes. Consistent with the new mathematics pedagogy, process writers work
cooperatively to analyze and edit their projects. For the first several weeks of
the course, specific assignments were given so that teachers could explore pedagogical issues and experiment with writing styles (e.g., transcribe a classroom dialogue and then write a narrative, based on that dialogue, about what
happened; describe a student who has revealed to you that he or she has
learned something that you are trying to teach; write about a student who expresses a mathematical idea that surprises you). Eventually, teachers determined the direction of their own writing and worked on final projects—15- to
40-page reflective narratives on topics of their choosing. Throughout the
course, teachers met in both small and large groups to share their efforts and
solicit feedback. All work was turned in to me, the project director and instructor, and I responded in writing. Upon request, I met with teachers in class
or in my office, or spoke with them over the telephone.

Appendix B is a compilation of reading and writing assignments given in
the three courses.

WHAT DID TEACHER-WRITERS LEARN?

The work of the teacher-writers enrolled in the MPWP provides an opportunity to learn about the possibilities and challenges of mathematics education reform. The process of writing provided *them* with a uniquely powerful
way to deepen their own understanding of the new mathematics pedagogy. All
participants had engaged previously in some kind of reflective writing process.
In SummerMath for Teachers courses taken prior to entering MPWP, they had
kept journals that were read periodically by members of the staff, and most

teachers had found this kind of writing an essential instrument of their learning. Some used their journals primarily as vehicles to explore mathematical issues; others emphasized analysis of their own learning processes; and still others found the autobiographical record the most useful aspect of journal keeping.

However, the MPWP was distinguished in several ways from the writing the teachers had done in the past: (1) teachers wrote concrete, detailed descriptions of classroom process, often in response to specific assignments; (2) they received regular feedback from their instructor; (3) they also met weekly with peers to discuss one another's work; and (4) the papers were written for a larger and anonymous public.

Teachers wrote concrete, detailed descriptions of classroom process

The act of narrative writing allowed teachers to revisit classroom events and, by viewing these events from a distance, to consider them from new perspectives (van Manen, 1990). Teachers could identify alternatives to the decisions they had made and spot opportunities for learning they had missed. Often student comments could be seen to have had different and/or greater significance than appreciated in the moment.

Many teachers found their new perceptions initially disconcerting. As one teacher wrote:

> I found the writing process forced a scrutiny of what goes on in my classroom that I have never experienced before—not from having observers in my room, not from being evaluated, and not from writing in a journal. When I first began, it was a painful experience to read what I had written. There were so many incidents and situations that looked different when I read about them that I began to question my teaching skill. Now that I have had a chance to think about the experience for a while, I realize that writing and then reading about what happened puts you and your observations some distance from the situation written about. It allows an objectivity in a more leisurely setting, which helps to clarify thinking. Consequently, it makes sense that other options and questions would occur.

Careful descriptions allowed teachers to return to decisions made in the moment in order to analyze their immediate responses and assess their fit to the situation that evoked them.

> Writing for this class helped me to focus not only on activities and responses but on my motivations and expectations. There are times when I seem to have settled into a rhythm and I do things instinctively: responding to a student or posing the next question. In writing [my pa-

per], I was forced to examine situations and try to clarify, at least to myself, why the response was appropriate. . . . Writing made me more aware of students' behaviors and provided a concrete record of my interactions so that I could and can review them by myself and with others to critique my teaching.

Many teachers found that transcribing dialogue—a task assigned early in the course—was particularly effective in highlighting for them the differences between the kind of listening habitual to the traditional classroom and that which encourages students to articulate their mathematical ideas. In her paper, Donna Natowich (1992) entitles a section, "Are You Listening, Mrs. Natowich?" and then answers her own question.

> No. I wasn't listening. At least I wasn't listening in the way I needed to listen. I hadn't been listening for years—I planned lessons instead. I worked hard at planning appropriate motivating lessons. I planned, unaware of a very basic component—what the children actually knew. I made assumptions based on my experience and knowledge of children and the curriculum.
>
> I listened for right answers, confirmation that the students understood what they had been taught. I was accustomed to listening for specific indicators that a student was following my line of thinking. I taught other people's lessons, those deemed appropriate by the experts, and listened for the answers to assessment activities designed by these experts.

Being assigned to capture their students' words quickened the teachers' sensitivity to what those words were saying, revealing thoughts and understandings—as well as misunderstandings—that frequently were surprising. Being asked to tell stories about classroom interactions had the effect, in one teacher's words, of "changing the lens."

> I know so much more about my kids now. By having to write down exact words, I had to slow down the whole process. I began to take much more seriously each question or look.

Another teacher wrote:

> The transcribing-dialogue assignment pushed me to *listen* to the children and to *think* about what they said. Taking notes during math class, I think, made the single biggest change in my teaching style. I needed to listen, not talk. I needed to slow the conversation down in my head, and therefore was able to process it more.

Furthermore, their teachers' sharpened attention became a model for students. As they realized how carefully their teachers were listening to their classmates, the children began to *really* listen to one another, too.

Teachers received regular feedback from their instructor

I collected teachers' writings each week and, every two to three weeks, returned their work with extensive feedback. In general, I tried to offer encouragement, pointing out strengths—both in the writing and in the teaching it described. Reading with an eye toward how weekly assignments might lead to coherent final papers, I suggested ideas that could be developed, asking for more detail and further explication. My comments frequently urged teachers to write more explicitly about their own decision making in their analyses of classroom process.

The challenge to be more explicit often led to deeper comprehension of the classroom situation. For example, after reading about a boy described as "learning disabled," I asked the author to provide a more detailed profile: What is this child's learning disability? What are the strengths he can call upon to support his own learning? How does he get along with classmates when they are not doing mathematics together? What are your learning goals for him? As she worked to describe this child more fully, his teacher came to know him better and so was able to define more clearly her goals and expectations.

At times I asked about the mathematics discussions being reported: "There is only one girl who spoke up in the discussion. Does this reflect the ratio of boys to girls in your class?" "Perhaps your attempts to protect your students from the embarrassment of their inadequate work interfered with the expectation that they critically analyze what they had done. What do you think?" Such questions invited teachers to return to events they had already interpreted, but to consider them from yet another vantage point.

When it seemed to me that individual teachers were stuck—either in writing or in their classrooms (at times both)—I gave individualized assignments. For example, during the first weeks of the semester, I realized that one teacher (who was just beginning to transform her practice) repeatedly expressed frustration over her class' poor behavior. She was trying to get them to work in pairs, use manipulatives, and talk about their thinking, but they simply were not cooperating. While her frustrations were understandable—are, in fact, quite typical—I felt that her writing did not convey a sense of what any of the individual children in her class were like. There was just a single, obstreperous, amoeba-like organism, "the class." Since the group was small (eight ESL students), I asked her to describe each of them—what mathematics does he or she understand? not understand? what else do you want to know about him or her? In the first piece she turned in after I gave her that assignment, this teacher could not analyze her students' understandings, but she did describe their appearance and personalities. In the weeks that followed, her ear became more attuned, and eventually she began to hear her students' mathematical ideas. At the end of the semester, she wrote:

> The one assignment that in retrospect was a turning point for me was the suggestion that I write short narratives about my students as individuals. I had been struggling with the group dynamics and several students who affected the entire atmosphere of the class. After completing the assignment, I felt more connected to the individual students and was able to separate each from what was going on in the group. "Community" still remained an issue but I started to pay increased attention to the mathematics and [do] less "preaching" about how to be a "group."

Teachers met weekly with peers to discuss one another's work

At each class session, teachers met in groups of three or four for one to two hours to read and discuss their work. While most teachers felt that this was an essential component of the process, for some it was also the most problematic. They found particularly difficult the expectation that they provide feedback to their peers and receive feedback from them.

Many teachers felt extremely vulnerable and did not want to hear anything that might be construed as criticism of their work. And feeling so exposed and imperfect themselves, they did not believe they "had a right" to be critical of someone else's writing. However, by the end of the course, some of these teachers felt they had lost a valuable opportunity: "Now that it's over, I wish that I had been challenged more."

But other teachers felt that the feedback they had received from their peers had not been helpful. One reported that when she was in need of direction, she found it confusing to try to sort through the multiple, often contradictory, suggestions she had received. Still others found simply irrelevant the reactions from peers who seemed to be operating under different assumptions about teaching and learning.

Despite these sentiments, the general feeling among MPWP participants was that focused discussions with their colleagues were critical to producing their papers. It was in their small groups that they could test out their ideas and receive the emotional support that kept them going. Here they could discover what needed to be clarified, what could be deleted, and where they had not communicated what they had intended. And here, too, teachers learned how to look critically at a piece of writing, how to ask clarifying questions, how to analyze what was strong and to suggest ways to make it stronger still.

> At first it was very difficult, but as I began to see [how to correct] weaknesses in my own writing, I felt more comfortable sharing those ideas and suggestions with others.

Equally important were small group discussions stimulated by the papers' contents. The writing course became a forum for exploring with colleagues the issues that were at the heart of their teaching. Participants found these discussions helpful in clarifying the dilemmas they faced and in working through instructional problems. Meeting with other teachers of the same grade levels was useful, but they also valued the opportunity—otherwise quite rare—to hear from teachers of all grades, kindergarten through grade 12. Karen Schweitzer summarizes the power of this collaborative work in her narrative, included in Chapter 2.

> Meeting with a group of teachers each week helped me not only by giving me feedback on my writing, but with the math that was happening in my classroom, as well. It also gave me a chance to read and hear about what was going on in other classrooms. Developing this habit of reflecting and sharing has been a pivotal part of my change. It has struck me several times that these are pieces that often are missing from teacher education programs and from our daily professional lives, and for me these were pieces that were essential.

The papers were written for a large and anonymous public

Keeping a journal is done mainly for oneself, and writing assignments are targeted at a different, though still singular, reader, the course instructor; but participants in the MPWP were writing for an indefinitely large audience of strangers. Granted, most of those were likely to be other teachers; the writers still could not make assumptions about their readers' beliefs about teaching and learning, or about their professional development experiences or the nature of their teaching contexts. Authors were challenged to convey their messages clearly and concretely, and especially to explain themselves without reliance on educational jargon (the word "constructivism" and its derivatives were essentially taboo).

Making descriptions of classroom events understandable to others required their authors to make sense of those events for themselves. One teacher reported, after an extremely frustrating and confusing lesson, that she had spent hours at her journal, trying to sort out what happened. However, once she took it upon herself to write a narrative about that lesson, she had to make comprehensible for others the sequence of events that had thwarted her.

> As I wrote . . . the frustration that I felt cleared. Although I ended saying I was frustrated, I wasn't feeling it as passionately as I was when I started. The writing of it cleared things up for me. I saw learning and a continuity that I didn't (and couldn't) see even after writing in my journal.

A particularly important task for the paper writers was that they analyze their own decision-making processes in the events they described. Early on in the course, they realized that on this score generalities would not suffice: They had to "analyze and explore each detail" in order to explain to the reader why they had done what they did—had to take ideas "at the back of [their] head[s]" and put them "in the forefront."

In writing her paper, included in Chapter 3 of this book's companion volume, Jill Bodner Lester (1996) had to face precisely this issue. It had been seven years since she began to center her instruction around her students' mathematical thinking, and so, that September, she quite confidently set about turning her latest roomful of second graders into a community of mathematical inquiry. And it was this transformation that she chose to write about. However, although she recorded classroom dialogue in order to track the emergence of a qualitatively different kind of classroom discourse, early versions of her paper conveyed the impression that her students had somehow, magically, learned to engage in the type of mathematical inquiry she was after. Her challenge became to explain to her readers why she had set up her lessons as she did, what particular interventions were intended to achieve, how she interpreted student behavior, and how her interpretations shaped what she next did. At the end of the course, Lester wrote:

> I have a clearer sense of what it means to establish a community of learners. Prior to working on this project, my ideas tended to be nebulous; it was intangible; it couldn't be described. While I still believe that the process is complex, I have more respect for the role of the teacher and the many clearly defined steps that provided a framework for respectful interactions among students.

Throughout the course, I stressed two overriding goals for MPWP: to produce a set of papers directed primarily toward teachers and to support the participants' professional development through an examination of their teaching through their writing. But, I emphasized, should the two goals conflict, their own learning would take precedence. In fact, it did prove necessary at times to set aside the first objective in order to break through writer's block or to promote greater honesty by reducing fear of exposure. In the end, however, the two goals supported one another. The teachers exceeded their own expectations and, with the recognition that their thoughts and experiences were of value to others, approached their professional activity with greater self-esteem.

SUPPORT FOR TEACHER WRITING

As each MPWP course began, participants were made anxious by the magnitude of the task set for them. They doubted their ability to create a significant piece of work, one that addressed a complex pedagogical issue and honestly represented their teaching. And they were afraid that others would scorn—or, at best, be indifferent to—their work. Thus, I thought it best to start with short assignments and to provide lots of feedback that pointed out successful writing and identified important ideas, so that I would help build their confidence. Writing week after week—for 14 weeks—with encouragement and suggestions from me and from their peers, the teachers slowly developed drafts of their final papers. They then had an additional 10 weeks to complete their projects, calling, as needed, on me and on one another for further support.

Clearly, such writing is time-consuming, exposing, and difficult. And in the absence of serious, well-conceived programs designed to encourage it, very few teachers will volunteer to do it. But I hope readers of this book and its companion volume will have been convinced that such writing represents a form of professional research uniquely suited to the project of reform they are intended to support.

REFERENCES

Atwell, N. (1985). Writing and reading from the inside out. In J. Hansen, R. Newkirk, & D. Graves (Eds.), *Breaking ground: Teachers relate reading and writing in the elementary school* (pp. 147–168). Portsmouth, NH: Heinemann.

Ball, D. L. (1993a). With an eye on the mathematical horizon: Dilemmas of teaching elementary school mathematics. *Elementary School Journal, 93*(4), 373–397.

Ball, D. L. (1993b). Halves, pieces, and twoths: Constructing representational contexts in teaching fractions. In T. P. Carpenter, E. Fennema, & T. Romberg (Eds.), *Rational numbers: An integration of research* (pp. 157–196). Hillsdale, NJ: Lawrence Erlbaum.

Heaton, R. M. (1991, February). Continuity and connectedness in teaching and research: A self-study of learning to teach mathematics for understanding. Presented to the University of Pennsylvania Ethnography in Education Research Forum, Philadelphia.

Hillocks, G., Jr. (1990). Teaching, reflecting, researching. In D. Daiker & M. Morenberg (Eds.), *The writing teacher as researcher: Essays in the theory and practice of class-based research* (pp. 15–19). Portsmouth, NH: Heinemann.

Lampert, M. (1988). The teacher's role in reinventing the meaning of mathematics knowing in the classroom. In M. J. Behr, C. B. Lacampagne, & M. M. Wheeler (Eds.), *Proceedings of the tenth annual meeting of the North American Chapter of the International Group for the Psychology of Mathematics Education* (pp. 433–480). DeKalb: Northern Illinois University.

Lampert, M. (1989, March). Arithmetic as problem solving. *Arithmetic Teacher*, pp. 34–36.

Lester, J. B. (1996). Establishing a community of mathematics learners. In D. Schifter (Ed.), *What's happening in math class?, Volume 1: Reshaping practice through teacher narratives* (pp. 88–102). New York: Teachers College Press.

Natowich, D. (1992). Learning the art of unteaching. Unpublished paper.

Schifter, D. (1993). Mathematics process as mathematics content: A course for teachers. *Journal of Mathematical Behavior, 12*(3), 271–283.

Schifter, D. (Ed.). (1996). *What's happening in math class?, Volume 1: Envisioning new practices through teacher narratives*. New York: Teachers College Press.

Schifter, D., & Fosnot, C. T. (1993). *Reconstructing mathematics education: Stories of teachers meeting the challenge of reform*. New York: Teachers College Press.

Simon, M. A., & Schifter, D. (1991). Towards a constructivist perspective: An intervention study of mathematics teacher development. *Educational Studies in Mathematics, 22*(5), 309–331.

van Manen, M. (1990). *Researching lived experience: Human science for an action sensitive pedagogy*. New York: State University of New York Press.

Writing and Reading
Assignments for MPWP Courses

For each session, MPWP participants were given writing and reading assignments. Over the course of three years, the specific assignments varied somewhat from semester to semester. They are consolidated here as a single list.

WRITING ASSIGNMENTS

Although I suggest a structure for your weekly writing, it is up to you to redefine assignments, if necessary, so that they are most helpful to you. If you have selected a topic for your final project, you might use the assignment to explore your topic and experiment with ways to address it.

- Frequently, when our students arrive in September, they are used to a traditional approach to mathematics instruction and don't know how to be in a class taught alternatively. What do you do to "acculturate" your students to a new kind of classroom? (What do you say? What activities do you set up? etc.)
- Transcribe a dialogue between you and a student or between two students. Then write a narrative, based on that dialogue, about what happened.
- Rewrite the same story, but now in first person, from the perspective of a student.
- Describe a student who has revealed to you that he or she has learned something that you are trying to teach. What did you want the students to learn? What was the context? What was the student's interaction with you? with other students? What process did the student go through? What were the words and actions that indicated learning? How does this learning fit with other things this student has learned? How does it fit with other things yet to be learned? What did you learn from your student?
- Write about a student who expresses a mathematical idea that surprises you. Why did it surprise you? What did you expect? (If the student's idea is not

177

consistent with conventional mathematics, explain why. Is there an element of logic in the student's idea?) How did you respond? What did the student learn? What did his or her classmates learn? What did you learn?

- Describe a teaching dilemma that you have faced. Then present two scenarios (at least one of which will be fictional) in which you respond to the dilemma differently. What was the basis of each of the decisions? What were the different outcomes?

- What does it feel like to discover one's own misconception? What is the process of resolving the disequilibrium engendered? You can write from your own experience as a learner or from the perspective of a teacher observing a student.

- Which of the articles I have distributed in this course do you think are particularly effective? Reread these articles to examine the writing. What techniques and strategies does the author employ to make the writing effective? How do these techniques serve to communicate the issues the author addresses? Rewrite one of your pieces (or write a new one) to employ these techniques.

- Select one of your pieces (or work on a new one) that you think could be strengthened by a specific story. Try to tell that story by "bringing the reader into the classroom," allowing the reader to hear and see what's going on.

- Select a piece of your writing that you would like to share with the class for feedback, and bring enough copies for your classmates.

- Write a statement to me about your final paper. What topic do you plan to explore with your readers? What ideas do you want to communicate? How do you plan to present your ideas? What will be the flow of the discussion. (You will not be required to follow through on exactly what you say here; you can still change your mind. Even if you're not sure, for the purpose of the assignment pick one of the topics you are considering.)

- Continue work on your project. The focus should be developing by now and your writing should be underway. If you are having trouble figuring out what you are writing about, please schedule a conference with me.

- You should be thinking carefully about the development of your final paper. At this point it won't "just happen" without some thoughtful work. As you continue your writing, I want you to identify the problems you face in trying to create a meaningful and coherent piece and work with me and your classmates to solve them. While the identification of the problems does not have to be a writing task in and of itself, you must be able to articulate them verbally so that others can help you.

- By now all of you are well into your final projects. Most of you are working to (1) clarify for yourselves the points you want to make, (2) make sure that those points are made clearly and strongly in your paper, and (3) make sure that everything that is written in the paper serves the purpose of making those points.

Here are a few minor issues to check.

Have you given the reader information about your class? What grade is it? How many students? What is the ratio of boys to girls? What kind of community does your school serve?

If you use the word "constructivism" (or a related word), does it really serve what you are trying to communicate in your paper? Consider making your points without the "c-word." Instead, say what you mean by it.

If you refer to SummerMath for Teachers, does it really support the points you are trying to make?

READING ASSIGNMENTS

- "Arithmetic as Problem Solving," by M. Lampert (1989); "The Struggle to Link Written Symbols with Understanding," by J. Hiebert (1989); and "Is the Algorithm All There Is?" by J. B. Lester (1996). As you read these articles, address the following questions: What are the three articles saying about learning and teaching? In what ways are the messages the same? In what ways are they different? What are the differences in writing style? What is the impact of the different techniques? What can be communicated using one style that cannot be communicated using another?
- Three articles on journal writing: "Math Journals: An Individualized Program," by J. B. Lester (1987), is about her use of journals in a second-grade class. "Mathematics Process as Mathematics Content: A Course for Teachers," by D. Schifter (1993), uses journal excerpts to illustrate the kind of learning that took place in a mathematics course. "School Days: A Journal," by D. Meier (1992), consists of excerpts from a teacher's own journal, raising issues about education. How do you respond to the content of these papers? Does anything in these papers spur reflection on your own use of journals? Are there aspects of the style of the papers that you would like to try?
- "A Year of Inquiry," by J. Szymaszek (this volume); "Making Graphs Is a Fun Thing to Do," by V. Penniman (this volume); and early drafts of each of these papers. How did Szymaszek's and Penniman's work develop? What ideas/issues are they able to communicate in their final papers that don't come through in earlier work? How does the writing change? How does the early work support the final papers?
- "With an Eye on the Mathematical Horizon: Dilemmas of Teaching Ele-

mentary School Mathematics,'' by D. Ball (1993a); and ''New Beginnings,'' by H. Gougeon (1992). Review the articles you have read in the
course thus far and consider the ones you have found most effective. What
are the techniques the author employed to carry the message? Can you identify what makes an article effective? Come to class prepared to discuss this.

- ''Down the Rabbit Hole: On Decimal Multiplication,'' by R. Horn (1991);
''Of-ing Fractions,'' by J. Moynahan (1996); and ''One Last Stab: High
School Kids and Arithmetic,'' by N. Koch (1996). These papers continue
on the theme of making meaning for mathematics or making mathematics
make sense. For some of you, this will be an opportunity for *you* to learn
some mathematics. If the issues about mathematics addressed in a paper are
a challenge for you, take the time to think it through. Remember that following a line of mathematical thought is not the same as reading prose. It
will take you quite a bit longer to sort out the mathematical ideas.

- You have received writing from other members of the class. Read and respond to as many pieces as you feel is a reasonable assignment for the
week.

- Two articles by D. Ball: ''Magical Hopes: Manipulatives and the Reform of
Math Education'' (1992) and ''Halves, Pieces, and Twoths: Constructing
Representational Contexts in Teaching Fractions'' (1993b). What are these
papers about? What do you learn from these papers about fractions and
about the questions that arise as children engage with fractions? How does
Ball use description of classroom events to communicate her points? How
does she include her own thinking, analysis, and decision making? Ball will
be in class on Thursday. In the first part of the class, we will observe and
discuss a video of her students working on fractions. In the latter part, we
will open the discussion to whatever issues you want to raise. Think about
what you would like to talk about with her.

- ''Teaching, Reflecting, Researching,'' by G. Hillocks, Jr. (1990); ''Writing and Reading from the Inside Out,'' by N. Atwell (1985); and ''The
Symphony,'' by N. Lawrence (1991). Analogies are frequently made these
days between language arts and mathematics instruction, and some of you
are bringing up such comparisons in your papers. I'd like you to read Hillocks's paper about writing instruction and Atwell's chapter about teaching
reading to think about issues of teaching mathematics. Then consider how
Lawrence uses her experience as a language arts teacher to inform her work
teaching mathematics. In addition, I'd like you to reflect on what makes the
papers effective or not.

- ''Continuity and Connectedness in Teaching and Research: A Self-Study of
Learning to Teach Mathematics for Understanding,'' by R. Heaton (1991);
''Pictures at an Exhibition: A Mathphobic Confronts Fear, Loathing, Cosmic Dread, and Thirty Years of Math Education,'' by L. Yaffee (this volume); and ''Adventures in Math Teaching: Educational Reform on a Per-

sonal Level," by K. Bridgewater (1991). I would like you to read these three papers, in which teachers describe their own experiences trying to transform their mathematics teaching.

- "Homogenized Is Only Better for Milk," by J. Hammerman and E. Davidson (1993), and "Beyond Stardom: Challenging Competent Math Students in a Mixed-Ability Classroom," by M. Riddle (1996). Consider how the papers are similar and how they differ. Consider both *what* is said and *how* it is said.
- "Building a Case-Based Curriculum to Enhance the Pedagogical Content Knowledge of Mathematics Teachers," by C. Barnett (1991). Although the basic conception is somewhat different, Barnett also has a project in which teachers write about what happens in their classrooms, and their writings are used for in-service instruction with other teachers. I'm interested in your reactions to what she describes.
- "Composing the Multiple Self: Teen Mothers Rewrite Their Roles," by S. Jonsberg with M. Salgado (in press). Although this paper is not about mathematics, I decided to have you read it because Jonsberg has used a very interesting approach in writing about her teaching (and also addresses important issues). I'd like to hear your reactions to it.
- During these last two weeks of the semester, I would like you to put your efforts into your writing and therefore am not assigning any specific reading. However, sometimes I find that when I am stuck in my writing, it helps to read. In that case, consider rereading some of the articles that you have found particularly helpful, or try reading an article you haven't yet gotten to.

REFERENCES

Atwell, N. (1985). Writing and reading from the inside out. In J. Hansen, R. Newkirk, & D. Graves (Eds.), *Breaking ground: Teachers relate reading and writing in the elementary school* (pp. 147–168). Portsmouth, NH: Heinemann.

Ball, D. L. (1992, Summer). Magical hopes: Manipulatives and the reform of math education. *American Educator*, pp. 15–18, 46–47.

Ball, D. L. (1993a). With an eye on the mathematical horizon: Dilemmas of teaching elementary school mathematics. *Elementary School Journal, 93*(4), 373–397.

Ball, D. L. (1993b). Halves, pieces, and twoths: Constructing representational contexts in teaching fractions. In T. P. Carpenter, E. Fennema, & T. Romberg (Eds.), *Rational numbers: An integration of research* (pp. 157–196). Hillsdale, NJ: Lawrence Erlbaum.

Barnett, C. (1991). Building a case-based curriculum to enhance the pedagogical content knowledge of mathematics teachers. *Journal of Teacher Education, 42*(4), 263–272.

Bridgewater, K. (1991). Adventures in math teaching: Educational reform on a personal level. Unpublished manuscript.

Gougeon, H. (1992). New beginnings. Unpublished manuscript.

Hammerman, J., & Davidson, E. (1993). Homogenized is only better for milk. In G. Cuevas & M. Driscoll (Eds.), *Reaching all students in mathematics* (pp. 197–212). Reston, VA: National Council of Teachers of Mathematics.

Heaton, R. M. (1991, February). Continuity and connectedness in teaching and research: A self-study of learning to teach mathematics for understanding. Presented to the University of Pennsylvania Ethnography in Education Research Forum, Philadelphia.

Hiebert, J. (1989, March). The struggle to link written symbols with understanding. *Arithmetic Teacher*, pp. 38–44.

Hillocks, G., Jr. (1990). Teaching, reflecting, researching. In D. Daiker & M. Morenberg (Eds.), *The writing teacher as researcher: Essays in the theory and practice of class-based research* (pp. 15–29). Portsmouth, NH: Boynton/Cook, Heinemann.

Horn, R. (1991). Down the rabbit hole: On decimal multiplication. Unpublished manuscript.

Jonsberg, S., with Salgado, M. (in press). Composing the multiple self: Teen mothers rewrite their roles. In L. Phelps & J. Emig (Eds.), *Feminine principles and women's experience in American composition and rhetoric*. Pittsburgh: University of Pittsburgh Press.

Koch, N. (1996). One last stab: High school kids and arithmetic. In D. Schifter (Ed.), *What's happening in math class?, Volume 1: Envisioning new practices through teacher narratives* (pp. 159–175). New York: Teachers College Press.

Lampert, M. (1989, March). Arithmetic as problem solving. *Arithmetic Teacher*, pp. 34–36.

Lawrence, N. (1991). The symphony. Unpublished manuscript.

Lester, J. B. (1987). Math journals: An individualized program. *The Constructivist*, 2(2), 1–7.

Lester, J. B. (1996). Is the algorithm all there is? In C. T. Fosnot (Ed.), *Constructivism: Theory, perspectives, and practice*. New York: Teachers College Press.

Meier, D. (1992, Spring). School days: A journal. *Dissent*, pp. 213–220.

Moynahan, J. (1996). Of-ing fractions. In D. Schifter (Ed.), *What's happening in math class?, Volume 1: Envisioning new practices through teacher narratives* (pp. 24–36). New York: Teachers College Press.

Penniman, V. (this volume). Making graphs is a fun thing to do.

Riddle, M. (1996). Beyond stardom: Challenging competent math students in a mixed-ability classroom. In D. Schifter (Ed.), *What's happening in math class?, Volume 1: Envisioning new practices through teacher narratives* (pp. 136–148). New York: Teachers College Press.

Schifter, D. (1993). Mathematics process as mathematics content: A course for teachers. *Journal of Mathematical Behavior*, 12(3), 271–283.

Szymaszek, J. (this volume). A year of inquiry.

Yaffe, L. (this volume). Pictures at an exhibition: A mathphobic confronts fear, loathing, cosmic dread, and thirty years of math education.

About the Contributors

Christine D. Anderson has been a teacher in the Holyoke (MA) public schools since 1972. She has spent most of her career working with kindergarten children, first as a city teacher and presently as a Chapter I teacher. She has always loved math, but never really felt that math was her forte. She enrolled in the SummerMath for Teachers Program in the summer of 1990 to increase her understanding of the process of working with numbers. She feels that her role as a teacher-facilitator empowers her students as learners.

Deborah Loewenberg Ball is Associate Professor of Teacher Education at Michigan State University. With elementary school mathematics as the primary context, her research focuses on the challenges of teaching for understanding and on efforts to support such teaching through policy, reform initiatives, and teacher education. Her publications include articles on the role of subject-matter knowledge in teaching and learning to teach, on dilemmas of teaching for understanding, and on challenges of systemic instructional reform.

Ruth M. Heaton is an experienced elementary teacher who, after nine years of teaching, made an effort to change her mathematics teaching. Her recently completed dissertation is a study of the learning that was demanded of her as she worked to change her teaching practice. She is currently a research associate with the Mathematics and Teaching Through Hypermedia Project at Michigan State University. Her research interests include the learning of teachers and teacher educators.

Stephen Lerman taught mathematics in secondary schools in Britain for a number of years, and in a kibbutz school in Israel for a short time. He completed his doctorate in 1986 and since then has pursued his interest in theoretical frameworks of mathematical education, working in the areas of philosophy of mathematics, equal opportunities, action research, and cultural perspectives. He is Head of the Centre for Mathematics Education at South Bank University, London, where he teaches both initial and in-service teacher education courses.

Deborah Carey O'Brien has been teaching elementary school since graduating from Smith College in 1985. She has participated in a variety of courses through SummerMath for Teachers since 1987 and is currently part of the Teaching to the Big Ideas research project.

Anne Marie O'Reilly graduated from the University of Massachusetts in 1969. She earned her Ed.M. from Smith College in 1991. Most of the years in between were spent raising her four daughters. She has taught in the Southampton (MA) public schools for the past three years in a multi-age 3/4 classroom and in grade 6.

Valerie Penniman began her career as a kindergarten teacher, became a tutor of junior high special education students, and then returned to elementary school where she has taught second, third, and fourth grades. She has been a participant in the SummerMath for Teachers Program since 1989 and became an instructor in 1994.

Jessica Dobie Redman has taught second and third grades for four years. She first became involved in SummerMath for Teachers in 1992. Currently she is participating in the Teaching to the Big Ideas mathematics education project.

Susan Jo Russell is a senior project director at TERC, a nonprofit organization that works to improve mathematics and science education. Her work focuses on the development of mathematics curriculum materials that connect elementary students with significant mathematical ideas and on understanding how practicing teachers can learn more about mathematics and about children's mathematical thinking.

Karen Schweitzer lives in Massachusetts with her partner Mitch, her son Ethan, her housemates, and her cats. In 1981, she began teaching Chapter I math and reading, grades kindergarten and 1, and currently is teaching second grade. She became involved with SummerMath for Teachers in 1992, and remains connected through a research project called Teaching to the Big Ideas.

Janice M. Szymaszek has been teaching young children in independent schools since 1979, first in New York City, and since then in Massachusetts. In 1992, she moved from teaching kindergarten to teaching grade 3. Pursuing her interest in mathematics and teaching led her to SummerMath for Teachers for the first time in the summer of 1990.

Nora L. Toney has been an educator in the Boston public schools since 1978. She taught at the elementary level, all grades except first, for 15 years and is currently an assistant principal. She was introduced to the philosophy of SummerMath for Teachers in 1991 and excitedly became involved as a participant and intern. She is also a participant in a four-year collaborative project with SummerMath for Teachers, TERC, and EDC.

Lisa Yaffee was a classroom teacher for nine years: two at the preschool level, three at a high school for students who were invited to leave Boston public schools, and four as a choreographer of fifth and sixth grade. She is now a senior research associate at TERC in Cambridge, MA.

ABOUT THE EDITOR

Deborah Schifter, who works with the Center for the Development of Teaching at the Education Development Center in Newton (MA), is currently directing the Teaching to the Big Ideas project. She began working with the SummerMath and SummerMath for Teachers programs at Mount Holyoke College at their inception in 1982 and served as the director of SummerMath for Teachers from 1988 to 1993. She has also worked as an applied mathematician and has taught elementary-, secondary-, and college-level mathematics. She co-authored, with Catherine Twomey Fosnot, *Reconstructing Mathematics Education: Stories of Teachers Meeting the Challenge of Reform.*

Index